RUFF PUP

Phil Tompkins

ISBN: 1460913671
ISBN-13: 9781460913673

LCCN:

1

Foreword

Many of the guys who have been in combat have later said that war in Vietnam "consisted of endless hours of boredom punctuated by a few minutes of sheer terror".

Our lives in the villages and militia outposts were far different. We were always on our guard – anything could happen and often did. Those day-long sweep operations might have ended up being uneventful but at any moment things could go sour. There was no "rear area" for us to relax in. If you got too lax in security you would pay the price.

But once we made contact and a "manageable" firefight broke out it was exhilarating-and we then knew what to do and how to do it. The actual combat was a relief from the worrying. And when it was over – you couldn't wait for it to happen again. I know it sounds crazy but it's true.

So I would say that our lives in the district "consisted of endless hours of being on edge punctuated by a few minutes of sheer excitement every once in a while".

And our five-man team of Americans did this as part of a new culture to us. Every day we depended on, and lent some kind of help to, our brothers in arms – the local militia soldiers and South Vietnamese government officials in this small part of a historic fight for the very survival of the Republic of Vietnam. But we did this for only a year, while our counterparts had been at it for almost two decades. We did it 12,000 miles from home, while they did it in the midst of their very home towns and right in front of their own families.

So this is the story of that experience. It is about them and their homeland that, sadly, would eventually disappear. They fought the good fight and I salute them for that – always will.

CHAPTER ONE

It was chilly at the San Francisco International airport when we landed, but not as cold as the welcome we would receive as we individually transferred from commercial flights to the bus that would later speed us the 100 miles or so to Travis Air Force Base. Travis was the main jumping-off point for charter flights carrying hundreds of troops to Vietnam every day, and it was also the arrival point for those lucky souls getting back to "The World" after a year of duty in the combat zone. While we all would debark from there, not all of us would come back in the same condition - some would not come home at all. These kinds of thoughts were on everyone's minds; some of us would share, unashamedly, these innermost feelings.

We were hurriedly ushered onto a couple of greyhound-type buses, then sat on them for what seemed like an hour before all the assigned people had made their way from various airlines to this one spot. Why didn't they let us just hang out in the airport - preferably the bar - and be on the bus at a designated time. At the time - March of 1969 - we didn't realize what concern the Army had about the public's potential treatment of soldiers in uniform. I had in fact noticed some cold stares from civilians and furtive glances away from eye contact as I had walked through the airport. Later stories, and our own experiences upon receiving our "welcome home" the next March, revealed the Army's reasoning at the airport. They just knew that there would be problems, fights, or even bad psychological effects of raw treatment of the individual soldier by our so-called "fellow Americans" who chose to protest everything about the war. In later years we would be convinced that the protestors weren't really against war, but were against the draft.

They were afraid they would wind up in our shoes - or in a body bag!

At long last, about sunset, the bus convoy took off toward San Francisco, across the Bay Bridge through Oakland, and north toward our final stateside destination - Travis. Since we were all Army - both enlisted and officers - we were once again under the control of Uncle Sam. Just about everyone had just come off 30-day-leave - a vacation at home which made it that much tougher - and commercial airline flights from all over the country with orders to report for military flight such-and-such at Travis. We would now be back in the cloistered environment where we felt secure as long as we did our jobs. Most were apprehensive, but excited, about a new adventure. Some who were going back for a repeat tour were soon recognized as the authorities and drew lots of questions. They didn't seem to tell "war stories", though - just some helpful hints about the "Vietnam Experience". Some were very solemn about it. They knew what war was about at their ripe old ages - a few were almost 30 ! - and now they were going back! One Sergeant Major in a Green Beret was ready to start his third tour!

On arrival at Travis we were surprised to see about a dozen DC-8 and 707 passenger jets with the colorful markings and logos of almost as many different airline companies. They were all chartered to make these runs from the U.S. to Vietnam and back on a regular basis. I thought the civilian crews must get tired of that. Here they all were lined up on the tarmac and being fueled for tonight's departures on the 2-stop, 20-hour run to Saigon. Each plane would be rigged for 268 seats with no first class section. That full Colonel would have to ride with the rest of us. Other than that, these were just like normal jetliners with full crew, stewardesses and, we would soon learn, lots of food that all tasted the same. Still, it was a much better idea to travel this way than a 30-day ship ride would have been. Uncle Sam was good to us at this stage of the war. One of the hot rumors was that your tour in Vietnam -

scheduled for 365 days each - began when the plane took off, and our departure was set for tonight, 28 March at 2350 (11:50 P.M.) so my Date of Estimated Return from Overseas (known as DEROS) would be set for 28 March 1970. I was now 365-and-counting. To top it all our 20-plus hours of travel would take us west across the International Dateline, so our arrival in Saigon would be early morning on 30 March 69. We would set foot on Vietnam's soil with only 363 days to go!. Of course we were over-playing this whole thing as a joke. People didn't actually count the days when they had important and challenging work to do, did they ?

After we milled around the Travis terminal for what seemed like hours - it was actually at least two- our TWA flight was loaded. Officers first, of course, so we got the best seats and had a chance to sit next to someone we knew or had just hit it off with. 20 hours would be a long time otherwise. I sat next to one of the new Captains that - small world - had been the Senior Tactical Officer at 56th company (Officer Candidate School) when I was a candidate. Bob - funny that I now called him just Bob - had been seriously wounded on his last tour with the 1st Cavalry Division and after a long convalescence stateside he had been senior 1st Lieutenant at OCS and then just made Captain before getting orders for his second tour. He had done his thing as a rifle platoon leader with the Cav and was now slated to be an Adviser with Military Assistance Command Vietnam (MACV) just like I was. Joining us in the middle seat of our row - neither Bob nor I wanted the middle - was another good guy I had just met,another 2nd Lieutenant, who also had orders like mine and Bob's. We would all be assigned to various Mobile Advisory Teams (MAT Teams). We still didn't know what that was, but it didn't sound like a cushy rear echelon job - good ! We would find out soon enough what a unique role we would have the opportunity to play in the Vietnam War.

*   *   *   *   *   *

I don't remember what day of the week it was, but for sure the date was 30 March 69 when the TWA charter crossed the beautiful coastline where the South China Sea met the eastern coast of South Vietnam. Finally! After 20 hours of flying,punctuated only by brief refueling stops in Honolulu and Okinawa,we would be getting off this cramped plane. We were in enough of a descent pattern to see that the country was absolutely lush and seemingly untouched, but as we neared Saigon and *Tan Son Nhut* airfield the steep final dive of the DC-8 "stretch" jetliner revealed a closer look. From my vantage point the occasional smoke plumes rising from the jungled mountains were too big for cooking fires. On a sharp turn I could see similar signature columns of dark smoke coming from a few random squares on the neat patchwork of rice paddies leading back to the coast. I wondered what was going on near the origins of these markers, but I was sure it wasn't a series of friendly cookouts or random brush fires. Here we were, about to land a bright red-and-white painted airliner as if in a vacation haven while somebody was fighting not too far away. It was the first of many bizzarre paradoxes I would witness in my first trip outside the U.S. Now we were minutes away from starting a new adventure literally half-way around the world. This promised to be a year I would never forget!

Making my way down the outdoor mobile stairway from the DC-8 to the tarmac below created those first-impression memories of a wave of intense morning hot air blown by a fury of activity - aircraft of every size and description going everywhere at once - steady noise levels making it impossible to hear myself think, and the incredible smell. As we were sorted out by sour but generally efficient clerks at the outdoor replacement clearing house, many of us - officers and senior non-commissioned officers (sergeants) - were loaded on buses and whisked to the nearby MACV compound. The non-air-conditioned bus had chicken wire stretched across open windows to prevent a grenade from being tossed in on the short but wild ride to MACV HQ, better known as the Pentagon East. Through the open windows the smell mixture changed from the aifield environment to that of rotting garbage, raw sewerage, and one very strong overpowering scent that smelled like a blend of rotten fish and soy sauce. Come to think of it, that one strain had also permeated the air at the airfield. The source was the now-famous "*nuoc maum*" or fish sauce that was the universal seasoning,dressing,dip,and sauce used on every and any food by all Vietnamese. The whole country smelled like it! In a few weeks I would get to know how to use *nuoc maum* like everyone else and enjoy it, but right now it made me almost sick. *Nuoc maum* is made by piling dead fish on a rock in the hot sun, letting the rotting fish drip oil into a bucket, then adding some pretty hot spices and,I swear, a soy sauce. After a few days in the sun this stuff was right! All you needed to do then was to break down the supply into little baggies for individuals to tie to their belts and you had ever-ready seasoning for your rice,meat,noodles,or vegetables or any combination thereof. The only analogy I can think of would be to imagine being in Italy and being able to smell garlic 24 hours a day no matter where you were. I'm not saying it's true in Italy as I've never been there, but try to imagine.

We spent a couple of days hanging around the transient housing area at MACV, getting new jungle fatigues, jungle boots, and other things we would need, like web gear - a kind of harness attached to a wide pistol belt from which everything you would carry on a field operation would hang,snap,or tie. Most important we were each issued an M-16 rifle as our personal weapon. This toy-looking weapon would be ours for a year and once we got to the field we would go nowhere without it. The gruff supply sergeant and his Vietnamese hired helpers loaded all but the M-16 in a laundry bag and gave us a paper to sign listing all the items we should have received. I noticed that the proper quantity of jungle boots was 2 pair while they had only issued one pair. I was nonchalantly told that they were short of the green canvas boots developed specially for the hot, wet Vietnam duty that I was about to enjoy. The sergeant offered nothing, but one of the old Vietnamese laughed and told me in pidgin English that I could buy the second pair in downtown Saigon from a street vendor. Wonder how that happened ? I had heard about the black market for U.S. goods and would soon experienced it first hand if I wanted a second pair of boots - something that no self-respecting Infantryman would think of doing without.

Those of us who were destined to be advisers to South Vietnamese field troops learned that we were scheduled for a two-week in-country training course - the Advisers School at *Di An* (pronounced "zee on" in the Saigon dialect) which was located not far from Saigon. Actually, the distance was about 20 kilometers(12.4 miles), but everything between Saigon and *Di An* was like a major metropolitan area and was relatively safe now.Further down the highway was *Bien Hoa* ("bin wa").It was at that time the largest U.S. military installation in the world and had an airfield that launched or landed some kind of aircraft every 20 seconds day and night. There were well over 25,000 Americans there - it met the classic definition of "The Rear". So we would be going to school to learn how to be advisers, but there was the weekend to kill before Monday's start of training. We were given temporary quarters in a barracks at MACV with concrete floors, running water, and air-conditioning by nature (screen wire on the top half of the plywood-and-sandbagged walls) - and real bunks. For the record, officers were in separate buildings but got no special amenities, but separate quarters and separate social activities were still a part of this environment - a dead giveaway that we were still in the rear.

Four of us decided to venture into downtown Saigon,the famous "Pearl of the Orient", on Saturday just to see what it was like. I was a little apprehensive since the weapons had been locked away in the barracks armory and we would be going to town unarmed. But a visit to Saigon turned out to be like downtown New York - just a little bit more unorganized and smelly but probably not too much more dangerous. The military shuttle bus dropped us off in the center of the city right near the famous Rex Hotel - once home to visiting French dignitaries and colonial rubber magnates and now filled with senior officers and U.S. government officials on short-term assignments. The Rex also had a rooftop restaurant, which at night hosted the high society clientele of all nationalities, with a breathtaking view of the city and sometimes of the war going on in the distance. Our small gang favored a stroll in the afternoon down *Tu Do Street*. This place reminded me of Bourbon Street in New Orleans but was probably a lot more sinister. If it was this way in daylight, I didn't want to be there after dark. Street vendors were everywhere, hawking everything from Zippo lighters with American military insignia to lacquer plates and wall hangings to U.S. issue uniforms. I easily found that extra pair of jungle boots I needed and paid the Vietnamese equivalent of about 20 dollars for them.

Immediately upon landing in Vietnam we had been relieved of any U.S. money - our "greenbacks" had to be changed to a sort of monopoly money called MPC (Military Pay Certificates). This phony currency could be used in U.S.-run establishments only, such as the PX (general store) or one of the many bars or snackbars that were found on U.S. installations. If you wanted to buy from Vietnamese, you had to exchange MPC for Vietnamese money - called *piasters* - at the U.S. facility. The rate was officially set at 118 *piasters* per U.S. dollar. The idea was to keep U.S. dollars out of the Vietnamese economy as they would cause uncontrollable inflation , so naturally a huge black market in U.S. currency flourished. Americans in the rear were often caught in elaborate scams to make huge money just by playing the complicated money exchange game. In addition, if you as an individual happened to have squirreled away a real U.S. greenback dollar, that " 20 dollar " pair of boots might be sold by the Vietnamese vendor for the one greenback. That's how much they wanted the dollar. Or you could probably get the boots for only 10 dollars in MPC. Even the monopoly money was valued by the Vietnamese. But if an American got caught doing either there were severe consequences

- even being caught with greenbacks in your possesion would get you a long jail term. Meanwhile, the Vietnamese entrepreneurs would just get richer.

Tu Do Street was most famous for its bars and brothels - hundreds of them-that now catered to the lonely American soldier. We four straight-laced officers did stop in a couple of bars, but could barely get seated before being approached by the famous bar girls who begged us to buy them "Saigon Tea", which was supposed to be Champagne but was probably ginger ale, for which the bartender would collect at least 3 dollars worth of *piasters*. More commonly the price would be "400 P'" while your beer would be "200 P'" (almost 2 dollars worth). After a few rounds most soldiers would lose track of the exchange rate, which the bartender or "b-girl" would be happy to help with. Actually they would help themselves and split the spoils. Often the b-girls would ask soldiers what unit they were with or where they were assigned and more. They say "loose lips sink ships" and I'm sure there was much valuable military intelligence gained at those bars, and informers were well paid by the enemy. After this scene began to look like a re-run to us in the second and third bars, we decided to move out and take in more tame entertainment. We didn't want to be in Saigon after nightfall - we were too new for that! The next move was a *cyclo* ride up to the Chinese section of the city, called *Cholon*. There was a huge American PX in *Cholon* and we had heard it was like a stateside department store. The *cyclo* consisted of a seat with its driver just behind the seat riding almost a bicycle. This human powered transportation was about the safest in town, although the endless motor scooter, bicycle, and even car traffic moved around seemingly without regard to rules or safety precautions. The rule of the road seemed to be " if you make eye contact, you relinquish the right-of-way or any other rights you may have thought you had". An interesting 15-minute ride soon found us at the *Cholon* PX. Dozens of American soldiers were going in and out of the huge building as hundreds of Vietnamese loitered outside. Some of them were probably friends waiting for a soldier to buy something for them, while some were hoping to take advantage of green soldiers like us and swindle or rob anyone who had some inviting packages. It was not a pretty sight. At this point I began to wonder if all Vietnamese followed the example of these big-city street people. If so, I would be watching over both shoulders for a year - one at the real enemy and one at the "friendly" South Vietnamese. We spent a couple of hours in the PX. I bought a new 35 mm camera real cheap, and by then it was time to catch another shuttle bus back to the MACV compound by the airport. So much for my first impressions of Saigon. I was glad for many reasons that I would be going out to the field. The cities gave me the willies!

That night I slept OK back at the compound and didn't even hear some distant incoming rockets that some of the other guys were awakened by. There was also the steady racket of aircraft going in and out of *Tan Son Nhut* to provide a covering background din. This may have been the last night of complete, sound sleep of my life. Next morning, Sunday, was spent writing letters and repacking gear into the huge duffle bag that would follow me everywhere. That afternoon about 30 of us loaded on a bus for the short ride to the school compound at *Di An*. While the highway was paved it was still a very dusty ride past intervals of mud-hut squallor and fancy new American military setups. We were past the old French villas and town homes and into what used to be the country. People hurried everywhere mixed with convoys of U.S. and Vietnamese government vehicles streaming in both directions. Along the way I noticed *Tu Duc*, which was the Vietnamese Army's Officer Candidate School. I wish I had gotten a chance to visit there to compare it to Infantry OCS at Ft. Benning - my old stomping ground. We also passed *Long Binh*, another big U.S. installation. It was famous for being US Army, Vietnam HQ and for the *Long Binh* Jail - better known as LBJ in clever imitation of the initials of the President who had pushed the gradual buildup in Vietnam to over 500,000 Americans. Nobody wanted to visit the LBJ. Eventually we pulled in at a large guarded gate with markings that indicated this was the division base camp of the U.S. 1st Infantry Division - the

"Big Red One" as it's shoulder patch proudly depicted. This was *Di An* all right, but the old village by that name was completely dwarfed by this base camp. In one corner there was a small compound of barracks and other permanent-looking buildings that was loosely known as the Advisers' School - our home for the next two weeks. It looked like we were in a relatively tame area again, so we could concentrate on cramming everything we could learn into our brains in two weeks - including many hours of studying the Vietnamese language. We spent almost half of every day trying to learn this very difficult language in a lab well equipped with audio tape teaching systems and complete with a Vietnamese instructor. None of us got very good at it. We did a better job of absorbing the lessons-learned offered by countless classroom visitors - guys who had been there. Most of them were American Officers but several were Vietnamese and one was French. That's right, French! This guy had been living and working with the Vietnamese for over 20 years, and he had an awful lot to offer about the country, the people, and their unique culture. This Frenchman was not the ugly colonialist that the communists had chased out in 1954 ; he may have been the ultimate adviser. Other visiting instructors supervised training on old and home-made weapons, some of which we would see the enemy use and some of which would be the newest thing some of the people we would be advising could get. Some of these weapons dated back to World War I . We also learned from an enemy terrorist, who had defected, how to look out for and handle booby-traps and mines, the reality of camp defenses against infiltration, and how to pull our own acts of terrorism in areas that might not include friendlies or civilians.

A South Vietnamese Major who had been a District Chief in charge of both military and civilian affairs in a District - one of about 240 divisions of South Vietnam that might be equivalent in size to a County in the U.S. - spent a good deal of class time with us. As Mobile Advisory Teams (MAT Teams) we would have a District Chief as our primary "Counterpart", or opposite number. He would be in charge of the Regional Force Companies and Popular Force

Platoons that were the backbone of the territorial forces recently mobilized by the Government to take over local defense of every District in the country. Our job would be to support these territorial forces with tactical training, fire support, logistics help, and anything else we could do to increase their effectiveness. We would also be trying to teach their leaders how to use their own system of logistics and fire support so that someday they could handle it without us. This was the most important part of our mission. There were American advisers with the Vietnamese fire and logistics support organizations as well. Hopefully we would all be working in concert to get the South Vietnamese to be able to stand on their own - and win !

Our District Chief instructor gave us very valuable insight into his viewpoint and the things that he as a District Chief had expected and appreciated the most from his Advisers. I could tell that he had developed a special relationship with many of his American Counterparts. He really gave us a head start on our jobs. Most encouraging to us were his apparent strengths as a military leader, his command of English, and his honest desire to help us to help his fellow officers accomplish their missions. He spent many hours after class with us, answering as many questions as he could. I hoped that I would be fortunate enough to have Counterparts like this to deal with. Soon I would find out for myself - and the make believe of school would be over.

Last but not least, we learned about the structure and mission of the MAT teams we were about to join. Each District already had a District Advisory Team that worked more on the civilian/political side under a District Senior Advisor (DSA) whose counterpart was also the District Chief. The District Team had 3 or 4 members, usually army types, who supported the DSA with logistics, handled communications, and ran the advisers compound at District Headquarters. Now each district was assigned a MAT team to handle the military forces buildup that had just started in 1969 under Nixon's Vietnamization plan. The MAT team organization called for a Captain as Team Leader, a 1st Lieutenant as Assistant Leader, and 3 senior sergeants who each had a military specialty - one light weapons, one crew-served weapons (machine gun & mortar) , and one medic.

The Officers were to be the senior military advisers to the District Chief and his subordinate officers and would help in their training in infantry small unit tactics and leadership while the weapons sergeants would be responsible for training riflemen and machine gun or mortar crews.

The medic had several roles. First, he was responsible for the team's medical needs because if we were not kept in good health we would be useless to our counterparts.Secondly, the medic was the medical advisor to Vietnamese soldiers assigned as medics within the Regional Force and Popular Force units we advised, and last, he would be responsible for civilian medical programs in support of the district team. Often we would support what was called a MedCAP, or Medical Civic Action Patrol, to provide medical attention to a remote village or refugee camp. While training was all-important, our role included the task of coordinating fire support, aircraft, and some logistics (supplies) support during tactical operations. As I have said, this was supposed to be Vietnamese support whenever possible, but more often than not we were calling in pure American might when we got in a firefight. We had to. We wanted to win - and to survive!

Most of the people initially assigned to MAT teams were experienced soldiers re-assigned from the Infantry divisions. Once the teams were in place, normal one-year rotations for these veterans began to necessitate assignment of people directly to teams on their initial orders to Vietnam. Many of us - most of the officers - were on our first tour, while most of the sergeants were coming back for a 2nd or even 3rd one-year tour. On balance the experience level was pretty good. Even a 2nd Lt., new in-country like me, could gain experience under the wing of the senior Team Leader for a few months before he would have to move up to take over the team. The Army wasn't stupid. They didn't endanger teams or the mission by putting inexperienced leaders in charge before they were ready. In the course of our two weeks at *Di An* we would get to meet a few MAT team leaders who tried to tell it like it was. It would be a tough job and living conditions would be only as good as our initiative and scrounging ability could make them. Supply channels were nil, but fire support was usually abundant if you could establish good relationships with the support units. We were also told that the mostly rag-tag units we would be working with - affectionately called "Ruff-Puff's" because of their RF(Regional Force) and PF(Popular Force) designations - would sometimes run away in a firefight or even defect to the other side. We also learned that nearly half of the first MAT teams deployed in the last year had been overrun and wiped out as units. I hoped the program would be a little more successful than that this year. It had better be!!

All-in-all, this Adviser School was well-conceived and executed. They crammed a lot of good info into our heads in the limited amount of time available. Living conditions weren't bad either, with minimal distractions to cut into class, lab, or study time. There was challenge volleyball after dinner, which was hot food by the way, and usually a movie or one of the clubs on the base camp was available. Only a few night rocket attacks fairly close by would remind us that we were actually already in the combat zone, but they did teach me how to sleep much lighter - just to be on the alert.

The two weeks were over before I knew it and it was almost the end of March. I had met a bunch of good guys who were now going to their various teams in Districts all over the country. As with any group that I was associated with, the question of how many of them made it still haunts me. I do know of one officer, that same 2nd Lt. I had ridden all the way from California with, who was assigned to a Team near mine. He didn't make it - and for the life of me I can't remember his name. I can almost picture his face but the name won't come to me. It was time to move on. I was eager to get to my assignment. After a year and a half of getting myself trained to do this job, I was finally about to get a chance to actually do it!!

CHAPTER TWO

It was time to get to work. Two of us - my new buddy from the overseas flight and I - were finally scheduled out of Tan Son Nhut airfield on a military hop north to Da Nang. South Vietnam was divided into four Military Regions,also called Corps Tactical Zones,starting with I Corps(or "Eye Core" as we knew it) in the northern part of the country and going all the way to the Mekong Delta,IV Corps,at the southern tip of the country. I would join the Mobile Advisory(MAT)Team in a District in I Corps,in Quang Ngai Province - the southernmost Province in this northern Region. Region Headquarters and the largest city and airfield were in Da Nang, actually a beautiful port city on the South China Sea. Da Nang was dominated at the time by the huge airfield with its twin 10,000-foot runways - second busiest in the world during the war - and by the U.S.Marines, who pretty much controlled the U.S. military effort in I Corps. This was probably due to tradition, as the first regular U.S. ground troop unit sent to Vietnam was a Marine Battalion (600 men) that was sent to secure the Da Nang airfield in the spring of 1965. From there the U.S. commitment started to grow until it reached its peak in ' 69 of nearly 550,000 troops. So the Marines still ran I Corps.

The flight to Da Nang was over 2 hours on an Air Force C-130 Hercules transport rigged with "jump seats" for paratroopers. These jump seats were nothing but a few straps and weren't very comfortable on a short flight, let alone the two hours from one end of the country to the other. No wonder it was so easy to get paratroopers to jump! This flight had the added attraction of several Vietnamese families crammed into the cargo section with us. Many had brought a live chicken or two or even a fat pig stuffed headfirst into a cone-shaped basket,leaving his worst side showing out of the open basket. This was an ideal way to get acquainted with average Vietnamese citizens and their most prized possessions - all crowded into this airborne boxcar. One of the things I found interesting was that while some of the new Americans like myself were a little nervous about their first flight in an old cargo plane over a combat zone, none of the civilians seemed phased by the experience. They had all had much more harrowing experiences and maybe faced worse in the future. They had become hardened to all this. I never figured out where these people were coming from or going. I just knew the U.S.Air Force was doing a good deed for the day – one of many.

We landed at Da Nang airfield in late morning and caught a Marine shuttle bus downtown to the compound occupied by the Corps advisory team. We signed in there and were both told to catch another military flight from a smaller nearby airfield to Quang Ngai City, the Capital city of our assigned province. We wouldn't have to even stay the night, which was just fine with me. I got enough of a look at Da Nang - much smaller than Saigon but still a city - that I didn't really care to hang around. I wanted to get to my final destination and get settled. Luckily the small airfield was located only 10 minutes by jeep from the compound. It was a busy little place - lots of helicopters taking off and landing or being refueled, reloaded and sent out somewhere. I thought one of them might be our ride, but it turned out to be a really old, single-engined Army observation plane called a Beaver or an Otter or something like that. At any rate it was another giant step downward in both size and speed as far as aircraft go. As long as it took for this pig to get airborne and even clear the short runway, I imagined it would take til dark to get to Quang Ngai City, which was less than 100 miles to the south. It did take over an hour of low but uneventful flying. The view was great, though, as we headed straight to sea on takeoff, over the port of Da Nang, and then paralleled the coast - "feet wet" as it was called - down to Quang Ngai. That's pronounced "kwong nye" by the way. There were only the two pilots and an older sergeant on this plane, and nobody talked because of the noise and vibration. Here was another reason to want to be a paratrooper. You got to jump out after flying only halfway, and no sweating through a landing. The coastline on the South China Sea was beautiful. Broad expanses of rice paddies worked their way up to very attractive beaches in some spots ; in others the mountains came right down to the shore. We spotted dozens of fishing villages on the tranquil Sea and I wondered which ones were mostly friendly and which were overtly enemy. None would be 100% safe. That much I already knew. The busiest place I saw was the American base at Chu Lai right on the coast. Chu Lai was the HQ for the 23rd Infantry Division - better known as the Americal Division. Also here were a Marine Air Wing and an Air Force wing for close tactical bombing support, the 91st EVAC Hospital and the 27th SURGE Hospital for the obvious reason, lots of helicopter units, Navy, Seabees, etc. It was big. I didn't know it at the time but Chu Lai would be the source of almost everything we could scrounge for our remote teams. It looked like it would be a great place to rest someday,too, with its beaches actually inside the property. Some of these Americans had it pretty good. At the speed and altitude we were flying, I got a pretty good look at how the other half lived.

At last we cut back inland at the mouth of a river and headed due west about five miles til we neared a decent-sized city - I would guess the population at about 25,000 .Most of the buildings looked to be made of block or stucco but here and there on a side street there was a grass shack. The Quang Ngai City airfield was on the west end of town, so we got a good look at the busy main drag and its shops and open-air markets as we skirted the city by air.. We were met at the airfield by a private in a 3-quarter ton army truck, and he drove us to the Province advisory team's compound,which was located near the center of the city at what was known as "the soccer field". This really had been the town soccer field in earlier days. All the high school games had been held here until the custom became too dangerous. These public gatherings were a favorite target for communist terrorists, and there were plenty of them, organized by the Viet Cong, around here. The compound included the soccer field, which served as an excellent helicopter landing area with its high outer walls, and several bungaloes for living and office space for the Province Team. They didn't get out to the "boonies" very much, but I still didn't envy them for living in the "luxury" of the city. I thought it was too easy to be off your guard and have someone drop a grenade in your pocket or, worse yet, to get kidnapped some evening while enjoying a nice 7-course Chinese dinner. Actually, during the famous Tet Offensive of 1968, this soccer field was penetrated by Viet Cong (VC) terrorists who hung on for several days. The Province team spent a few hairy nights as the enemy's 83rd VC Main Force Battalion had occupied the city center for about 5 days before being driven out in bloody house-to-house fighting.

We met several of the members of the Province team and got scheduled to formally meet the Province Senior Adviser the next morning. Then our respective MAT teams would come from the field to pick us up and haul us "home". That night we took temporary quarters in one of the bungaloes and had dinner with a couple of the staff Lieutenants who tried to give us an outline of the Province as they saw it from here in "the rear". Any other briefings would be handled at our final destinations, which made sense, as these two had never seen a shot fired in anger with the impersonal exception of a rocket attack on the city now and then. They sure knew how to get to their protective bunkers when that happened. I don't mean to lessen the importance of any of these "rear echelon" people I've referred to so far. They were important in their roles - they just didn't get the lucky field assignments like we did. I'm told that it was a practice in the American combat Divisions that officers served 6 months on the "front lines" - with combat units - and then were given staff jobs in the rear. With MACV you were assigned to a team and you stuck with that team for the full year you were in country. I think this made more sense from the learning standpoint. Then there were the guys who never got a field assignment. At the time I felt a little sorry for them. To come all this way and then miss out on the excitement must have been frustrating. If you were a career man, the lack of combat experience could also be career-limiting.

Next morning we met with the Lt. Colonel who was Province Senior Advisor. We actually saluted as he greeted his two newest officers. I think that was the last time I saluted an American in Vietnam. The colonel actually knew a lot about the personnel throughout the province, especially the officers, and shared quite a bit of folklore with us. What started out formally turned into a cordial meeting . The Colonel liked his MAT Teams - probably envied them a little. The MAT teams were considered renegades, swashbucklers, even the poor-man's substitute for Green Berets. (I doubted the latter.) The MAT Teams were very independent and used their own initiative for everything. As I would learn, this could often be a disadvantage, but being independent and somewhat autonomous was fun. Our Colonel seemed to wish he could be out there again but he had a job to do back here in the relatively secure Province capital.

We parted company with the Colonel. I wouldn't see him again until about four months later at my own promotion party when I made 1st Lieutenant. The personnel officer then introduced us to a couple of 1st Lieutenants. They were our respective Team Leaders who had come in this morning from their District compounds to pick up their new assistants. After a few minutes small talk, my team leader, Ron, and I piled my gear and ourselves into an old beat-up jeep for the 10-mile ride "home". A young corporal from the District team,Rich, was waiting in the jeep. He had ridden up to the city with Ron - Americans didn't travel alone. As I parted company with the young 2nd Lt. with whom I had gone through the whole experience since California with, I wondered where and when we would bump into each other again. Surely we would. We were both sharp guys - too good to get hurt.

Rich jumped in back, I rode shotgun, and Ron drove the jeep at break-neck speed until we got out of town. He didn't like the city either. He felt safer out in the boonies. Ron had been team leader for about 2 months. He had been transferred from the 101st Airborne Division after 6 months in the field as a platoon leader. Instead of going to a staff job with the division, he had been selected to go to the MACV advisory program. I like to think it was because he was good, or maybe it was because he didn't play "staff politics" and they didn't want him in a higher headquarters; or maybe it was because he wanted to be here. I learned later that it was a combination of the three. We seemed to hit it off from the start, although there would always be a senior-subordinate relationship. That's the way the Army worked - and it usually worked well - particularly in the field. Ron was tall, skinny, and blond-haired. He was also sort of a yankee, louder than most people, abrupt and impatient, but still fairly easy to work with. He was always conscientious about his secondary mission - to make sure I would be ready to take over the team when he rotated back to the states. This would happen in four months. Right about the time when I would be promoted to 1st Lieutenant, I would be taking over the 5-man MAT Team for Tu Nghia District.

We pushed our way east on the main street of the city to get to the highway that would take us south to our district. Quang Ngai City was not bad looking, except that all of the stucco houses were in need of exterior repair due to bullet and shrapnel holes - a brief reminder that there was a war going on from time to time and that certain repairs could wait. Some of the buildings had been French villas for the rich, some were obviously office buildings for Province officials and countless U.S. advisory groups - most of whom were civilian, para-military, or so secret we didn't want to know. We turned south at the major intersection which included the official Province capital building and dozens of shops, restaurants, and a large open-air market. From here we could spot the headquarters of the 2nd ARVN Division of the South Vietnamese Army and its adjoining MACV advisory compound, where we could occasionally visit a very small PX for supplies and an even smaller bar for short periods of relaxation with other Americans. Of course this compound was also home base for the military advisory team that worked with the ARVN'S. We didn't stop for anything, as we wanted to get to our district HQ before lunch. Ron said that even the gate guard there would lock up and take siesta until 2:30, leaving us out in the cold - no,actually the heat, which already seemed unbearable !

The road south of Quang Ngai City was called National Highway #1 (QL1). It consisted of hard-packed dirt and was wide enough for two trucks to pass carefully. Eventually this highway would be paved by American Army Engineers and American contractors all the way from Saigon to Da Nang, and by the time I got there the paving process was making its way from the south toward our District. By the end of summer the paving would be complete all the way north through Quang Ngai City and up to the base at Chu Lai, making it easier and safer for our occasional scrounging trips. It would be safer because the VC would not be able to bury their land mines in the dirt any more. Clearing the road every morning would be a much easier job for the Engineers. During daylight hours this section of QL1 would be freely traveled by military convoys (our side) and civilians on foot and in every conceivable mode of transportation imaginable. Since Uncle Sam was doing the work, we inadvertently started to call the highway "US1" at times. (Not very good.)

On this first drive to Tu Nghia I was amazed at all the people moving quickly up and down the highway, all carrying something to or from the market. Most common were the "chogey" sticks, which were long bamboo poles balanced on one shoulder with a basket of goods at each end. Even the oldest man or woman could and would trot along, or "chogey" along looking like they had a solemn purpose in life - to get the goods to market or home. The goods would be rice , meat, fruit, and sometimes even small pigs-in-a-basket like we saw on the big transport plane. Also on the road were lots of bicycles, Honda motor bikes or scooters, and an occasional overloaded Lambretta mini-bus. This was a busy road during the day but it was deserted at night. I noticed that the people were either very old or very young. There were no young men anywhere, unless they were in uniform. The General Mobilization order had succeeded in getting almost every able-bodied man into the Vietnamese armed forces. Any young man seen not in uniform was immediately suspect of draft-dodging - or worse - and would routinely be arrested and questioned. This seemed to be the prevalent function performed by the National Police, who were known as the "white mice" because of the white uniform shirt and hat they wore. So here was a country that had mobilized 100% of its men between the ages of about 16 and 35 to fight this war for freedom. By way of sharp contrast, the ratio of draft-age American men that actually ever served in Vietnam was less than 10 per cent. The other contrast, for background, is that each American soldier would serve just the one year in the combat zone, while these Vietnamese soldiers were in it for the duration - or as long as they could stay alive. So it wasn't a case of the Americans fighting someone else's war for them as some Americans seem to think, or would like to think. These people were very deeply involved in the fighting for freedom in their country. Even if they had begun to get too dependent on our wealth, they were committed to the personal sacrifice each of them had to make.

The Tu Nghia District Headquarters was right on Highway I, which bisected the district on its north-south axis. The HQ was almost exactly centered geographically in the District. I would get a chance to explore it all soon enough. The actual District compound was on the west side of the highway with the main entrance only about 50 meters down a heavily barricaded dirt driveway. Just inside the gate and centered in the compound was a large stucco building with a flagpole outside - obviously an official building that served the purpose of a "town hall". Inside this main building and down the northeast leg of the perimeter were lots of offices. The southeast wall was also offices, but the southwest quadrant of this compound looked different. This section had its own inner fence and heavy barbed wire that separated it from the rest of the compound. This was Home - the American advisers' compound. I could tell because over the gate hung a sign that, in addition to a drawing of the black profile of a rabbit's head, announced that this was "The Playboy Club - Tu Nghia". There must be a sense of humor that infects all men at war. This didn't look too plush to me!

Our part of the compound must have been only about 25 by 25 meters in total, while the whole District compound was probably 100 by 100 meters. Our living quarters,which we called the "team house", was a row of block/stucco running the length of our southwest boundary, which also the inner boundary of the whole compound. The one-story building was partitioned to create 4 sleeping rooms, a kitchen/dining room and a bathroom - well,sort of a bathroom. Several screened windows looked out on the outer perimeter and at the world beyond. Across from our team house was a huge , mostly underground bunker which served as a command and communications room all the time and as a safe haven from mortar or rocket attacks when they occurred - which was frequent. Looking through the fence I could see that the northwest quadrant of the main compound was living quarters - and bunkers - for the District Chief, a few of his key officers, and all of their families. The main residence building looked like a normal house except for the multiple antennas on the roof. The rest of the compound was a hardpacked dirt circular drive that wound around the main office building. Three jeeps and a 3-quarter-ton army truck were parked behind the main building. This was about it - this would be home for the next 11 months. (Surprisingly, I already had a month in-country and only 11 to go!) This would be home base anyway. Most of our time would be spent out on combat operations or visiting various villages and their defense forces or actually conducting training for the local troops. But our activities would be controlled out of this District compound and we would return here to sleep on many nights.

I stowed my duffel bag in the team house room I would be sharing with Ron. This was like being back in college again, learning to live with a stranger in a strange place, but it didn't take long for me to get acclimated to the whole team and the environment. We really didn't have time to waste. "School" would open right away ! Our room was comfortable enough, with a screened window that looked out on the perimeter which, I quickly noted, was set up to be guarded by some of the Popular Forces troops assigned to the District compound security. By this time there was no sign of life. It was after 12 noon! This made me a little uneasy, but I soon learned what all this meant.

Most surprising about our room, which was good-naturedly referred to by the rest of the team as the "Officers quarters", was that we had electric lights and a ceiling fan !! Yes, this compound was the proud owner of a scrounged diesel generator that powered everything including perimeter lights. This was a huge surprise ! A set of bunk-type beds had been separated and set on each side of the room with the foot end against the outside wall closest to the screen door out to our little compound. A frame of heavy timbers around each bed supported an overhead shelf that in turn was topped by a couple of layers of sandbags with a piece of plywood nailed over them. While the sandbags were to protect us from shrapnel should a rocket or mortar come through the roof, the plywood made a great spot to stow junk. Each of us had an old school-type desk for reading or writing letters and after-action reports. The screen door opened outward and to the right because that would provide the easiest fast exit to the bunker just across the small yard from us in case of emergency. I would learn to make that move at Olympic speed.

First order of business was for Ron to show me around the defensive perimeter of the compound itself. The whole place seemed deserted, but Ron explained that as it was after 1:00 now, it was still "siesta" time. I remembered hearing a little about this custom at the Advisers School, but I had thought it was an exaggeration. It wasn't. At 12 noon everything stopped for the Vietnamese so they could cook lunch, eat fast, and then sleep until 2:30 when everything started again. The Americans living with them also adopted the custom. While Ron and I were touring, about 100 Vietnamese soldiers and their families and at least 8 Americans were fast asleep in this compound. One might think this was tantamount to inviting attack by the enemy, but he was Vietnamese, too, and enjoyed the break like everybody else. Besides, most of the dirty work was done at night anyway. So in the quiet time I got a look at what turned out to be a pretty sloppy perimeter. Fighting positions were appropriately placed all around, but the barbed wire and mine-fields out front of them looked old and poorly maintained. The French had laid this minefield 20 years before and nobody knew where the mines were. Now I knew why the barbed-wire and other barriers were not updated. Nobody could pick his way through an unmarked minefield to repair the barriers. This barrier system wouldn't slow anybody down in an attack. The best we could hope for if we were attacked by a large force some night would be early warning and fast action. The good news was that a solid ring of floodlights were mounted high above the heads of our defense force and their bunkers. These were the perimeter lights that some genius (a resourceful American) had scrounged and erected years before. As long as the defense line kept a good watch - and as long as the diesel generator and its fuel held out, we could expect any enemy approach to be spotted fairly far out from our positions. Then, with the superior firepower we Americans could deliver with artillery, helicopter gunships and even jet bombers, this compound would probably withstand a fairly large ground attack. That was the theory, but nobody knew what would really happen. For some reason, this District compound had not gotten hit hard by serious ground attacks even during the 1968 Tet

Offensive, and a District Headquarters was almost always a favorite target for the bad guys. It would mean a lot to their attempts to take over politically if they could show that the government forces, with all the American might behind them, couldn't even hold their own District capital. A serious ground attack would have to come sooner or later. It was inevitable. I hoped we would really be ready. I felt a chill down my back - even in the heat. My instant mental picture was of a few Americans and their South Vietnamese friends defending this compound and their very lives in the darkness. For years I had heard stories from Bill and his friends at Ft. Bragg about the Special Forces camps being overrun, whole A-teams being wiped out, and the heroic acts of some who fought to the last or led daring rescue and relief operations to save the camps. Ironically, here I might have the chance have the same kinds of experiences here in 1969 that they had had in the early to middle 60's. It was exciting!! And it was frightening at the same time!

CHAPTER THREE

Finally, just after 2:30 pm, the compound started to come alive again. There had been real people here the whole time - I just hadn't seen them! Vietnamese and Americans came out of their hooches, presumably to pick up where they had left off over 2 hours ago. I noticed that the Americans almost all stopped by a large box cooler inside our compound and next to the bunker entrance to grab a can of beer or soda- mostly beer. It was still hot and stifling! From the perimeter, Ron and I watched an American in civilian clothing head out through our gate and across to the office building. Ron pointed out that this was our District Senior Adviser (DSA), Ken, to whom all the Americans in the district reported - including our new MAT Team. Ron told me that Ken was in fact a civilian with the State Department(Foreign Service) and that he had been in Vietnam and this Province for over seven years. He must have loved it! He had just recently become the official DSA as the previous DSA, an Army Captain, had to go back to the states on emergency leave and was so "short" (so little time left on his one-year tour) that he probably wouldn't be back. So the Province Senior Adviser, the Lt. Colonel I had just met, had placed his confidence in Ken to run the advisory effort in *Tu Nghia* District. This would turn out to be an excellent decision, including its effect on the District Chief, who had known Ken for a long time and now was happy to have him as his official trusted adviser.

As more people stirred around, it was a good opportunity for Ron to introduce me to as many of members of the team as were here today. Later this evening I would get to meet our Counterparts - the key Vietnamese officers, including the District Chief. We started out in the little office at the back corner of the "town hall" in the middle of the compound. Here I met Ken, the civilian DSA, with his long full beard and otherwise non-military look. He said he was glad to see the MAT Team finally building up and threw a couple of good-natured barbs Ron's way, as if to jibe him for the inactivity of the Team. I could tell right away that Ken was a sharp guy with a sharp wit to match. His assistant was a very straight-looking 1st Lieutenant named Paul who looked and acted like a career type. I found out that he was an ROTC officer out of one of the colleges in Virginia and indeed was planning to be a "lifer". Paul had lots of time in grade and time in-country and I could already see a good deal of competition between him and Ron. Nothing serious, but the MAT Team concept was in need of proving here, and Ron had been sent here to get it started. I quickly surmised that I would have to push it all the way once Ron left country and I took over the Team. We spent quite a while with Ken and Paul while both of them outlined their expectations of the MAT Team and gave some helpful insights about the District Chief and some of his subordinate officers. I also sensed that Ron was hearing some of the latter for the first time. Could it be that he had not made much personal progress in building relationships with our Counterparts in the South Vietnamese hierarchy? It occurred to me that this must be one of the first orders of business for any adviser - building credibility, trust, and a good personal working relationship with your counterparts. I made a mental note, promising myself that I would stay conscious of this priority as long as I was out in the field doing this job.

The more I think about it, I was being placed in an ideal position. Ron had been here only about 2 months and had still only received 2 added people, including me. We were supposed to see two more sergeants come on board over the next month or so, but by the time the Team was up to full authorized strength, Ron would only have a month or so to do anything with it. I on the other hand, would have the opportunity to accomplish a great deal - or what would feel like a great deal compared to other frustrating experiences I had heard so much about (and still hear about, unfairly, today). I would start with the benefit of a full-strength Team to do it with - or at least I thought that was the case. Right now we would have to do the best we could with the personnel we had.

Ron and I went back to our own compound to meet the rest of the District team and the only other member of our MAT Team. This individual would provide the shock I didn't anticipate. Ron introduced me to a very senior Sergeant First Class whom I'll call "Crusty". This guy was the prototypical old salt who was bitter about his assignment, the living conditions, and the Vietnamese. How could he be an asset to this team with the attitude he had? Thankfully, I found out he was "short" too, with only 3 months to go. It would become obvious that he was suffering from the short-timers fear as well when the first operation came up, and he would prove to be useless to our efforts. It might as well have been just Ron and me on this team. I had never seen such a whiner in the guise of a career soldier! I just couldn't wait for "Crusty"'s replacement to show up.

So much for our under-strength MAT Team. The district team included Rich, who had been with Ron to pick me up at Province HQ, a young hard-working jack-of-all-trades whose primary job was to serve as radio operator and gopher. He was mentored by another career senior Sergeant First Class I'll call Johnny, who had been a Platoon Sergeant in combat and with the 25th Infantry Division all his life. He was a Hawaiian, as most of the 25th people had been, and he served as First Sergeant or "Top" with the district team. Johnny was a good man who made sure everything was ship-shape in our compound, took care of supply (scrounging), and lent his experience to all young, inexperienced team members like me. Like most senior non-commissioned officers he did it with humor and respect for our rank at the same time. I would learn that it was good to have him on the horn at the district base when I needed help or stability in support of our later rag-tag adventures out in the boonies. Johnny of course maintained the "duty roster" for radio watch,etc., in the compound and made sure that officers pulled their weight like everybody else. This was good for the team and gave all a sense of comfort that somebody was keeping things together. There was one more sergeant in camp today whose name escapes me, but he would turn out to be a good man. He was part Hispanic, from New York, and was responsible for support of the Phoenix program in lieu of an officer on hand. I would learn more about Phoenix later, but I liked this guy right away. One more sergeant was not in camp this afternoon. I'll call him George. He was laughingly pre-viewed to me as the "town drunk" who was today at his favorite hangout - the Engineers' compound about 3 klicks (kilometers) south of here. The engineers were our friends and were working on paving of "Highway 1" through the province. They worked hard from first light in the morning but they tended to spend most evenings guzzling beer and this was right up George's alley. Fortunately he was "short"' too.

So, this was it for now. The team of Americans that Uncle Sam, Richard Nixon, and South Vietnam's President Thieu had charged with the job of "Vietnamizing" the war in this district in 1969. And there were about 200 teams just like this one in country. This many-faceted group was responsible for the security and development of a strong South Vietnam at the rice-roots level. Was this what I had anticipated? Was my mind playing tricks on me, or were we for real ?

Could we turn the local forces and civilian village government into a self-sufficient organization that could turn the tide against Communist take-over? And could we do it in one year? At this point it seemed like a monumental task, but I would learn to take the approach recommended to anyone setting out to eat an elephant - "do it one bite at a time".

We spent the rest of the afternoon squaring away my gear in the team house while Ron briefed me more on what the team was charged with doing here. Reality seemed to be that we weren't doing much training or unit development yet, but that was one of the objectives. Most of Ron's time had been spent trying to get supply methods set up for newly organized Popular Force platoons and Regional Force companies. The rest of his time had been spent supporting daytime operations with artillery and occasional air strikes, as the operations almost always made some sort of contact with small units of VC Main Force troops, who were ever-present in one Hamlet or another. The enemy was intent on continuing chaos as close to the Province flagpole as possible and *Tu Nghia* was the "gateway" district to Province HQ. In addition, the improvement of highway 1 was a key element in the pacification effort and the VC attempted to disrupt progress on this project as much as they could. This included sapper (terrorist) attacks on the many bridges along the highway in our district. Ron then casually dropped the bomb I wasn't expecting. It seemed that the PF platoons he accompanied on operations had a distinct tendency to retreat under fire. Simply stated, they would run in the face of the enemy, leaving an adviser out there alone if necessary! It was bad enough to be the only 6-footer in a gaggle of 5-foot Vietnamese soldiers - a target sticking out like a sore thumb - but if they turned and made a hasty retreat in a firefight it could get dicey for the "*co vans*" (advisers). The good news was that the District Chief was a warrior who didn't want to lose one of his advisers and assigned special bodyguards to the Americans during operations. They were called PRU's (Province Recon Units) and were mercenaries who had been paid with release from jails,etc., on the condition that they would fight for the government. They were used for many of the hairy missions in the Phoenix program and in our case were also used as bodyguards. The PRU's would not lose an adviser at any cost. It was comforting to know that in the heat of battle I could count on a hired criminal to keep me safe at the risk of his own life. Things were starting to get interesting.

*   *   *   *   *   *

At about 5:30 everyone made their way to the kitchen/dining area in our team house where we would find an impressive spread of baked chicken and powdered mashed potatoes ready for us. This imaginative meal had been prepared by our " hooch-maids", one who was old and in charge and one who was young and supposedly retarded but strong as an ox. She did all the hard work. The chicken had come from the large freezer - a luxury for this kind of a team - and had originally been scrounged from the Americans at the division base camp at *Chu Lai*. We must have had about a hundred pounds on hand, because it's all we had for dinner for a month. We counted our blessings, though. It could be a lot worse. We could be eating Army C-rations. When we weren't being fed and entertained by our counterparts, we were always able to get pretty good food here in the team house. And, it didn't cost much. Almost everything was scrounged or traded for and we each chipped in $5 per month to pay the women to cook. Another 50 bucks a month went into the kitty for beer and soda purchases for the compound and any other incidentals that couldn't be gotten through the "supply system" - the scrounging and trading network that took precedence over any formal system in Vietnam.

During dinner there were informal updates on the day's happenings and tomorrow's plans from just about everybody around the table. Ron's plans for next day included a briefing tour of the district for me by helicopter, as he was fortunate to have use of the Province chopper for a couple of hours in the morning. I learned that you had to request use of this valuable resource several days in advance unless, of course, you had a dire emergency - which could get a chopper diverted from the American division or other users in the province. Once in a while we would get the "civilian" Air America chopper, which was a story in itself - CIA and all. So tomorrow I would get my first look at the district, and what better way to get an overall picture than from the air. Ken said he would like to go with us, and suggested we invite one of our counterparts, perhaps even the District Chief. This sounded wise to me, and it also gave me a sense of the importance Ken was placing in the MAT Team and my training to take it over shortly. He wanted to be involved in forming my impressions and in the priorities that the Team would operate on. I liked his hands-on approach, particularly since he was a civilian in charge of military operations. I also knew his years of experience in Vietnam would help me a great deal.

After dinner and updates there was about an hour left til darkness would fall on my first night in the District. Ken had invited the District Chief over for a beer and to meet me and asked him to bring any of the officers also. They showed up at about 7 pm while Ron, Paul, Ken and I waited and talked in the room in the team house that Ken and Paul shared. Paul was cleaning his M-16 rifle while we talked. We were all in our jungle fatigues as if this were a formal meeting (except for Ken, of course) and I soon found out why. When the District Chief arrived he was dressed in sharply starched fatigues as were the two Lieutenants who accompanied him. I was introduced first to the Lieutenants and last to Captain Hoa, the District Chief. Paul had called in his favorite interpreter, Phuoc, who politely translated the small talk between me and the Lieutenants. One of them was *Trung Uy* (1st Lieutenant) Cahn, the assistant District Chief for military affairs. Cahn spoke only a couple of words of English and not very well. I would always have to use an interpreter with him. He was rather reserved, or humble at this point, but I would find out that he was quite a character in his own element. The other officer was an "Aspirant", actually more like a Lieutenant-in-training, thus he "aspired" to be given command. I don't remember the Vietnamese word for Aspirant, but he would soon become officially a *Thieu Uy*" (tee wee) like me - a 2nd Lieutenant. Aspirant Hahn was sharp-looking, serious, and maintained a strict military bearing as he was really in training at the time. Later on, after he made it to 2nd Lt., he still kept his serious side and became a good leader. Hahn would always be around for operations with the PF platoons, but when we ran larger operations with multiple RF companies and PF platoons *Trung Uy'* Cahn would come along. In most cases, larger operations were almost always commanded by the District Chief himself.

Now the formality of meeting the District Chief was at hand, and there was a surprise in store for me. Captain Hoa shook my hand, smiled broadly, and in almost perfect English welcomed me to *Tu Nghia*. The Vietnamese for Captain is "*Dai Uy*" "(die wee) and I would address him that way until his next promotion. He re-iterated the jobs of the officers with him, led us in a small toast with beers, and then paused for his officers to excuse themselves to their work. Hoa then turned to more social talk as Ken invited all of us to sit and relax. The *Dai Uy'* was taller than most other Vietnamese - about 5'8" - and boasted a much harder-looking face - even with the big smile I now noticed. I was still in awe of his command and execution of English. I could also pick up on the close personal relationship he had with Ken and, to a similar extent, with Paul. He and Ron exchanged courteous hello's but you could see that the warmth was not there - they hadn't had time to become close yet. I guess Hoa looked at me as the new guy who would have a lot to learn, but his first reactions seemed very positive. I knew, however, that he wouldn't laugh and joke with me like he now did with Paul until he and I had gone through some tough battles together. Obviously, the bond here was that they could share the common bond of having been in close-up combat together and of both having survived. This was the kind of thing that two buddies sharing "war stories" could do. And that's what these two were doing, reminding each other of the excitement and the danger they had shared and conquered - what a bond that makes, almost to the exclusion of others who do not share the same experiences. How true this is, even in later life - perhaps even more so now. I find that

I have a much easier time talking to or bonding with someone who has been there and understands.

Ken mentioned the Visual Recon Ron had planned tomorrow in the chopper, and Hoa gladly agreed to come along. I was flattered that he took an interest, but I also guessed that he wanted to check some things out, too. Hoa wanted to stop off if possible at two locations, an RF Company outpost in the southeast corner of the District and at the "Junk Base" in the northeast corner. Ron and Ken agreed, and the plan was set for mid-morning. *Dai Uy'* Hoa then excused himself, welcomed me again, saying he looked forward to tomorrow's mission, and left to go back to his house. It was then that Ken filled me in on the *Dai Uy'* 's very impressive background.

Hoa was originally a North Vietnamese! His brother, who had not migrated south to freedom a decade earlier, was still an officer in the North Vietnamese Army (NVA) - the regulars that were invading South Vietnam by the tens of thousands. When asked about this situation Hoa would tell you that one day he might have to kill his own brother in battle. He had spent a lot of time in the early sixties in local defense positions at village, district, and province level, and had risen to a staff job in Saigon by 1964. At that point he was promoted and sent back to the field and worked extensively as a field unit commander running joint operations with the famous 1st Cavalry Division, who engaged the NVA in the first major battles of the war. It was here that *Dai Uy'* Hoa felt he had the greatest chance of meeting his brother across the battlefield. After a couple of years at this, he was given the job of District Chief here in *Tu Nghia*. He had viewed this as more political/civilian administration than military although the pesky local Vietcong organization was quite strong then. By mid ' 68 the Allies had just about wiped out the local *Vietcong* organization - a result of the *Tet* Offensive ' 68. While the news media in the U.S. portrayed the *Tet* Offensive as a major loss for us, it actually was the decisive blow to the southern military capability of the Vietcong. In order to re-mount a serious military threat to South Vietnam, North Vietnam stepped up the infiltration of division-sized regular units into the South. This meant that once again the primary military threat to us here in *Tu Nghia* by 1969 consisted of NVA units or old VC Main Force units re-populated and led by North Vietnamese replacements. Once again *Dai Uy'* Hoa faced the possibility of meeting his NVA brother in combat. Ken also pointed out that Hoa was a very tough but fair leader who would not put up with poor performance from his subordinates. One of the problems with South Vietnamese troops in general was thought to be the lack of leadership, but we seemed to have a jewel here. The difficult task Hoa faced was the newness of so many of the troops just mobilized into PF platoons and RF companies. Subordinate leaders were incredibly green. Hoa's handling of civilian matters and the civilian government - Village Chiefs on down - was similar to the way he handled military subordinates so I got the impression that we were supporting some kind of martial law here. It was almost that. It had to be.

Dai Uy' Hoa, being from the North, had been brought up Catholic and educated before he had migrated to South Vietnam as a youth. He now had a family of his own - a very attractive wife and two cute kids about 8 and 12 years old. He was fortunate to have his family living with him here in the compound, and they lived well. Hoa had been able to put aside a good deal of money during his rise in the South Vietnamese Government and he had survived not only combat, but also the many bloodless coups that changed the unstable government situation in the early and mid-sixties. He had gained the respect and admiration of the general in charge of the Ist Military Region during his field exploits with the 1st Cav, and when a District job came open, General Lam quickly gave it to *Dai Uy'* Hoa. So this upper-class officer was put in charge of thousands of working-class and peasant farmers in a coastal district - half rice paddy and half mountains - and had to work through an organization of Village and Hamlet Chiefs whom he was not sure he could always trust. He also was responsible for two large refugee camps filled with people who had been unwillingly uprooted from their homelands by the war and stuffed into shanty-towns here in the lowlands. Amongst all this he was responsible, of course, for the development of the Territorial Forces that I would be working with, including the PF Platoons, Regional Force Companies, and hamlet-level People's Self Defense Forces(PSDF) - the most pitiful, rag-tag of them all. It was clear that *Dai Uy'* Hoa had his work cut out for him. He would need help at both war and "nation-building" at the rice-roots level, and we would be doing our best to give him most of that help. Maybe we could make some headway and have a small sense of accomplishment in our relatively short tours here - tours that I knew would be over before we realized it.

We spent another hour or so listening to Ken's good advice and some funny stories about happenings in the district before any of us had been here. Then we broke up and I prepared to spend my first night in the team house. First Ron introduced me to Phu, the mortarman for the compound. Phu was old and apparently senile, but he could fire illumination rounds from his trusty 81 mm mortar any time the compound was under fire. Phu was brave if not accurate, proven by the legendary story of him firing an illumination round a little short so that it fell in the back of one of our jeeps. Phu had had the presence of mind to scoop large piles of sand into the jeep to put out the fire before it could eat through the floor and into our gas tank. If we took any incoming fire during the night we could run to the bunker, get on the radio, and wait just a short time before we knew that Phu's illumination was on the way, helping to turn our outer perimeter - beyond the reach of our perimeter lights - into daylight. Sharp eyes would then scan the perimeter for any sign of ground troops, giving early warning of any ground probe or full infantry attack. With this comforting thought I retired to our hooch and wrote a quick letter home. I tried to convey the bright side about the people I had met and the unusual things this compound had, like electricity. I didn't want to give any hint of danger - that would be non-productive.

That first night, actually at about 2:30 A.M., we took about 8 rounds of incoming mortar fire from the southwest. I followed Ron out the screen door and into the bunker and waited to see what happened next. A radio report had been forwarded to the Province team in the TOC (Tactical Operations Center) by Johnny, who had been on radio watch at the time, letting them know we were under mortar attack. The moment the second round hit, all of us were in the bunker with him. We counted the incoming rounds with each explosion. A few hit inside the main compound on the dirt drive, but we didn't think any came into our area. After a few moments of silence and a last radio conversation, Johnny announced "all clear" and we all carefully returned to our hooches. He had made sure that he had an all clear report from the District Chief's bunker before we ventured out, so we knew that the troops on the line had reported no sightings of enemy ground troops under the perimeter lights and Phu's illumination rounds. Everything was pretty routine in this kind of harassment mortar attack - we didn't even try to set up counter-mortar fire. Perhaps we would in the future. I made another one of my many mental notes and went back to a light sleep quickly, but not before checking the time at 2:43 A.M. Only about 3 hours' more darkness to cover any sneaky moves by the bad guys. I think I woke up twice more to check the time before first light came. This had been my first night of the real thing, and I must have been anxious for it to be over. It was almost like the bad guys had done this as a welcome for the new guy - me! Was it possible that they knew there was a new adviser officer in camp and wanted to show me their presence and their ownership of the night? By now I knew that anything was possible in Vietnam !

CHAPTER FOUR

First light came, suddenly, just before 6 A.M. (or 0600, as I should be referring to the military time system). I was up and out in the compound once my mind had adjusted to the surprise of waking up in a new environment. This was home now and, in spite of its primitive and relatively dangerous makeup compared to other places I had been in Vietnam, I sensed that there would be days or nights that I looked forward to being here rather than in some of the situations that awaited me. People were again stirring, stopping off for a beer or soda, and heading to the kitchen for light food and small talk before the day started in earnest. The aroma of rice cooking, mixed in with that unmistakable smell of *nuoc mam*, drifted in from the perimeter and from all over the Vietnamese part of the compound.

Although the sun had only been up for a few minutes, it was steaming hot! We didn't have a thermometer - didn't want one, I guessed, but one of the team had turned on AFVN (Armed Forces Vietnam Network) on his radio and announced the current Saigon temperature as 95 degrees and rising. That was enough for me! It was already hot with a whole day left to get hotter!

There were only three seasons here : hot-and-damp, hot-and-dry, and warm-and-wet. Since it was April we were in the long hot-and-damp season in I Corps. The hot-and-dry would run about July to September and the real rainy season would be September till late November. In other areas of South Vietnam the seasons could be completely different. So we were now in hot-and-damp which meant that there were frequent but brief showers followed by bright sunshine that caused a steamy feeling. The humidity itself must have stayed close to 100% all the time and at night I'd guess the

43

temperature rarely got below 80. The high temp every day had to be well over 100 "in the shade" and, since our district consisted of lots of open rice paddy, there wasn't much of that shade to go around. All this leads up to is the fact that to this day I can't stand to be hot! Of course it also meant that the working conditions were less than ideal for softies from "Back in The World" where air conditioning had become quite prevalent during the sixties. Fortunately, after all the training we had gone through, most of us were in pretty good physical shape by the time we got here. I thought I was rather trim at about 170-175 pounds when I left the states.

Ron and I grabbed a cup of coffee and a smoke with Johnny, who had stood that last radio watch that included the brief mortar attack. He indicated nothing else had happened that night - no reports of attacks on any bridges or villes and no good news like a friendly ambush sprung on the bad guys. Obviously the team (probably just one VC) that lobbed in the mortar rounds on us last night got into and out of position - usually within 500 meters - without being caught in one of our night ambushes or even detected by an observation post or listening post (OP or LP). There were supposed to be several of these in place every night all over the district and, of course, in different locations every night. Johnny scoffed at the idea that the PF(Popular Force) Platoons were even setting out patrols - let alone whether they were effective or not. If they were out there he suspected they would be in the same predictable, safe places every night. You didn't want to set any kind of pattern or routine or the bad guys would be sure to figure it out and use it against you. This didn't sound like a good sign. Were these people disobeying orders or just bending the rules? If so, sooner or later someone would pay. Mental note time again. I wanted to dig into this subject of night security patrols before I myself started to accept the status quo with a shrug of the shoulders as many of the more seasoned advisers had. I had a lot to learn.

Ron helped me get a map of the district and some acetate to cover it with. I would use the thus waterproofed map - folded up in the leg pocket of my jungle fatigues - for my whole time here and would even save it as one of the few items I brought home. Before covering it, I needed to outline in red magic marker the various village boundaries and locations of key outposts and such. I also hi-lighted in orange the longitude and latitude numbers on each grid line. This would make it easy to quickly identify map coordinates when they needed to be called in when we needed help. The map was already laid out with easily identified terrain features like rivers, roads and hills. Each small Hamlet was identified by a clump of dots and a name such as "*La Ha* (4)". This was in turn a part of the Village of *La Ha*, whose boundary I had marked in magic marker. As we went through this map-updating process Ron gave me some comments about each village and referred occasionally to (of all things) a computer printout as his backup. We would have a chance to go over this computer stuff later, but right now it helped to have Ron characterize each village. This was a very helpful exercise - going through a briefing by the map even as I was updating it. This could then be reinforced on the helicopter ride with a bird's-eye view of the same areas we were discussing. I thought this would be an excellent way to get things put in perspective, at least from a geographic and demographic standpoint.

By the time we finished the map work and briefing it was almost time for the chopper to pick us up. A radio call alerted us to the fact that they were inbound and about 5 minutes out. As we ambled across the compound, weapons and radio in hand, we were greeted by *Dai Uy'* Hoa and *Trung Uy'* Cahn on the dirt drive, and almost immediately by Ken - ready to go in his Hawaiian shirt, cowboy hat, and shoulder-holstered revolver. My first reaction was that of alarm at being out with someone dressed so brightly, but I later learned that this didn't always matter. As we made our way out to the highway for pickup, Ron explained that soon we would have a real chopper pad built by the engineers but that right now we had to pop smoke to stop traffic on the busy road and allow the helicopter to land safely. I could hear the wop! wop! of the Huey's rotor blades beating the thick air long before I could see it, but soon it low-levelled its way down the highway and landed right in front of us. Hats in hand to avoid losing them to the rotor wash, we all piled on past the door gunners and crew chief and settled in on canvas seats behind the pilots. I looked back at the highway and was greeted by a scene of total chaos. Many of the civilians traveling QL1 on foot and bicycle had failed to heed the smoke grenade's warning of a landing helicopter, and all I could see was dust, conical straw hats, and even chicken feathers flying all around. Both pilots - neither of whom could have been more than 19 - smiled and then turned to the task of getting this bird off the ground, rising up to a low hover and then dipping the nose into the wind for maximum lift and increased forward speed. I had not had a ride on a Huey since training at Fort Benning and now remembered what a thrill it was!

We lifted to about 200 feet and started a long westerly turn to get a look at the mountainous part of our district, then swooped south at 90 knots past the engineers' hill location, and on to our southern border with the next district. Ron pointed to a hill just below the border that looked occupied - then pointed to its location on my new map. I had marked it as "LZ Snoopy", which was the artillery firebase that would become all-important to us in support of every operation and firefight we got involved in. It would be important to keep a good relationship with these guys. They were in place to provide artillery support to the units of the Americal Division operating in the western part of our area, but they were secondarily able to fire for us if we got in contact. In reality we would monopolize their time in the months to come, which upset the Division staff - but so what! A slow turn to the east along the district border started us toward the coast. From this vantage point I could see the beauty of the South China Sea and the beaches where it met the coast of our district. There seemed to be just enough wooded areas to make it interesting here and there. The whole district was webbed with what appeared to be meandering, sampan-navigable streams. This view of the sea past the patchwork of rice paddies sharply contrasted the bright greens and blues in a way I had never seen before. Quite a sight! But my enjoyment at the view was short-lived. All the time Ron, Ken ,or *Dai Uy'* Hoa were intermittently shouting to me over the din of the chopper, each pointing through the open doors at something they thought was of interest. *Dai Uy'* seemed to often repeat "very bad area" as he indicated one spot or another. This was comforting. I took notes - for sure.

About halfway between the highway and the coast line, my attention and that of the pilot was called to a small fortress-looking arrangement down below. Ron gestured downward as if to instruct the pilot to land. The Huey started to lose altitude and slowly corkscrewed down for a landing among some yellow smoke just outside this camp. We were welcomed on landing by a young Vietnamese Lieutenant who turned out to be the company commander of Regional Force company 119 who occupied this outpost and was charged with providing security for the four villages surrounding it. Right after we all hopped out and cleared the blades the chopper took off and circled at about 500 feet while we made a short inspection of the outpost. They didn't want or need to be sitting ducks on the ground out here. We could call them on the radio in a few minutes when we were ready to go.

This was apparently *Dai Uy'* Hoa's first visit to this outpost since 119 company occupied it. He was not happy with what he saw. I wasn't too thrilled either. The first thing that struck us, more significantly than the general disrepair all around, was the fact that someone had constructed a ten-foot high bamboo fence around the outside of the camp and at a distance of less than 50 meters out from the main defensive perimeter. A solid fence!! This monstrosity did nothing but take away the most important asset of a defensive perimeter - clear, long-range vision of the area in front of it. It would provide concealment for the enemy all the way to within 50 meters of the camp !! They could then breach the fence and be on top of the camp in almost the same motion, having been protected from any kind of observation or defensive fires. This could not have been more backward if the enemy himself had designed it for an easy target. If this RF company could not get this fence down by sundown, we would be back tomorrow with some of our engineer friends to take it down! I was sure that the little company commander got the message and would comply. *Dai Uy* was making his thoughts perfectly clear. Right then I knew we would be back soon to try to get this unit squared away. This visit was over.

With a nod from *Dai Uy* we headed out of the camp with an entourage of RF soldiers in front of us. One of the things that he had pointed out in his "instructions" to the RF leaders was that even as we met inside the outpost, the VC - sensing an opportunity to get the District Chief, all of his advisers, and a helicopter to boot - could have deployed a small group armed with Rocket Propelled Grenades (RPG) to blow the chopper as we took off loaded. If they were alert, they could have done this in broad daylight without their preparations and movement being detected because of that ridiculous fence !! The perimeter guards would never see them moving into position from the wooded areas south and east and about 200 meters away. The RF troops spread out to check out the area to a safe distance from the camp. Then, and only then, were we ready to call down the chopper to pick us up. I was very impressed with the way *Dai Uy* handled this. His example made the point unmistakably for the young lieutenant, but did it without embarrassing him in front of his troops - at least not too much. Hoa also showed his great caution where the lives of his advisers and helicopter pilots were at stake, a trait we appreciated - to say the least!

Up we went again to continue our push to the coast, now only about 3 klicks east. I was getting a good perspective of our area of operations now. I also had the sense that all of the others felt very little concern for ground fire now - except maybe the pilots. It was as if our Vietnamese friends knew there would not be much happening enemy-wise today. I realized that I was the only one who brought his M-16 assault weapon, but I didn't have a sidearm anyway, and none of us would ever go anywhere completely unarmed. Otherwise I had fit in by just wearing a broad-brimmed bush hat. No steel helmet for me. I hated the things, and only kept one in the bunker because it had been issued and now I was stuck with having to account for it. Before the year was over it would become a flower pot. So, with only the security of knowing the land - and of course the two door gunners with their M-60 machine guns mounted on either side of the doorless passenger compartment - we confidently continued the flight to the coast and then turned northward. Right at the turn, I saw *Dai Uy'* signal with an upward motion of his thumb, and the chopper started to climb. He smiled at me and yelled "bad area" again as he pointed to the entire coastline. Just north of our turn, Ron pointed out an hourglass-shaped island. I would learn later that this island was a major problem for us. At the point where our coastline intersected the River I had followed up to *Quang Ngai* City on the flight down from *Danang*, the district ended. Directly below us was a Vietnamese Navy "junk" base that we also wanted to pay a call on. As the Huey circled down for a landing my attention was drawn to a peninsula in the district north of us (*Son Tinh*), where it looked like an air strike was in progress. We had a ringside seat to this aerial ballet about 5 klicks away. Troops of the Americal Division had gotten into another pretty good fight that day in *Son My* village. The name of the village would become somewhat significant in a few months when its most famous hamlet - *My Lai* (4) - would hit the news media in a big way. The world was just beginning to learn what had happened here one year earlier. Also unknown to me at the time was the fact that a young Lt. Colonel had just taken over the battalion operating in that area with the mission to clean up its act. His name was H.Norman Schwarzkopf.

The Huey settled in at the Junk Base and this time the pilots felt secure enough to just sit on the ground. They knew that there were American advisers here permanently on this small compound. They didn't completely shut down the jet engine - just let it idle very low. We would only be about 5 minutes here. We actually were able to hand the American Navy Lt. a small sack of mail that someone had thrown on the chopper before it had left Province this morning. Our short visit gave them a chance to make that delivery. Another small bag of papers - letters from the 4 other Navy guys on the advisory team - was ready to be thrown back on the chopper. It wasn't that sophisticated, but somehow the mail got to and from spots like this from halfway around the world!

We got a quick tour - mostly for the "new guy" (me) - then spent a few minutes talking about that hourglass-shaped island just south of the base. I could look out at the 4 old "junk boats", each armed with a 30-cal. machine gun at either end. These 30-foot wooden junks represented the entire Vietnamese Navy contingent here where the Province's major river met the South China Sea. The navy , small as this group was, was charged with interdicting the movement of enemy supplies and personnel by the coast and river. They would stop and search boats by day and shoot at any they spotted by night. Innocent civilians were not to be out on the waters at night. If it moved - it was enemy. It was our hope that the navy could generally hold back infiltration into Tu Nghia from the district above us. That was, as Dai 'UY would put it, a very bad area. We made sure that there was nothing this group needed before we left. If they needed anything, we would go get it for them. Here were 5 Americans, stuck out here with a courageous little navy, trying to do a job. As usual, we respected the "other guy" as having it tougher. A few months later we found out just how tough it could get out here. Just before loading back on the chopper, Ron and I offered any help we could give with fire support coordination for the junk base. They apparently had not learned of the availability of the artillery support from LZ Snoopy. Ron told them he could help get immediate support if they needed it, and later we would help them form a more direct working relationship with the army artillery. Ron could say all this with the full confidence that even though the artillery was not "officially" there to support the navy, any Americans out in the boonies would do anything to support their friends – inter-service rivalries and rules would not get in the way! Those would only apply back in "the rear".

We pulled out of the junk base and rose to over 400 feet to get a view west to Quang Ngai city and the foothills further west. One prominent hill stood out about 5 klicks west of the city. It was known as LZ 411, or Hill 411. This name simply reflected the number shown on all maps at the summit of this small mountain, which on a map would reflect the elevation in meters. Hill 411 happened to be the battalion base camp of yet another unit of the Americal Division - this one having responsibility for the mountain areas in our district and farther west to the district of Nghia Hanh - an enemy stronghold for years. The Americal battalion was supposed to keep large NVA units from operating there or any further east. While we would often be in touch with the American unit and its leaders and would occasionally run a joint operation, Ron explained that we didn't plan on taking our local forces into the hills to any extent. Chasing large numbers of NVA around jungle mountains was not the mission of our RF's and PF's. That was for the big boys.

It was about time to circle back to the District Compound and home - just in time for lunch and siesta! And maybe a little cleanup? Actually, I wasn't that hungry. It was too hot, even after the relatively cool ride in the chopper, I thought I would probably skip lunch. We landed in the highway outside the District compound with the same result - people and things scattered in the blowing dust and grit - then back to normal as if nothing had happened as we walked back inside the gates. It had been a productive morning as far as I was concerned. I now had a good physical picture of the district - at least from a few hundred feet up. I thought that *Dai 'Uy* felt he had learned enough during the short stopovers we made to make the time worthwhile. Now he let us know that he wanted to talk. He invited us to have lunch on the veranda of his house - a rare treat, I was told. So, hungry or not, I would not think of turning down an invitation. That would have been an insult, and also I wanted to take as much advantage of these opportunities to learn as possible. After all, I would be taking over the team in a couple of months, and I wanted to have a head-start on knowledge as well as the beginnings of a good relationship with my new counterparts.

Lunch on the District Chief was quite an experience. Actually it was the first time for me to sit down for a meal - Vietnamese style. This wasn't to be a family meal. It was a business lunch just like any you would have in the U.S., complete with small talk, rapport-building, and the discussion of business at hand. We were served by young, junior soldiers who scurried about to make sure everyone was satisfied with the food and beer. We had offered to bring some cold beer over, but *Dai 'Uy* had cold American beer of his own to serve us. The meal consisted mainly of a noodle soup with beef broth and chicken parts cooked in. I learned it was called *"Pho'"*, and was the staple food of all Vietnamese. It was great! A side order of rice was always available, and it could be eaten with chopsticks because it was stuck together - plus you forgot about manners and kind of sucked it in while guiding it with the chopsticks. The *pho'* was served with a china spoon for the broth, but chopsticks were used for the meat, noodle and vegetable ingredients. Most of the people at the table added a generous quantity of *nuoc mam* just for added flavoring. I tried a little of the fish water and it didn't seem too bad - it tasted a lot better than it smelled! As we ate, there was discussion about what to do about the 119 Company outpost and its ridiculous fence. *Dai 'Uy* was visibly angry just talking about it, probably a little because of embarrassment in front of his advisers. We decided then to go back in 3 or 4 days to check it out. This would give the company some time to get the fence down and the perimeter shored up while still allowing them to provide regular security patrols in their area of operations. What we planned to do was to run a major sweep operation in the outer edges of their territory and down to the district's southern border. This operation would include 119 Company and 3 PF Platoons assigned to the villages directly. After the sweep we would circle back to the outpost and then "casually" inspect. All of this would allow the Company Commander to make corrections and then show them off to the District Chief and to us, thus allowing him to save face. During our visit today he had lost face, and now he could gain it back. This was a lesson to me. I was excited about going out on my first major operation in a few days! I would be able to observe while Ron would be the main tactical adviser for *Dai 'Uy* Hoa.

As lunch was now over it became obvious that Hoa had work to do and then would join his family for siesta. He shook hands and thanked each of us with a broad smile. When he got to me he called me by name for the first time and asked what I thought about 119 Company. Concerned that I would say the wrong thing if I was too careful with my answer, I blurted out the truth - that I thought this was a very good way for the Company Commander to learn and that I was happy to help in any way I could. It must have been the right thing to say, or Hoa knew I was just speaking my mind truthfully and appreciated that. With a huge smile he shook my hand again and thanked me, saying that he very much needed my help. I felt pretty good about the beginnings of a relationship that would flourish.

CHAPTER FIVE

It was now early May, 3 or 4 days after my joining the team at Tu Nghia District. This morning I would have the chance to go out on a company-sized sweep operation - after a month in-country, this would be my first combat operation ! This first time I would observe only. Ron would be the senior military adviser on this day-long mission. Ron had made old "Crusty" go on this operation also, along with Tu, one of our interpreters. Crusty started out the morning bitching that he had to carry the radio - actually both Ron and I would share in the load - and our turns would come when it was hotter and livelier. Right now, at 0600, it was pretty cool as we started out - had to be under 90, but it would get much hotter.

The troops included 3 Popular Force (PF) Platoons who would be joined by most of 119 Regional Force company as we neared their outpost late in the morning. Captain Hoa was in charge, directing the young Platoon Leaders and keeping an eye on their actions. Our plan today was to sweep south to 119's outpost area, then bear southeast toward the district border, hoping to clean out a rumored force of platoon-sized strength consisting mostly of North Vietnamese Army regulars that was supposed to be playing both sides of the border with Mo Duc District. When and if we made contact, our "Ruff/Puff's" were to engage and destroy the enemy using fire support from their trusted advisers. With any luck, this could be my first firefight !! I wondered how I would react under fire. Sure, all the training would pay off, but would I be able to emotionally react the right way - would I be able to make the right decisions fast enough even as an observer - let alone later when I would be in charge ?

*   *   *   *   *   *

Careful observation of my fellow Americans helped me to prepare my gear. Since this was just a "day-trip" we didn't need much - a webbed pistol belt with shoulder harness could hold two canteen pouches, two first aid bandages, several ammo magazines in pouches, and a couple of colored smoke grenades each. We wore standard jungle fatigues and jungle boots, no sox or underwear, *yes* and a broad-brimmed bush hat. Most field troops in Vietnam didn't wear sox or underwear because of the moisture - humidity, rice paddies, streams to cross, and torrential rains. The jungle fatigues and boots would dry out fairly well, but sox or underwear would not. Too much moisture in certain spots would cause any number of skin ailments. But, as hard as we tried to keep dry and clean, I still have jungle rot 40 years later. On this operation, Crusty and I carried our M-16 rifles, while Ron carried an M-79 Grenade Launcher. I learned why he preferred that weapon and later took up that habit myself.

The PF soldiers were dressed in fatigues and steel helmets and most were armed with M-16 rifles. They also consistently liked to load their belts down with baseball type fragmentation grenades - so many of them that it was a little scary. While the Americans carried no food, all of the PF's had a small backpack with their own supplies of uncooked rice, *nuoc mam*, some dried fish, squid or other non-descript meat (maybe dried rat), and most had an individual cooking pot and bowl. Even though we were only out for a day, these guys were taking no chances of being hungry. We knew that we would get to eat with the troop commanders whose food would be provided by village or hamlet officials wherever we were in the district. This would include rations of American beer and soda - and it was usually almost cold when they served it!

As we moved out of the District compound, across the highway and off into the rice paddies, I couldn't help but be alarmed at the lack of any semblance of a tactical formation and at the racket made by these 80 newly-trained Vietnamese soldiers bunched up in single file, with their 3 American advisers tagging along, off to fight the war, again! We would wander this way for about two kilometers (kliks), over rice paddy dikes and trails, passing near two or three small and friendly villes, until we came to a river that needed crossing - its narrow point being only about 50 meters wide. The crossing was handled easily - we only waded up to our armpits in the slow stream - but I noticed as we emerged on the other side that the troops spread out, correctly on a line - a much more tactically sound formation. In spite of keeping too close to each other, they looked pretty good from a security standpoint, although sloshing through the wet, open rice paddies still left us very exposed. It was obvious that this was known bad territory and the transformation from slack to alert was almost magical. One more klick and we would be joined by 80 more troops from 119 company who would come from their outpost (the one with the ridiculous fence around it) to continue the sweep south with us. The enemy platoon had been reported in a wooded area just this side of our border, about two more klicks to the southeast. I wondered why they would still be there if they were there yesterday or the day before. Weren't these the stealthy guerillas that would terrorize an area and run away, avoiding contact in the daytime? Or were they determined North Vietnamese Army regulars who would depend on local hamlets for some of their supply while being guided by local Viet Cong guerillas, but would stand and fight a pitched battle day or night? Was it really a platoon (about 30 people) or had someone misjudged the size of the element? We wouldn't know until it was too late to be guessing!

At the prescribed rendezvous location we stopped for a break and to wait for the RF company to join us. The break was most welcome. I was hot and tired and soaked to the skin. Ron suggested I take a salt tablet with lots of water, so I did. I knew I was in shape and the going had not been rough or fast, but I was close to being worn out by the heat and humidity.

The RF company was late, so we got a long rest. Finally they arrived in a radio-coordinated approach. *Dai Uy* Hoa led this operation like a pro, leaving very little to chance. The last thing we needed was for his troops to get mixed up and start fighting each other. Stranger things had happened in Vietnam. After a quick chewing out for the 119 company commander for tardiness, administered by the *Dai Uy,* the troops saddled up to move out toward the border. The formation was now a sort of wedge shape as the terrain turned from rice paddy to light woods. The adviser team moved with *Dai Uy* Hoa's command group in the center of the formation - probably 50 meters or more behind the point element. Within the command group we tried to maintain enough spacing to avoid multiple casualties with a single incoming mortar round, but we had to stay close enough to maintain good voice communications with each other. *Dai Uy* had a radio for communicating with his unit leaders, while the advisers' radio was used to contact the outside world - our district team back at the compound, the province network, and the all-important fire support elements that we depended on. So, all communications with our Vietnamese counterparts was by direct voice and through interpreters. Comparing this operation and formation to the school solution (as we used to call it at Fort Benning) I was more pleased than I had been when we first moved out in the morning. It was obvious that some contact with the enemy was expected and we seemed to be doing most things right in that situation.

Following our movement on my folded map, I noticed that we were now crossing through one of those areas that *Dai Uy* Hoa had pointed out to me from the helicopter a few days ago as he had frowned, shaken his head, and said "bad area". Now suddenly Hoa, seeing that I was studying my map as we moved slowly on foot, stepped over next to me and pointed to where we were on my map as if to help me along with it - then once again frowned and said "bad area". Normally I would have laughed at the coincidence, but I couldn't. He had made his point! I took a sip of water. For some reason my mouth had become very dry.

Waiting for something to happen is as nerve-wracking as the real thing - perhaps even more so in its own way. We continued to work our way across the wooded area as it gradually got thicker. This was not jungle by any means, and the underbrush was not that thick, but more and more concealment for the hunted and the hunter was developing as we moved deeper into it. Because of the disposition of the wedge formation, we ran little risk of a classical ambush, but we could expect harrassing sniper fire and other delaying tactics like booby traps and mines. The other danger was to stumble on a dug-in enemy force at close range without knowing it. But the purpose of this whole exercise was to find the enemy and engage them. This was not just a clearing operation to chase the enemy from inhabited areas - we were to find "Charlie" and fight.

We seemed to be stopping for a break about 1100, so Ron took the time to remind me what we had available for support today. The artillery battery on LZ Snoopy had two of their guns pointed in our direction and ready. A call to Province would divert to us a FAC (Forward Air Controller) in his prop-driven spotter plane to circle over the location of our firefight. From up there, the FAC could bring in Marine or Air Force jet fighter-bombers for air strikes. Ron indicated that as usual we would not be able to get any helicopter gunships because the Americal Division was hogging them for some operation in the mountains. Other support such as Med-Evac and resupply choppers were always available through the Province network. If things were too busy all these calls could be relayed through the District team back at the compound. They always kept a close watch by radio when we were out in the bush. Of all the support available, the artillery guns were the most used and the fastest. We could get heavy indirect fire in less than a minute in a pinch. And the artillery guys at Snoopy were always willing to give it all they had. Our relationship with them was good, our team had credibility, and they loved to fire. After all, that's what they were up there for.

Tu, our interpreter, came over to Ron and me to tell us that we had not stopped for a break. It seems that the point element had come on a small clearing in the woods and were looking 75 meters across it to the next tree line. They were convinced that the far edge of the tree line was a perfect place for the enemy to be dug in and waiting for us. Right now they were just observing but nobody wanted to make a move. These troops were very cautious! *Dai Uy* started to yell over his radio. From my 2 weeks in language school I could tell he was urging the point to move up. At almost 100 meters behind, the command group could just barely see the clearing's edge. I could then see about 10 PF's walking slowly forward, spread widely across the clearing. As this movement started, the command group started to move toward the front line for a look while the right and left trailing edges of the wedge formed flank protection for us..... And then all hell broke loose!! *ARTillery prep?*

It sounded like the finale of a fireworks show! A heavy long burst of small arms fire broke out all at once in front of us. I could instantly tell that half of the fire was coming in our direction, and as I hit the ground with the rest of the command group I could glance toward the clearing to see most of the PF's that had ventured reluctantly into the open were going down, too. 3 or 4 of them looked like they went down involuntarily. At that range they were probably dead before they hit the ground. A couple of the others were scrambling back to the "friendly" side of the clearing - hell bent for cover and relative safety. All in all, those first few seconds stick in my mind's eye like a snapshot picture of total chaos!

In a few seconds the firing settled down to steady and heavy. For the first time I could distinguish the most distinctive sound in the world - the sound of the enemy's AK-47 assault rifle's bullet as it cracks over your head. There was no other sound like that. We could also detect the different sound of at least two enemy machine guns involved, so this force had to be a re-enforced platoon at minimum. They were also obviously NVA regulars. As I caught my breath for once, I observed Ron had the radio handset in one ear and was listening to *Dai Uy* Hoa with the other. He was reporting to the district bunker and then was ready to call in artillery support. It happened that Ron had relieved old Crusty of the radio for a turn just before everything hit the fan. In a brief moment he explained *f60* what I had already figured out - that the PF's would stay on this *LATE* side of the clearing while he pounded the other side - less than 100 meters away from our front line - with all the artillery we could get. The district had relayed an additional request for an Air Force FAC who could direct air strikes from his spotter plane. The FAC was on his way and about 15 minutes out.

This would be the way over 100 of our PF's would handle this one - stand fast and in contact with a significant force of 30 or so well-armed communist regulars, keeping them "pinned down" while the U.S. Army and Air Force tried to destroy them with technology and firepower. I hoped that at some point our troops would move forward to finish the job that the Infantry is supposed to do.

While Ron was finalizing his plan for a fire mission for the artillery, we were startled by a couple of incoming mortar rounds just behind our front and very close to the command group. At first most thought it had been errant artillery rounds from "Snoopy", but we could then hear the thump of a mortar tube somewhere out front. It was unmistakably an 82 mm mortar, which could mean that we had grabbed a tiger by the tail!! We may have locked horns with a full company-sized NVA unit, which would mean about 150 troops! This would mean they had as many people as we did and were better armed - and probably better disciplined. The only thing they lacked was the Air Force! Get that FAC in here in a hurry!

Just at the right time, Ron got the fire mission to LZ Snoopy and within half a minute they were pouring high explosives all over where we thought the bad guys were dug in. This silenced the mortar at least and significantly slowed down the small arms and machine gun fire. Meanwhile I noticed that the NVA weren't the only ones who had their heads down. Our own PF's were hugging the ground, afraid of our friendly artillery. I hoped they would be ready if the enemy decided to counterattack! Instead, the exchange of small arms fire deteriorated rapidly. Could it be that the enemy had broken contact and successfully gotten away? Ron seemed to think they had only pulled back enough to regroup - possibly for a stronger counterattack. During the lull, would our PF's pursue on foot or would we have to make do with other ways to find them. I got my answer very quickly. While Ron continued on the radio, calling off the artillery and trading shouts with the district team, I noticed that there was a flurry of activity on our front lines. I assumed the PF's were busily reorganizing their gear, reloading cartridge magazines, and maybe even rebalancing the ammunition distribution. Well, I was wrong. They were cooking!!

NO!

The excitement of the firefight had put time out of our minds. It was high noon, and, coincidentally, both sides had broken contact and were relaxing. They would cook some rice, eat it with some dried meat and *nuoc mam,* and then would nap until 2:30. Sensing my concern, Ron came over to update me. It seemed that the Air Force FAC had been diverted for now. So, with both sides of the *No!* ground troops taking a break, no spotter plane, and no other way to find out exactly how far the enemy had retreated, we had to follow the lead of our Vietnamese friends. Just as an aside, it was obvious that the FAC probably decided that he could do us no good during the noon-to-2:30 "siesta", so he went home. He presumably knew the drill, having worked in support of our rag-tag teams and their troops for some time. Even the artillery people knew that the war would stop at 12 and laughed about it. This was certainly a strange war. I had heard about this before, but didn't believe it until I experienced it first-hand. *BS!!!*

While some of the Vietnamese soldiers busied themselves with cooking chores, a small detail assisted the medic in sorting out the casualties. We had four dead and seven or eight severely wounded - all this in less than 30 minutes of fighting. We had no idea if we had scored any casualties against the enemy. A Medivac helicopter was already on its way. In a few minutes "Dustoff 16" came in to land near the yellow smoke grenade that Ron had thrown well behind our position when the Medivac pilot had called in for guidance. These U.S. aviators and their on-board medics would go almost anywhere to save a life. All of us, including the Vietnamese soldiers, knew that this kind of quick access to great medical attention - with surgical hospitals only a 10-minute flight away - might save one of us from certain death at any time. This time the seven wounded we loaded on the chopper with the big red crosses all over it would survive. It was too late for the other four. Their bodies would be carried by their comrades to their homes nearby. The Vietnamese believed that if they were not buried at the very place of their birth that their souls would wander for eternity. Soon we would face the additional administrative task of following up on the wounded at U.S. field hospitals as well. We couldn't let them get misplaced. At this point I reflected briefly on my first experience this close to death. I felt for these young Vietnamese boys who in a split second had lost all their tomorrows, but I wasn't as shocked at the reality of instant death as I had always thought I would be.

*   *   *   *   *

We were treated to a fine lunch. There weren't any nearby villages, but out of nowhere came a few civilians with hot *Pho*, the staple noodle and meat soup for the District Chief and his command group, which included Ron, Crusty, Tu and me. It suddenly occurred to me that there was little communication with Hoa during lunch. Of course Crusty and his dour face sat up against a bush by himself. Ron and I were in the circle of the command group, but Hoa did not say much to us, so I decided to chat with him a little. This suddenly opened up a great deal of chatter about what had happened and what would happen next. Hoa, to my surprise, seemed resigned to the proposition that the enemy would not want to engage us heavily as the afternoon wore on. He sensed that they had not yet made a complete retreat, but that we would end the day in frustration. This sounded like it might be a self-fulfilling prophecy to me, but since I was the new guy I'd have to wait and see. We needed to be ready for any eventuality at 2:30, the magic ending of the siesta. I hoped that we would move forward in a more aggressive search with the FAC plane overhead. I was in for a letdown.

Things began to stir about 2:15. I just couldn't believe that a culture that seemed rather laid back about some things was so precise about the timing of its rest period. Most intriguing, of course, was that both sides played off the situation to their advantage. While I pondered this scene, I heard the increasing noise of an airplane coming closer at fairly low altitude. It actually sounded more like a bumblebee or one of those model airplanes with its high-pitched buzz. As the plane reached overhead of us I noticed that Ron was talking to him on the radio. This was the Air Force FAC we had expected earlier. He had waited out the siesta and hoped there was now something for him to do here. His call sign was JAKE 40 (four-zero) and he flew alone in his O-2 Skymaster aircraft. The O-2 had two engines, but they were arranged differently than on most prop planes. There was one at the front of the fuselage and one in a direct line at the tail end of the fuselage. The tail itself was raised up above this rear engine, which actually pushed the aircraft while the front engine "pulled". Apparently this gave extra speed and maneuverability, which, judging by some of the antics I saw that afternoon, were essential to the effectiveness, not to mention the longevity, of the JAKE FACS. "Push me—pull me"

The FAC's job was to find and mark the targets for the jet fighters that he would then closely direct. The FAC would occasionally direct artillery also, so they were plugged into the artillery supporting each area they went into. The airstrike would be delivered by a set of 2, 3or4 Air Force or Marine jets loaded with various combinations of bombs, machine guns, and Napalm - the most frightening, and therefore most effective, weapon at our disposal. Napalm strikes consisted of the dropping of large drums of a jellied gas substance that, on contact with the ground, would release a huge, spreading fireball which not only dispersed the flaming jelly over a large area, burning anyone in the open, but also deprived its coverage area of its oxygen supply for long enough to suffocate anyone hiding from the fire in a hole or a bunker. The heat generated by one of these Napalm strikes was intense enough to be felt at more than 100 meters, and that was much closer than you wanted to be when the stuff came in. One other rule of thumb - air strikes were preferably brought in across, ➔ *yEs* parallel to, your front and not over your head in either direction. This was to avoid bombing your own people in case of a long or short drop. While ground leaders would occasionally bring in a bomb run perpendicular to their front for some good reason, I don't think anyone would risk making that exception with Napalm. It was too dangerous - and too final. All in all, the power of an air strike was awesome! I have often reflected on how thankful I was to have this firepower on our side. In other wars the troops had the threat of an enemy air power, but not in Vietnam. We were very lucky!

So the FAC had arrived on station and started searching the area working from our "lines" to the southeast. He started with lazy circles, sort of like a sea-bird searching for fish near the ocean's surface. In a few minutes he added a steep, powerless dive to his repertoire, looking more like a pelican diving in for the kill every minute. What a show! The last trick was for the FAC to fly as slowly as he could and low enough to entice even the most disciplined of enemy troops to take a pot-shot at him. And it always worked! With a great deal of patience and guts, JAKE 40 finally got someone to try to shoot him out of the sky. That was all he needed! He pulled up and was now waiting a couple of minutes for the first set of "fast-movers", the jet fighters, to get on station with him. I thought it was time for us to sit back and relax and watch the fireworks. Wrong again.

Just as the FAC pulled up out of his last dive which successfully drew small arms fire, the whole world exploded again in front of us. This time the incoming mortars got too close for comfort! We had no cover to speak of except a small pile of rocks where the command group gained partial concealment and cover. Our front line was being pounded unmercifully by small arms, machine gun, and hand-held rocket fire. Our PF's gallantly tried to return a volume of fire, but were just outgunned. The North Vietnamese had re-grouped and counter-attacked! For some reason - just as it started - I glanced at the watch dangling from a button-hole in my fatigue shirt. It was exactly 2:30 PM (1430 hours) on this side of the world. Siesta was definitely over! CRAZY!

I noticed Ron was tied up on the radio and was talking to the FAC overhead. I wished I could do something like call in artillery or something, but without a second radio and with planes flying around it was impossible. Besides, the FAC could offer great support with the view he had and with the ordnance that the now-arriving jets would have on board. I just wished they would get started. We needed to pour it on to stop any possible advance of the NVA company on our forward positions. Ron had mentioned in the middle of all this that if the NVA moved toward our line, the PF's might drop everything and run - toward us! Not a comforting thought! Visions of getting overrun on my first operation - when we had started out being on the offensive - weren't too appealing.

Fortunately the air strike was about to begin. This would not only repel the attack, but hopefully catch them out in the open long enough to do some real damage. JAKE 40 circled once more at about 500 feet, then started a steep dive and fired a smoke rocket into the ground before pulling up out of his dive. The white smoke raised by the white phosphorous tip of the rocket on impact would give a reference point for the jets. JAKE would then tell them what he wanted done, which direction to make their bombing runs in, and which direction to pull out of their runs. One at a time the jet would make their runs while the FAC gave them feedback and possible corrections. I was about to witness close-up the use of millions of U.S. tax dollars being put to good use to destroy enemy troops in the open - a show repeated scores of times every day throughout South Vietnam.

The first F-4 Phantom jet with its camouflage paint began its run at about 200 feet up and, in a fairly gradual descent, dropped four 250-pound bombs on the enemy position. The scream of his engine caught up with the close-up sight of him just as he pulled into a steep power climb. He wanted to be as far away as possible when 1000 pounds of bombs exploded. He just made it. In a burst of fire, smoke, and thunder all the bombs exploded right in front of us. Actually we were about 100 meters away and the front line had somehow gradually moved closer to us. Or maybe we had naturally crept up close out of instinct to get closer to what was happening. If the fighters were hitting their target, the bad guys were less than a football field away through the sparsely wooded area. I hoped they weren't enjoying the show as much as we were. It just occurred to me that I still had not seen the enemy we were engaged with in quite a nasty little fire-fight. Surely we would see them when we moved forward to sweep the target area.

After two bomb runs by each of the three fast-movers, we were warned by JAKE 40 to get our heads down - the Napalm was next. The flight leader barreled his F-4 across our front line at what must have been 500 miles an hour. As he approached the target area, I glimpsed what looked like a 55-gallon drum ,but pointed on each end, hurtling end-over-end toward the ground. The jet screamed skyward out of reach of the impending holocaust. Almost immediately I saw the woods in front of us erupt in a 150-yard long fireball whose flames licked at the air overhead about 100 feet high. The pilot had used what was called a low drag approach which maximized the length of coverage of the fire. I could feel the heat and smell the gasoline even at this distance. I could only imagine what was happening to the enemy troops out there. In spite of all the other noise of the battlefield one could imagine hearing screams of anguish from anyone caught in this rain of fire from above. Then, just as the heavy black smoke had nearly cleared our view, the next fighter came along to add insult to injury with yet another canister of the deadly Napalm, followed almost immediately by the third and last pilot with his canister. This one dragged his a little closer to our own troops. The heat was too much and we all hugged the ground, hoping it would subside quickly. It did, bringing an eerie silence to the scene. The jet fighters were well on their way back to base at Chu Lai. They had done a good job and would wait for word of any casualties they had caused. In reality, they had succeeded in getting the enemy off our backs and that was enough for us. We would be sure to try to get word back to the jet flight leader through JAKE 40 as soon as we could assess the results.

The quiet continued, punctuated only by the return of birds chirping - now a comforting sound as if normalcy had returned to what was hell just minutes ago. It was a feeling of serenity and relief and called for a smoke break. But then, as these emotions waned, I realized that I was forgetting what we had come here for. We should not be satisfied with just breaking contact and letting the NVA unit get out of our district. We needed to get after them and hopefully apply the finishing touches - to render them an ineffective unit. That's why the infantry fights battles.

On our side the casualty count had increased slightly - 1 more dead and 4 slightly wounded. A Medivac chopper would not be needed this time. The PF medic used the training our medics had provided to tend to the wounds while others took care of the dead soldier, preparing him for return to his family right here in the district. These citizen soldiers were never far from home.

I asked Ron when we would pursue. He didn't know but would ask *Dai Uy* Hoa as soon as he got off the radio. Hoa spent a long time on that radio yelling at his subordinate leaders who were now spread out in a long line in front of us. Once again he was urging them forward - a task not unlike pushing on a string. Finally, in frustration, Hoa swaggered forward and began to lead his men across the scorched earth. We didn't find much. A few seared body parts - enough to claim maybe 10 kills - but lots of blood spores and drag trails that indicated the enemy had recovered most of their dead and wounded. We couldn't find much evidence of how well they had been dug in. The bombs had bulldozed the area pretty well and there were pieces of trees everywhere. One of the most bizarre sights was that of a freshly roasted pig still tethered to a tree. Apparently the pig had been brought along alive on a leash - perhaps to be the main course in a celebration feast that would not be enjoyed by the communists tonight. The Napalm roast pig would instead be retrieved by our Vietnamese - not theirs. My instant reaction was to hope that I wasn't invited to join them for dinner.

*   *   *   *   *   *

It was time to go back to the district compound. The operation was over and we didn't have a lot to show for it, but hopefully we had made one company of North Vietnamese regulars think twice about boldly setting up shop in our district. We had brought the fight to them, pounded them with Uncle Sam's firepower, driven them across the border into *Mo Duc* District, and of course ruined their planned bar-b-que. In fact, with our Napalm attack, we might have made the thought of bar-b-que pretty sickening to them too. The ones who survived must have witnessed the incineration of close friends and comrades in arms - a sight they would always be haunted by. These were human beings, too.

Our movement back to the compound had to be carefully tactical. Troops returning from an operation and sharing the euphoria of combat survival were always the most vulnerable to an ambush. The returning column grew more rowdy as we got closer - everyone smoking-and-joking about the days events. It's a normal human reaction to the dangers of combat after its over. It's all part of the process of recovering from sheer terror - jabbering and making light of everything that happened. It helps to erase the other normal reaction, which is to ponder the what-if's. "What if I had been standing where the other guy was when he was hit.".......and, of course, the survivor's guilt - "why did I survive when others didn't"

Back in the compound Hoa joined us for a beer while we briefed the rest of our team on the operation. He left shortly to see his family, but not without thanking us for the support. He didn't have to. We knew how important it was to him, but he said it anyway. Just as he turned to leave he winked slightly to Ron and me and said "good operation". Even though we had taken as many casualties as the bad guys, I think Hoa felt we had done more than just survive. We had pushed a major threat out of that part of the district for now - and his troops had not panicked and retreated as they must have done in the past. He was satisfied with small improvement.

*   *   *   *   *   *

Later that night Ron and I shared another beer with Ken in the District Senior Advisor's hootch. It was then that I realized how worried Ron had been at one point in the firefight. When we got hit hard just after siesta, he said, there was a critical point where he expected to see the whole thing fall apart in a mass retreat followed by onrushing communist troops - whose goals included the capture of an American adviser or two. What an impact that would have had in the district! Ken and Ron probably noticed that I suddenly became silent - and stayed that way until it was time to turn in. Now my inner thoughts were providing the private reaction to what had happened and what could have happened that day. I probably dwelled too much on it then, but tomorrow would be another day - and I wasn't a rookie anymore! I had been shot at and missed. I had watched violent death at close range - and escaped it. What a feeling!

.

CHAPTER SIX

The operation we had just completed against the North Vietnamese company had signaled the beginning of what would be known as the May Offensive of 1969. During the month we had several attacks on the many small bridges that dotted our district and provided land communications and travel for farmers to the markets in Quang Ngai City. These vital links of the local civilian economy had long been favorite targets of the local Viet Cong and now the North Vietnamese had virtually taken the local guerillas' place. Operating in small units, these NVA regulars would hit 3 or 4 bridges a night while coordinating harassment of our District headquarters with mortar attacks and probes of our perimeter. Night observation and ambush patrols by both Popular and Regional Force units were increased at this time, but we were never sure if they were really out there. The solution to our doubt was to step up the participation by American advisers on night operations with the Regional Force companies. At least two advisers would go out at dusk with 50 or so RF soldiers and the officer leading them, ready to provide fire support when necessary. This would be pretty risky business because of the poor noise discipline of the Vietnamese troops. For some reason they would always tend to make as much noise as possible. Perhaps this was their way of avoiding contact with the enemy. Maybe if they made a lot of noise the enemy would run away. Wouldn't that accomplish just as much as getting in a firefight with them in the middle of the night? Probably not, but if a unit lacked the confidence in its ability to defeat the enemy, why would they try to force a contact. Perhaps the secret to making them more effective was to increase their confidence level. Our job was to figure out how to do this without causing anyone to lose face.

The night "operations" we went on consisted of little more than moving to a relatively tame position just at nightfall and setting up a night defensive position until first light in the morning. What we probably were accomplishing was to add an element of the unknown to the concerns of any would-be infiltrating enemy units. They would know there were medium-sized government units out in the field, adding another hazard to their movement. That was about as far as it went. On the couple of operations that I went on - again as an observer of the advisory tactics of my experienced team leader Ron - I found that noise and light discipline were sorely lacking. One night I watched one of the Popular Force troops we were with kill a chicken with a lit flashlight at 4 in the morning. (Yes, I was awake then, too.) On second thought, maybe the idea was to make your position known as a kind of comforting thing to the villagers. Wrong again. I would later see how the villagers reacted when they thought a fight might break out in their midst. (Americans haven't experienced that in a hundred years - in Vietnam it had gone on for a thousand years!) So, the static night positions we set up away from the normal outposts and compounds never really made any contact with the bad guys, but perhaps the show of force helped to discourage some enemy actions. It sure kept the population on edge and provided an interesting experience for me. It was really eerie to be out in the open in the middle of a perimeter of 50 or so Popular Forces just waiting for something to happen .Every time I heard a dog bark in a nearby quiet hamlet I imagined movement by the enemy. The smells and sounds became very important to me, as did time. I wanted to know how much time was left until the sun came up! Strangely enough, I still wake up often in the night and just have to know what time it is. If it's close to dawn, I'll sometimes stay awake just to watch it get light. Mornings are special to me. They bring with them a sense of security - peace.

*   *   *   *   *   *   *

As a result of the May Offensive, we concluded that nothing had been won and nothing lost. The whole thing was a stalemate. The way we drew this conclusion was the rating system that all District and Mobile Advisory Teams had to use country-wide - the dreaded computer reports. This system, probably a throwback to the MacNamara days of "paralysis by analysis" required the advisers to fill in the blanks on two huge computer printouts that would be delivered by helicopter on the first of every month. The reports were called the "Hamlet Evaluation Summary" (H.E.S.) and the "Territorial Forces Evaluation Summary" (T.F.E.S.). The H.E.S. required A-F ratings for each of about a dozen questions about the security of each Hamlet in the District. Questions like: "Do civilians readily move their produce to the district town for sale without fear of attack..... or "Do District officials safely visit the Hamlet day or night?" The answer choices would range from something like "always" to "never". One question was particularly ominous: "does the Hamlet Chief sleep in the hamlet every night?" On the T.F.E.S. report each PF platoon and each RF company was rated on their ability, personnel strength, armament, discipline, and cooperation with the advisory effort. The report also wanted to know if the unit had been bloodied lately (in a firefight) and if they stood and fought or ran away.(more encouragement!) So, once a month the District Chief joined us in completing these two reports. The Officers would gather in Ken's hooch for a few beers and discussion about how to fill in the blanks on the report. After it was completed, Ken would break out a bottle of room-temperature cheap Champagne to toast progress - progress sometimes being only the completion of the drudgery of the reports. We guessed that the reports would be used to paint a picture of progress in the hinterlands - like " x percent of all Hamlets are declared "pacified(peaceful)" etc. Somewhere in the "Pentagon East" - MACV (Military Assistance Command,Vietnam) headquarters in Saigon, some staff officer would be massaging the numbers before briefing the commanding general and forwarding the good news to Washington. The goal was to show that the "Vietnamization" program was working and that we were making progress in turning over the war to the South

Vietnamese. From what I could see, the South Vietnamese were *already* running the war here in the districts - and doing as well as they could. What occurred to me was that in none of these reports did anyone ask how the advisers were doing or - more importantly - what resources they were painfully doing without! We could have given Saigon an earful if they really wanted to know ! They didn't.

*   *   *   *   *

One thing that came out of our May "reports" meeting was the fact that in the first week of June, 3 more PF platoons would be trading in their old weapons for brand new M-16 rifles sent from the U.S. We needed to set up a training program as soon as possible to help these troops get used to the far superior M-16. Ron asked me to take on this particular task. The plan was to first help them "zero" their weapons to correct for mechanical sight variations, then to give them experience in automatic fire techniques and ammo discipline, and then to cover the all-important cleaning instructions. We had to convince these soldiers that the M-16 could be their best friend as long as they kept it clean. If they didn't, it might jam and leave them basically unarmed at just the wrong time.

One of the things that gave my training task a boost was the arrival of an important replacement on the MAT team. A new Sergeant First Class I'll call Lew arrived just in time. We could then let Old Crusty go back to the rear to bother someone else until his time to leave Vietnam came. He had proven useless to our team in my estimation. Sergeant Lew, I quickly found out, had just arrived for his third tour in Vietnam. He had been on a District advisory team the last time and we learned that he spoke fluent Vietnamese! Lew was a light-weapons infantry specialist and could take on the M-16 training right away. I'd work with him but he could be the chief instructor and teach the class in Vietnamese. This would be a definite plus and would solidify relationships in the district. When I talked it over with Sergeant Lew he had an even better idea. What if he worked with one of the district's young Vietnamese officers and the two of them taught the class together? This would go much further toward establishing the Vietnamese officers' leadership structure. I agreed. Already I had a great deal of respect for the experience of this senior sergeant and would use his savvy for the good of the team and the district. Any 2nd Lieutenant worth his salt learned to utilize the backbone of the Army - the non-commissioned officer corps - without relinquishing total control. I already knew I would be able to handle this when I took over the team.

The "classroom" we would use for M-16 training would be in a dry area about 500 meters across the highway from the district headquarters. I talked the engineers into bulldozing a 50 meter berm, or sand dune, that would serve as the backdrop for a firing range. Yes, right here in the middle of a war zone we were setting up a firing range with safety rules,etc. We ran the firing range just about like you would run one at Ft. Benning or any stateside training post. There was one major difference. Here we were playing for keeps. Right after qualifying with his M-16 on our makeshift firing range, our local force soldiers would be expected to be battle ready - in fact they would prove it the next day on a real combat operation. No blank ammunition here! Oh, and by the way, just to add a little realism to the situation, one day out on the range we took a few incoming mortar rounds. "Charlie" Cong just wanted us to know that he knew what we were up to. About that time I guessed that Vietnam would be one of those "never a dull moment" places for our little team of Americans.

*　　　*　　　*　　　*　　　*　　　*

Our team was growing, too. In mid-June we were thankful to welcome two more members to our MAT team. One was our new medic - we called him "Doc" from the start - and a heavy weapons sergeant I'll call Sergeant El for now. Both happened to be black

Staff Sergeants on their first tours in Vietnam. It would become amazing to watch how smoothly they worked their respective ways into the swing of things, including the relationship with our Vietnamese Counterparts and the civilians that we came into contact with every day. Doc used his southern charm and a strong knowledge of his medical skills to "win the hearts and minds", while Sergeant El used a calm, patient demeanor and some quickly-earned credibility with the mortar.

It turned out that Doc would become our best scrounger. He could get anything we wanted from the American supply sergeants at the American Division base camp in Chu Lai. One day Doc and sergeant El took off in 3/4 ton truck for Chu Lai - a 30-mile trip through questionably pacified country on QL1 (National Highway #1). The mission - among the orders for food, beer and something sweet for evening dessert - was to bring back an 81 millimeter mortar tube that sergeant El could use for mortar training classes and then turn the weapon over to the most deserving Regional Force Company in the District. I'm not sure how he did it all, but Doc was successful that day. The two set out with one captured Soviet weapon and about 6 Viet Cong flags that he would trade as captured enemy flags. Before leaving, Doc and the housemaid who had sewn the flags spread a few drops of chicken blood into the pile of flags and then Doc fired one round from a .45 pistol through the pile. This would randomly add battle signs to these homemade fakes, and Doc could trade them one-at-a-time as "one-of-a-kind" combat souvenirs. It worked. The rear echelon troops (REMF's) loved them and would trade anything for the war souvenir they would not have to risk their lives to get. Today, in dens across the US, there are such souvenirs displayed and storied about by "Wannabees" all over the USA. But that's OK. Everybody had a job to do, and we appreciated the moral and material support we got (however illegal) from our countrymen who were "in the rear with the gear". By late afternoon Doc and Sergeant El arrived back at the District compound with the truck loaded down. The spoils of their trip included not one but two 81 mm mortar tubes, enough mortar ammunition to last for the duration of the war, and, of course, tons of food and several cases of beer. It had been a successful scrounging trip. Later that night we learned what multiple trading steps Doc had used to get all this stuff. It was kind of a triumph for a couple of "New guys" to be that successful on their first scrounging mission. They had so earned the honor of being our chief scroungers for the rest of their tours!

Anyway, Sergeant El was ecstatic to have his two mortars as training aids. He asked me how fast we could get the District Chief, Captain Hoa, to bring in the weapons platoons of each of the 3 Regional Force companies in our district for training. We posed the question to *Dai Uy'* and got a quick response and quick action. He would have them come in the next day. This sense of urgency was refreshing and it sure perked up Sergeant El, who had heard when he first came in country that the Vietnamese would be lazy and that he was in for a bum tour. He was excited to be contributing so quickly and worked hard at getting ready for his first training class. He didn't speak Vietnamese like Lew did, but would work closely with *Trung Si'* (Sergeant) Kinh, our chief interpreter, and do all the instruction through him. Sergeant El did a great job! I observed every minute of his training session and was so impressed with his built-in soft, sincere way of delivering his instruction through Kinh and his way of show-and-tell with the mortar weapon itself! This critical indirect fire weapon, our own organic form of artillery - would prove to be an asset for a long time. Sergeant El, one of my favorite guys in Vietnam, had earned his keep in just a few days. What could be next? I was pumped up! We were really doing a job over here!!

*   *   *   *   *   *   *

Well, I found out what came next! We sat up one night in the team house - the whole team this time - and brainstormed about the Regional and Popular Forces that it was our lot to advise. I could not have been more pleased with the honest, constructive, and positive ideas we all shared that night. We were all in this together, and, as the officer soon to be in charge of our team, I was thankful for the group that we had been blessed with and, quite honestly, with the coaching I had received from Ron, who was about to rotate out and leave me in full charge of the team. During this discussion I could tell that Ron was counting the hours til his departure, or DEROS, but I knew his heart was in the right place. Actually, I sensed that he felt unfulfilled. I tried to tell him how much I had learned from him and how I would use this knowledge in the future, and this seemed to cause him some relief. As much as I might question Ron's methods, I will always revere his efforts to do what we were assigned to do. More power to you, Ron !!

*　　*　　*　　*　　*　　*　　*

The rest of June was consumed with extended-stay visits to Regional Force outposts in the District. The first was to 119 Company's camp - the one that had previously had the 6-foot fence around it. This camp had changed quite a bit from what it had looked like on our brief visit a few weeks ago. And the 119 Company had been bloodied in the May Offensive and were a lot tougher and more experienced. The few nights we spent here were quite uneventful. One exception was the first night medevac that I would experience. In this case, one of 119 Company's night patrols had made contact and had one man severely wounded. They begged for a U.S. helicopter medevac. Ron and I both took their pleading seriously. They needed help! The trick was that the patrol's location was about two klicks (kilometers) away and they couldn't move the casualty. At the same time, the "Dustoff" pilots would be crazy to go anywhere unless an American adviser were already on the ground with the Vietnamese casualty or would go out to the site on the chopper. We agreed to be picked up at 119's outpost, fly out to the patrol site, retrieve the casualty, and then be dropped off back at the outpost. The Medevac could then take the patient on to the U.S. Evac. hospital about 10 minutes flying time away. All this in the middle of the night!

A few minutes after our call, Dustoff 15 came up on our radio frequency and announced that he was about 5 minutes out and flying "lights-out". About that time we could begin to hear the "wop-wop" of the chopper's blades as it came closer. Ron readied a hand-held flashing strobe beacon lite to guide the pilot down. As the sound grew louder and louder we had to trust that the pilot could home in on our beacon safely and the pilot had to trust that this signal was really us and not a trick. Good radio communications helped to minimize the risk, and soon the chopper was hovering at about 50 feet over us, turned on his bright floodlight and quickly lowered himself til the skids touched the drying rice paddy we were standing in. Ron and I jumped on, and the pilot immediately roared out of there. His ground time must have been 10 seconds! We headed southwest to a point about 2 klicks away and our interpreter called down to the patrol on the chopper's radio. They in turn lit a small fire in the brush as a signal and we landed. Two of the RF troops carried their wounded comrade over to us and loaded him on the chopper, which again took off in a shuddering roar. These pilots didn't want to waste any seconds on the ground. The medic went to work immediately and indicated to the pilot that this was a severe wound, but that he felt like the victim would survive and that was stable at this point. There was time to drop Ron, me and Kinh back at 119's outpost on the way to the Evac. Hospital at the Duc Pho base camp down south. We were met at the outpost by the company commander with the strobe light we had given him. After the Medevac left on its continued mission of mercy, the 119 Company Commander thanked us profusely for the medevac, letting us know that once again, the American technology and support that we brought to bear sure had a positive effect on the morale of his troops. He hoped it would provide the edge they needed to win this war - at least to drive out the communists once and for all. We agreed that this would be the real test. While day-to-day accomplishments were at least as numerous as the problems, would we be able to pull off a long term success. I guess we thought so or we wouldn't be doing this, would we?

The night medevac was good training for me. What a weird sensation - flying around in a helicopter in the dark. The only light available was that of the stars and a very dim red glow of the chopper's instrument panel. We could see very little below us, and had to trust again the radio communications between two Vietnamese to get us down in the right place. I almost felt like Ron and I were just along for the ride, but the pilots knew that if we would go that they should, too. It was a strange phenomenon in Vietnam - perhaps it was that way in all wars. Americans from very different backgrounds and job assignments would work hand-in-hand and would take chances as long as the other guy would. We would often spend time trying to convince the other guy that his job was tougher and more dangerous than ours. This just led to more willingness to work together and sometimes to do things for teamwork that you would never consider doing before or after it happens - not consciously at least. Taking calculated risks became commonplace. We would have to guard against taking totally foolish ones. As it would turn out shortly, one of the most foolish chances Ron and I would take would almost be our last!

The day after the medevac, we had finished our visit at 119 company's camp. Amid a ceremonious lunch hosted by the company commander and the local Hamlet Chief, we bid goodbye for now. The Province chopper came to pick us up shortly after lunch and back we went to the District compound. Now to get cleaned up for a change and relax over a beer or two. In a couple of days the next visit to an outpost would be my first mission without Ron coming along. He wanted me to start working the operations by myself - both for the obvious training reasons and because he needed to slow down a little as he got "shorter". He now only had about a month left on his tour.

On arrival back at District HQ we learned that *Dai Uy'* Hoa's promotion had come through and that he was now a Major. From now on I would call him only *Thieu Ta'* (Major). A grand party was planned for that night, complete with visitors from Province Headquarters and some of the women that the more senior civilians had taken to entertaining. This would really be strange - a formal celebration with champagne and finely dressed Vietnamese dignitaries at our little compound in the boondocks. It was quite a party, but was called to a halt before 10 p.m. for security reasons. Most of the Province types hurried back to Quang Ngai City. It was interesting to note that the civilians mostly went by surface vehicles while the senior military had their helicopters come pick them up. They also complained that we didn't have a chopper pad in a safer place than right on Hiway 1.

When the party was over *Thieu Ta'* stopped to greet me once more. He remarked that he was looking forward to my first mission to the Montagnard outpost of RF Company 711. He would take me out to introduce me, but would then leave the team out there for a week. He felt there were many things that our team could do to help these Montagnard tribesmen. I would learn for myself what he was talking about in a few days, but right now the Major wished me good luck, assuring me that my upcoming visit to 711 Company would be one of the most interesting experiences I would have in Vietnam.

CHAPTER SEVEN

As the old Huey helicopter shuddered down to a landing just outside the outpost, I was aware of a different environment than we had experienced at other outlying camps. The perfectly triangular fort was surrounded by wide expanses of barbed wire and concertina, and further out by remarkably clear land for fields of fire. No enemy could move within 500 meters of the perimeter of 711 Company's base of operations without detection. The saffron and red- -striped flag of South Vietnam hung high above a well-manned watchtower in the center of the compound. Firing positions along the earth-and-sandbag walls were alert, and an overall sense of organization and military sharpness prevailed. This first impression would be reinforced many times during that year as we learned more about this particular unit.

We landed without fanfare this early morning, except for the obligatory smoke grenade that had been detonated by one of the two sharply dressed soldiers now greeting us at the landing point. A smoke grenade was routinely used to indicate wind direction (and often actual location or positive identification of friendlies), so that the chopper pilot could land into the wind if possible. Wind direction wasn't important this morning-there wasn't even the slightest breeze to be concerned about, and the yellow smoke hung in the thick, humid 95-degree morning air. What an appropriate spot for the familiar sound heard by tens of thousands of other American troops over armed forces radio : "Gooooood morning, Vietnam!" We didn't hear it, but it was time for this little team of two Americans (myself and Doc) and our interpreter, Kinh, to start off what would be a week-long stay with Regional Force Company 711, its 100 soldiers, and all of their families who lived in small grass and mud hooches around the inside of the fort walls. They were unique in the lowlands, as 711 Company happened to be the only Montagnard company in the province. These mountain tribesman and their people had been moved out of the central highlands of their birth for their own security, but had volunteered to serve as an intact RF company under the South Vietnamese military organization of our province and district rather than to be ensconced in one of the hovel-towns we called "refugee camps". Not only were they the most unusual, they were without question the best trained and most courageous unit we had in the district. While the South Vietnamese may have looked down on the Montagnards as second-class citizens, they could not deny the fact that every time the going got tough, the 711 Company was called upon and performed its mission with valor and tenacity. It was a comfortable feeling to be living in their outpost or accompanying them on even the most hazardous of operations.

Our greeting party at the chopper consisted of a young Montagnard Lieutenant and the company commander, Captain (Dai Uy') Hai. Our team that day was accompanied by my good friend the District Chief who would get a briefing from Hai before leaving us there to work with him and his troops. Of course the briefing , as always, would include a special and ceremonious brunch for the visitors, and nothing was held back in its preparation and serving. While one would think it was all for show, we quickly learned that this was a very serious part of the briefing of the District Chief by his direct report. As Dai Uy' Hai' described the situation, he and his troops had been harassed often by the local Viet Cong but as usual weren't able to pin them down for a decisive battle. This universal problem plagued every one of the Allied units in Vietnam. While Regional Force companies had the primary mission to provide quick-reaction support to any local force or hamlet security team that got in trouble with organized enemy units, their secondary mission was to regularly patrol the territory surrounding their individual outposts to provide geographic security for surrounding villages and hamlets. While there were no organized battles going on over the last few weeks -no Main Force or NVA (North Vietnamese Army) units to chase out - 711 company had been running security patrols and night ambushes. Their night ambushes had met with little success, but harassing mortar fire and ground probes of the outpost itself took place almost every night. These were always brief and hard to counter with normal measures.

Even daytime operations turned up little or no contact as the local VC melted into the population. Major Hoa suggested using some of the intelligence-gathering capabilities within the American-sponsored Phoenix program to pin down VCI (VC Infrastructure) cadres for arrest and removal from the population to neutralize them. This activity should reduce the current annoyance being perpetrated by these "local yokels" and allow 711 to go about its business of maintaining both local security and readiness for the next big operation when the time came. It would also help to temporarily cripple the political arm of the VC in that area. Too bad that was never a permanent fix, though. Thieu Ta then informed Hai' that Province Intelligence had indicated another major offensive would be coming soon, involving the 83rd Main Force battalion from the Son My Village area, in a District north of the river from our District, Tu Nghia. The 83rd was reinforced by tough NVA regulars and most of its officers were now NVA . Rumor had it that the enemy wanted to show that it could destroy the military assets of the district by crippling one or more of its best units. It sounded like potential trouble for 711 company, but Dai Uy' Hai took it as a personal compliment and a challenge that would be relished by his troops. They were itching for a good fight. But first, security would be the watchword for the outpost, its civilian inhabitants, and the surrounding villages. Then 711 Company , with the fire support that we advisors could call in, would be ready to take on the main force that was coming into our district ; but this would not be for a couple of weeks yet - at least that's what we thought!

*　　　*　　　*　　　*　　　*　　　*

The Province chopper returned shortly after the brunch meeting ended and picked up Major Hoa to fly him back to District headquarters, so we began setting up our home-away-from-home in the compound of 711 Company. We were invited to stay in a vacant hooch that was actually built into the bottom of the watchtower directly in the center of the compound. This seemed a little strange, but when you're a guest you pretty much go along with the sleeping arrangements. It just didn't feel right to be living on the first floor of the most prominent aiming stake that any enemy gunner could ask for. I also had visions of the watchtower being blown to bits and collapsing down on our little hooch at two in the morning. The fact of the matter was that I wouldn't be spending that much time sleeping in the designated spot at all. This would become obvious soon enough, as our first night here would fall suddenly in just a few hours.

*　　　*　　　*　　　*　　　*　　　*

We hadn't brought much gear with us for a week-long stay with the Montagnards. Of, course our personal weapons and radio were the only important items. Food was not an issue. We always ate with the Vietnamese troops or in the villages when on operations. In fact it would be an insult for us to bring our own food - the only exception being when we were in the "rear" at the District compound, where we did cook food scrounged off American units -

seemingly always chicken-ugh! At least in the villages we were occasionally offered duck for a change !

An extra set of jungle fatigues and boots and a shaving kit were about all I brought for myself. Doc brought an air mattress, mosquito netting, and other elaborate items; the kinds of things that you could expect a "newbee" to drag along. After a few weeks in-country, Doc would be just like the rest of us - traveling light. So, our setting up time was minimal, and as usual was closely watched by dozens of Montagnard kids and a few curious soldiers. The kids were always fascinated with these tall, fair-skinned (except in Doc's case) oddities, as they glued their eyes to our every move, apparently certain we would commit some bizarre act any moment. They did get a great laugh out of Doc's careful arrangement of air mattress, poncho liner, and overhead netting - an elaborate sleeping setup by Montagnard standards.

Our unpacking completed, it was time for the highlight of the day and a most essential task to complete before dark. We were to get a complete tour of the camp with Dai Uy' Hai. Gaining a feel for where everything was and who did what in an armed fortress was mandatory for anyone who wanted to survive the night without screwing up. The tour also would give me a chance to "inspect", although unobtrusively, the defenses of the camp so that I could offer suggestions and support for implementing them. After all, we were more of a support network than "advisers". On occasions when we did offer advice, it had to be offered humbly and was not always accepted. We found Captain Hai coming across the compound in our direction just as we stepped out of our borrowed hooch. He greeted us again with a big smile and, after a few words to interpreter Kinh, wheeled about and started off in the direction of one of the points formed by the triangular walls of the fort. Across the compound floor and up a steep ladder we followed and caught up with Hai at the top of one of the three "corner" bunkers. Here he beamed as he began pointing out features of the fortress he and his people had created from scratch. I was impressed, to say the least.

From the vantage point on top of the bunker and about 10 feet above ground we could look down the length of two of the three walls making up the legs of the triangle.Each leg wasn't much over 50 meters long, as I recall. At this corner bunker and at one other there was an M-60 machine gun with fields of fire that included a line parallel with either wall. This way the two guns could lay down a devastating shield of hot lead laterally right in front of any wall that was in danger of being breeched or scaled. Any VC that tried to put a bamboo ladder up to the wall of this fort would be in a world of hurt. In addition to the final defensive fires, each machine gun had good fields of fire that, with the proper discipline, could be coordinated well enough to leave no point around the camp uncovered by the crew-served weapons. One of the most impressive things about this little tour with Hai was the fact that while he talked, he referred us to an 8x10 overhead view drawing of the fort complete with a schematic of his lines and fields of fire. This was something I had not seen at any other outpost - or even at our District compound for that matter. Continuing along the outside walls, which were made of dirt with several layers of sandbags, we counted 10 firing positions on each wall. Each of the firing positions would be manned by at least one soldier in normal times including daytime and by two at night. Depending on the level of alert or during times of large daytime operations, this could change so that there could be anything from 10 per cent security to full alert. The point was that there was a well-conceived plan for all of this. What could I teach this guy?

In addition to the well-conceived external defenses , including freshly laid wire, booby traps and command-detonated Claymore mines, we noted contingency plans for pull-back and escape and evasion. Inside the compound a mortar pit at the center, complete with aiming stakes and barricaded ammunition pit , contained 711

Company's only real source of indirect fire - the 81mm mortar and its crew. They were practicing ! The Captain's command bunker was at another point of the triangle , where two large radio antennas were a dead giveaway. I got the feeling that Dai Uy' Hai didn't spend much time in there. If his troops were under attack, he was the type of leader that would be out there on line with them. With about an hour of touring and pleasant relationship-building under our belts, I suddenly sensed that there was something missing. Where were the kids, where were all the civilians? It became obvious that the Montagnard leader had put out the word that an important American visitor was going to be coming, and that while Hai was doing his formal presentation they were to make themselves scarce! Was I a lowly Lieutenant or was I General Westmoreland?? (Actually Gen. Abrams was in charge, but most of us thought Westy was still Mr. Vietnam).

Anyway, it was now almost dusk. It was time to inspect the ambush patrol teams and listening posts before they went out for the night. These brave souls would stay out almost alone (two to five per team)all through the dark night that was about to fall around us. I couldn't help but think of how little this method of active defense was used successfully by the regular South Vietnamese platoons and companies. Yes, this unit and these Montagnards were a breath of fresh air!

*   *   *   *   *   *

Nightfall creates an eerie feeling for anyone who is away from home, and the nights in Vietnam managed to outdo any feelings I had ever experienced. While half a world away most Americans were just waking from a peaceful, protected night of sound sleep, we were getting ready for just about any eventuality that darkness could conceal until it was time to spring it. Of course, the night belonged to "Charlie" in these parts. The VC could move about a "pacified" area in small groups at night, do their dirty tricks, and then disappear. Unfortunately the dirty tricks were not to be laughed at. People died or were maimed, bridges were blown, refugee camps were terrorized, and the continuous attempt by the local defense forces to stop it exacted a huge toll in government resources and attention. More time was spent patching up and rebuilding bridges, schools, and refugee camps and villages, than was spent on improving the quality of life or building the infrastructure to support a free people and the government to sustain it. Our team scarcely had time to actually perform the training mission we had been sent for - to train all the Regional Force companies and Popular Force platoons in our district on weapons, tactics, fire support. Using what we taught them, they were then supposed to take over the war effort at the rice-roots level, freeing up regular ARVN (Army of the Republic of Vietnam) divisions to take over the major battles from the U.S. units - allowing the Americans to go home - thus the term "Vietnamization". But we were too busy fighting a local war to do much real training.

*   *   *   *   *   *

Now 7:30 and pitch black, Kinh, Doc and I strolled around the compound for awhile. I spent my time observing the activity outside each hooch while Doc kept a keen lookout for the living conditions, sanitary practices, and any particular sign of disease prominence. Unfortunately most of the kids appeared to have various kinds of skin diseases such as ringworm,etc, the kind of thing that could scarcely be avoided when you lived on dirt floors and around lots of insects. I could sense Doc making some mental notes for his possible role in helping the Montagnards improve hygiene and treatment of these inevitable nuisance diseases. His work would begin in earnest tomorrow. He had been introduced to the camp bac si', or doctor, and the two of them had instantly started planning for a complete going-over for each of the civilians in the camp. No professional jealousy here - the bac si' would take all the help he could get, even if he had, not long ago, been more of a tribal "medicine man" than a doctor. Of course, Doc is an Army medic, not an M.D., but he had had more training on civic action programs than other medics. Doc was Medical Advisor on our team and, as far as the Vietnamese were concerned, he was The Doctor. During our brief walk-around,we became still more familiar and comfortable with the environment. Soft candle light generated from inside and in front of most of the dwellings, lending a warm glow to the whole place. At the same time I felt sure that the low light level was doing wonders for our night vision capability, in case we had to see what was going on in the complete darkness . Always on guard ? You bet!

There seemed to be industrious movement everywhere. Outside most of the dirt-floored grass and mud hooches, off-duty soldiers cleaned their weapons and gear while wives mended all sorts of clothing. Some older kids were engaged in a strange kind of domino game while several younger ones played their version of pick-up-sticks. Still others were amusing themselves just following us around , wide-eyed, watching every move. Many were catching the informal evening meal as most of the kids gnawed on gooey rice cubes. While lunch was a ritualistic thing for the people of Vietnam, the evening meal was catch-as-catch-can. This sounds strange when you consider the climate but, much like the old agrarian U.S., the Vietnamese made mid-day a major event. Actually it made sense because after a big lunch it was universal practice to sleep until 2:30.(Why work in the hottest part of the day?) I had even seen this happen in the middle of a fire-fight , where at 12:00 sharp the war stopped. Everyone cooked, ate, and slept until 2:30 and then the war would crank up again. What's $gs!$? more, it was evident that the bad guys did the same thing!

While out in the compound, we were once again tracked down by Dai Uy' Hai, who invited us to his command bunker for a drink of rice wine and a chat. Soon inside this bunker, we were quite ceremoniously introduced to an old man who was apparently a respected tribal elder from the old days in the highlands. These Montagnard's might be transplanted, but they kept many of their traditions. So, we all sipped rice wine through a straw - the same straw in one large urn - while Hai explained more about the tactical situation in this area. He spoke no English, but spoke better Vietnamese than most Montagnards ,so Kinh could translate well enough. We learned that Hai expected the Main Force movement into our district in a matter of days - not weeks - and that they would enter from the coast, stage on a barrier island we called "The Hourglass" for its shape, then move into the populated areas in the southeast part of the district. This would play right into Hai's hands. The Hourglass was the one place in our district where no friendlies, military or civilian, had set foot since before Tet of 1968. During the Tet offensive the 83rd Main Force battalion - 600 strong - had used the Hourglass as a jumping-off point for attacks in Tu Nghia and even into Quang Ngai City. At the height of the offensive they actually had held the Province Headquarters building in the city for a few days, still operating from the island base. When they pulled back to Son My up north, they left the most heavily mined and booby-trapped area in the province on the Hourglass. In this way the VC denied access to the Government and saved the island for a staging area in future offensives - offensives that were now going to start in late June of 1969. Dai Uy' Hai told us he expected an increase in harassment incidents in the villages and directed toward this outpost, and that he intended to step up recon patrols in daytime hours and double the number of ambush teams he sent out at night. Hopefully we could trigger some action and pre-empt the VC's plan. He asked me to consider how large amounts of American firepower could be used best in a possible bold move - an attack on the Hourglass. We agreed to review our thoughts in the morning, but now we would check the perimeter again. As we left the command bunker, I started to visualize a significant battle on the Hourglass, and I was at once both excited and frightened. If we didn't admit to fear in these situations we would be lying. We also had to admit a great rush of adrenalin and excitement just anticipating the exhilaration of combat. There is nothing more frightening and exciting than getting shot at - and missed !

On that note, I quietly accompanied the company commander on his perimeter check and we parted company to go to our respective hooches. Before coming down from the wall I took a long look out into the blackness, straining to see any movement. Nothing! All was quiet except for the barking of a dog in a nearby village. Wondering what was out there, I wandered back to our hooch and joined the others for the night.

We had decided to maintain radio watch by sharing 3 ways with Kinh. This was not our regular procedure, which called for one American to be awake at all times in even the seemingly safest conditions. This time we felt secure enough to allow our Vietnamese interpreter to stand a shift of 2 hours just like Doc and I did. We trusted Kinh and, besides, there was a Montagnard soldier on guard just out front of our hooch at all times. We were already growing to trust this group. The first clue had been when Major Hoa agreed with Hai' that we didn't need the usual entourage of P.R.U.'s (Province Recon Unit) to be bodyguards for the Americans while we stayed with him. Hai'was convincing and Hoa was very trusting of him. That was good enough for me.

The night was relatively quiet, punctuated only by a few stray and distant shots from rifles and at least one enormous rolling thunder-clap provided by a B-52 strike in the far-away mountains, compliments of the U.S. Air Force. I heard all noises, including the whispered hourly situation reports sent in by the watch man to the district hq. I learned to become a very light sleeper in Vietnam - still am. In fact, I have periods of time, especially when traveling on busines, when I will wake up once an hour, look at the clock, and go right back to sleep. The strangest part is that it doesn't happen on the hour or half-hour, but picks a different time each night - like 1:18, 2:18 and so on. This sounds frustrating, but I get enough rest even under these conditions. Of course the other habit is that I must have a clock that I can see easily for the times when I do wake up. I have to know what time it is and how many hours of darkness are left. Just one of the phobias left over from Vietnam, I guess. They will always be there.

Next morning we were up at first light, drinking some hot tea and eating little dried rice cakes that were brought to us by the door guards that had watched over us all night. It was a sort of honor to them to draw that duty and then to break bread with us to celebrate a successful, safe night. We did our best to thank them with universal signals - a smile and a double handshake. Then they went back to being ordinary soldiers. This ritual would be repeated with different guards on each morning that we awoke at the 711 camp. Actually, I felt safer and more among friends here than I did back at the district compound - at least for now. Our first night here had been unusually quiet - but why?

Mid-morning was the time that Doc and the bac si' had planned for the medical screening for the troops and their families. When it came time for the kids to be examined, I had fun helping with entertaining them. This would take their minds off what they might have feared in being examined for the first time in their lives by a medical practitioner like the big American sergeant as he gave each one a thorough going over. They were brought into bac si's hooch one at a time by their mothers who stayed and watched intently. Doc not only examined, but he also showed them a bit of western hygiene in a very polite fashion. Kinh interpreted as best he could to explain what Doc was trying to teach mother and child. As a reward, each kid received some candy saved from the "SP" packs we had scrounged from the American Division long ago and had saved for just such an occasion. Long since gone were the cigarettes, toothbrushes, soap , gum, and writing materials that came in these large "goodie boxes" that were regularly dropped off to American troops with the big units in the field. I made a mental note to try to get some more SP packs on our next trip to the Division base camp at Chu Lai and to save a whole one for the troops and families at this outpost. I knew they would appreciate it and that they would make good use of the contents - not sell them on the black market like some of the other Vietnamese were known to do. It seemed like I was getting more and more trusting of these people, and I was not surprised. After all the stories I had heard from the Green Berets at Fort Bragg back as early as ' 63, these Montagnards were living up to their reputation already. Before long I would have a close-range opportunity to witness their bravery in battle - the quality they were noted for...

*   *   *   *   *   *

One of the things I thought we could do for 711 Company would be to set up pre-planned artillery targets called DefCon's, or defensive concentrations, around their fort. This would allow our friends at the artillery fire base to get out maximum destructive firepower in minimum time, which could make a big difference in a ground attack on this outpost. With pre-planned targets, the computers in the fire direction center could take a target number and spit out firing directions to the guns in seconds. Rounds would be out in less than a minute from the first fire mission call. If the guns happened to be pointed in the general direction of the target area already, the first shells could impact in 15 seconds ! This could definitely ruin "Charlie's" day. So, after lunch, we started the process of registering these DefCon's in a ring around the outpost at a distance of 100 meters - rather close - and a second ring at 200 meters. In truth, in a desperate attempt to avoid being overrun, artillery might be adjusted in to as close as 50 meters from friendlies, then right on top of the camp if there were no alternative. My biggest fear was to get into that kind of situation. To this day the word "overrun" brings a chill. One of the Mobile Advisory Teams like ours, located in the next district North of us, had been overrun and lost the entire team - some are still missing. The team leader was my friend from the flight over here.

Since the majority of our district was not a "Free Fire Zone" and was heavily populated with innocent civilians trying to tend their rice paddies and raise families, we had coordinated with the local Village Chief, an elected official, to warn people to stay more than half a mile away from our position between 2:30 and 5 pm. Captain Hai sent out a small patrol to sweep the area one last time and when they returned we started the process. We called in single marking rounds for each of the targets we wanted registered, adjusted them as required, then recorded target numbers like YH1802 (this would be at 180 degrees - due south - and 200 meters) or YH901 (due East at 100 meters) as designated by the artillery people.Each target was then located and numbered on the fort's defense map. At the time firing was needed, one could call the artillery base, give the target number he wanted, and get accurate fast response. This would help us catch the elusive enemy in his tracks for a change. We set up the plan so that if no advisors were on site, 711 could call back to the District compound and someone on our team would coordinate the firing as if he were there by relaying the information to the artillery guys. Another mental note was made - how come we didn't have this set up to protect our own District compound ? We soon would! When the outer and inner circles of targets were registered and it was almost 5 pm, Captain Hai pointed to one more lone spot he wanted a DefCon for. It was about 300 meters out to the Southeast and was partially shielded by a slight rise in the land. (In this flat paddy country this would be called a "prominent terrain feature" by the Infantry School in Georgia - better known as Benning School For Boys - where most young Infantry Officers got their training.) At Hai's insistence, we registered this target as YH1203 and , thanking the artillery guys once again, we called it a day. That very night we would find a use for our afternoon's work, and my idea for this little exercise would earn us - his young advisors - instant credibility with the good Dai Uy', who had been fighting for 10 years already and would probably be fighting for another 10 or more, long after the Americans had left.

$$* \qquad * \qquad * \qquad * \qquad * \qquad *$$

So, after two days at 711 company, we had kept busy and accomplished quite a bit while getting acclimated to its unique environment. We were wondering when it would be time to get out and around the local territory and run some offensive operations. After all, this unit was not meant to spend all of its time in static defense of its own outpost. Their mission was to keep the enemy out of the area on a regular basis, and to hopefully disable enemy fighting units in the process. The only way to do that was to get out there in the territory. Just before dark we found the answer to our wondering - we were invited to accompany Dai Uy Hai' and most of his troops on a search and clear operation starting the next morning. I couldn't wait to work with them and see how they were on the offense.

At two a.m. my turn at radio watch was rudely interrupted by a loud explosion just outside the camp wall. Incoming ! As Doc and Kinh sat straight up, I grabbed a radio and ran out of the hooch toward the command bunker.Doc and Kinh followed. Given the poor protection the hooch offered, this move wasn't as dumb as it may sound. Of course, you don't want to be out in the open when mortar shells are lobbed in, but the few seconds it took to get to the command bunker didn't matter. In that short span of seconds, however, I was able to hear the tell-tale "chunk!" of the second round popping out of the mortar tube and sensed the direction of that sound at about Southeast. I got into the bunker to meet Dai Uy' Hai' before the second round impacted - this time near the interior center of the compound. Hai' quickly pointed to his defensive map and right at one of our pre-planned targets we had just registered, and nodded his head, indicating he knew that the gunner was right where his hand-picked target had been registered - just behind the rise about 300 meters southeast. I raised the artillery firebase on the radio - then yelled "fire mission, YH1203, fire for effect, clearance Papa Lima Tango" to the fire direction officer. The last phrase was the phonetic way to say my initials, indicating we had political and military clearance to fire, meaning if any friendlies were inadvertently in the way, they were the responsibility of my counterpart - the local Vietnamese commander - and myself. Within 20 or 30 seconds - which felt like a lifetime - a voice rang out over my radio : "YH1203 , rounds out, battery 2, over". This meant that four guns had just fired one round and would fire a second round each immediately. As the sentence completed we could hear the guns go off. Four huge high explosive shells from these 155 mm howitzers would land in a few seconds. The sound of a speeding train followed by a deafening, sharp explosion and a ball of fire and debris at about 300 meters to our southeast was the result. This sequence was repeated quickly and then everything went silent except for the sound of small bits of dirt raining down around the camp. It was all over and it had lasted only about a minute from the first incoming mortar to the end. Now there were no more mortar rounds being fired. Occasional flares fired from hand-held launchers lit up the area around the perimeter of wire and obstacles. Nothing there. Dai Uy' Hai' grabbed my hand and pumped wildly while Kinh came in to translate. It seems that every few nights this lone gunner would fire 6 to 8 rounds from his small 61 mm mortar tube, then disappear. Hai' suspected that this little nuisance often fired from behind the now-famous lone rise that tonight was ground zero for about 1000 pounds of TNT explosives and this time he only got off 2 rounds before our planning took its toll with near instant destruction. It was a one-on-one war sometimes.

At first light we saddled up for the planned operation with about 80 of Hai's troops and, after a quick briefing with the commander and his 3 platoon leaders, we moved out. Obviously our first mission was to find just what we had done to Nguyen-the-mortar-man. While we hoped to find his body and mortar tube , or parts thereof, all we saw was a few drops of very dark red blood and a set of sandal prints that led straight away with no signs of injury. To this day I wonder what happened to the little pain in the rear. My best guess is that even though he apparently got away, his eardrums were burst. The drops of blood would indicate something like that, and he had to be right next to the artillery impact point getting ready to stuff round 3 down the tube when all hell broke loose. If there were to be a next time for this guy, he would never hear the onrushing train again. Most important, we had stopped last night's mission and probably prevented any more of those stray mortar attacks for a while.

We continued on the sweep operation, advancing all the way to the coastline and a small fishing village before 10 a.m. with no enemy contact along the way. We didn't see any of them, but we knew the bad guys were always aware of our presence and were probably watching patiently our every move. In the village Hai' questioned the Hamlet Chief and learned that some V.C. had made a scrounging trip to his village last night and that they had paddled a sampan down for this mission. The old man mentioned their uniforms and we at once knew that they had been regulars from the battalion and guessed that they had come from the Hourglass, having been part of an advance party sent to set up and provision from the local residents before the main force of up to 300 filtered in. These scroungers were able to get rice and other staples fairly easily from villagers who responded to threats as well as kindness. Gone were the days when the V.C. tried to win the hearts and minds of the people in true insurgent fashion and then hold on to loyal "resistance" support. Now they would just come in, take the food, and kill or torture someone as an example to the others if the food wasn't readily given. Sometimes they would use these examples as a warning measure. I had met several hamlet chiefs who had had a hand, an arm, or a son taken from them as a warning not to cooperate with the South Vietnamese and the Americans. The hamlet chief in this fishing village was one of these. Over a rather filling but not too fancy lunch of - what else? -

baked whole fish and rice, we learned that in two nights the major offensive would start. One of the V.C. thieves had boasted of a total victory over the puppet local forces and reunion for the people with their real liberators - themselves of course. Oh, well, same old Communist B.S. I felt mixed emotions about this man and his leadership of the hamlet. Part of me was angry at him for giving in and seemingly working with both sides. Why didn't he take a stand ? At the same time, I realized how difficult it was for him and those like him to walk that fine line needed to keep his people and his own family alive. When he helped government he didn't get much of a deal and saw poor security - no matter what our computer reports said - and when he helped the communists he at least saved someone else from torture or death. But what a terrible existence! And to think it had been going on for 30 years! It's no fun when your neighborhood is a battleground and you just happen to be there trying to eke out a meager living while doing your best to survive the cross-fire. I know a baseball coach who, asked if it was always an advantage to be playing at home, said that the only game where you don't want to be the home team is war. I now knew why that was so true.

With the information we had gleaned from this village visit we felt a need to do some serious planning with the District Chief and to start coordinating with supporting forces we would need to pull off a major offensive operation against the 83rd Battalion now moving to the Hourglass. We would want to move fast to catch them before they were all set up on the island and would want to be able to cut off their retreat if possible. This would call for help by the 2nd ARVN (regular South Vietnamese army) Division, American fire support as usual, and this time a coordinated effort by the South Vietnamese Navy located at the junk base in the very northwest corner of our district. The American Navy advisors at the junk base were friends of ours and we had helped each other out on several occasions - mostly with supplies and scrounged equipment. These guys were really out on a limb if they ever got into a real coastal battle. While the junks they manned could control and interdict small movements of enemy supplies, they were not able to defend their own base very well without infantry help. (On a later occasion that year we would find ourselves using some of our regional forces as a relief column to help save the junk base.) Located not too far north of the Hourglass, the Navy would be needed to set up a blocking force to catch the enemy retreating from the island after our planned attack. With all these thoughts in mind our band of 80 circled back from the fishing village on an uneventful return - by a different route of course - to the 711 Company outpost. We had then completed a fairly common operation - a day's maneuvering with no contact, visits with civilian officials, a nice lunch meeting, siesta, and a calm return on the same afternoon. This war was conducted at the rice-roots level at a painfully slow pace interspersed with short periods of excitement and sheer terror followed by reflections of satisfaction with our small, incremental accomplishments or frustration with backward steps. But this day was worth more than most because of the information we picked up and the plans we were now working on. Maybe this time we were onto something big !

*   *   *   *   *   *

By the time we got back to the 711 area, we had learned that the District Chief was on his way out to meet with us. As we got within about a click (kilometer) of the camp we saw the province chopper once again come in and leave so we knew Thieu Ta would be ready to meet as soon as we got inside the compound. (Doc and I privately hoped someone had put a care package on that chopper when it stopped by the district compound to pick Hoa up.) After all the proper greetings and briefings on the day's operation, we sat down over a beer - Doc,Kinh, Hoa, Hai, and myself - and worked our way into a rough plan for an operation to pin down the enemy battalion at the Hourglass and hopefully to destroy it as an effective fighting unit - all before it could take the offensive in our district. What we didn't know was exactly how the enemy was planning his offensive moves, which would have been key to our success. We made the assumption that they were going to assemble on that barrier island and, feeling secure in that haven, would launch large-element operations against important targets like Hai's camp or a key bridge well inside the district, where they could do damage to important fighting units while damaging facilities like a bridge or a fort. What we ruled out was an attack on the District Headquarters compound. If our assumptions were correct, the battalion would mass on the island rather than disperse for small group actions. We had an opportunity to pound them with fire support and then get the 2nd ARVN people to send a large force from Quang Ngai City to augment our attack, and we could engage them and/or drive them north to be stopped and destroyed by a blocking force of more ARVN troops and the navy junks. We decided to start the next day with some bombardment and on the second morning push onto the island with the combined infantry units. During our conversation a thought came to mind for the first phase of bombardment - something new I had heard about and now called Province to get it arranged for the next morning. I thought I had a surprise brewing for "Charlie".

One of our intelligence group advisors at Province level had once suggested that we should try a new tool for finding, fixing and destroying enemy infantry in lightly covered positions. By definition, the water table on a barrier island would not allow the usual clever and elaborate digging of positions by the 83rd this time. They would try to prepare shallow foxholes with good concealment so that aircraft could not see them in the daytime, but if they could be found they could take lots of casualties without heavy cover. The new tool we would use was called "The Sniffer", but it actually was a heat-seeking device mounted on the belly of a scout helicopter - one of the smaller faster choppers we called a "loach". The loach would zip across the island at low altitude and high speed "sniffing" for likely locations for people based on different levels of heat generated by cooking fires and even gatherings of humans. After criss-crossing the island the device could amass a profile of the surface and point out some high-probability spots where people might be hiding. Then the innocent-looking unarmed scout chopper could transmit a "picture" to a team of 2 heavily armed "Cobra" helicopter gunships circling thousands of feet above the site. These terrors from the sky would then swoop down and unload everything they had on the suspected areas, and everything they had was a lot! Rockets, Mini-guns, grenade launchers!! When all the Cobra ordinance had been released, they would go back for more while the Scout, after waiting for the impact area to cool down, would try _3 Helos_ another pass or two using both the sniffer and visual observation. _or more_ About 15 minutes later another heavy fire team of Cobras would show up and bring maximum destruction again. The next day we were able to sit across the river from the hourglass and watch this "sniffer" team work the island over. My counterparts, Hai' and Hoa were amazed. What would the Americans come up with next? We watched this air show for a couple of hours, then asked the scout chopper to tell us if they could detect any results. They told us that they had spotted no movement at all, but that didn't mean anything. These bad guys could hide for days and they may be either all hiding and laughing or all dead. (We doubted the latter) The only way to tell would be to assess the situation with infantry troops. That would come the next day because our friends from the 2nd ARVN just weren't ready yet. We should have waited, but the sniffer was only available this day. That would be OK. We had lots of harassing and destructive artillery planned to go on all that afternoon and night before the ground attack would begin. Our artillery friends from LZ Snoopy would fire one round at a time in very erratic intervals and every once in a while would let go a barrage of 12 rounds, then go quiet, then back to the random single rounds. Of course, they would make slight adjustments in location of the target for each firing, so that anyone wanting to move around that island for the next 12 hours or so would have to be pretty brave. It would be like dodging raindrops - except these were of the high-explosive kind.

So we returned to the 711 camp again for the night, trudging carefully the 3 kilometer distance without incident. Thinking that the night would be quiet due to the fact that we had the bad guys basically pinned down on their island sanctuary, we grabbed a bite to eat, checked the camp perimeter with Captain Hai, and retired to our hooch for the night. Much later I was awakened by the loud but muffled explosion of a command detonated Claymore mine and considerable small arms fire. This had to mean that the perimeter troops had spotted something close to the camp, possibly in the wire. As Doc called in a preliminary sitrep to the District, I went across the compound to find out what was going on. This time I didn't find Captain Hai in the command bunker, but was able to make my way to the wall that had opened up firing and found him there talking to the squad leader on that wall. Apparently one of the homemade warning devices had indicated somebody in the wire and the appropriate bunker had blown the Claymore as a precaution and then fired their weapons in almost an individual "mad minute". What was amazing was that none of the surrounding bunkers had cut loose but maintained strict fire discipline. Again I was very impressed with the level of training and effectiveness of this Montagnard unit. Hai ordered a couple of flares fired off and we strained to see if there was anything out there either alive or dead. Nothing again. Someone or something had tripped a warning device and slithered off to tell about it. It could have been a stray dog, but we really thought it was a probe started by one of the enemy "sapper" teams that specialized in breaking down perimeter defenses so that their infantry comrades could have an easier time in attacking the targeted defensive position. The stories we had always heard about what sappers could do were legend, and our only close encounter so far had been when the Engineer compound near us had been hit. The only result had been 13 dead VC, three of which were sappers. Not very impressive!

Dai Uy' Hai put his troops on full alert for a possible attack. We stayed with him long enough to feel that this incident was over, then headed back to the hooch. Just as I arrived at the door we heard the unmistakable ruckus of a sudden but heavy firefight well outside the compound and probably a kilometer to the east. It was obvious that one of 711's ambush teams had made contact with a sizable enemy element and had sprung the full violence of the ambush on them. As the firefight continued for more than 30 seconds, we knew that the enemy was fighting back, but that only went on for a minute or so and then it was over. Back at the command bunker we learned that the ambush patrol team had radioed in its report. They had ambushed about 30 NVA regulars who had been hurrying down a trail headed straight for the 711 camp. After springing the trap they figured out that there were three times that many following but that they had turned and run when the firefight started. What was left of the first 30 fought fiercely but never charged the ambush position. Fortunately for the 8-man ambush patrol the enemy must have overestimated the size of the patrol and had broken contact, leaving 8 dead and 3 badly wounded behind. Several others had probably run away with slight wounds. Our dire need now was to recover the ambush team while it was still intact and to get those wounded enemy soldiers in for questioning. We would also tend to their wounds and then turn them over to South Vietnamese authorities. We wanted to question them right on the spot to get the best, freshest information we could before the rear intelligence community had a chance to water it down or doctor it at all.

A platoon of 711 company was sent out in the darkness to help. While night movement was to be avoided in almost all cases, Hai felt that the area between the camp and the ambush site was clear for now and that the enemy elements that had infiltrated had run back to the Hourglass to fight another day. The entourage of friendlies, carrying the wounded North Vietnamese in litters, was back in camp within an hour and it was now about an hour from first light. The 711 medic and Doc made evaluations of the 3 enemy wounded and concluded that one was dying quickly but the other two could survive with the proper care. They were both conscious, so Kinh explained to them that we would call for a

Medevac helicopter to take them to the U.S. field surgical hospital at Duc Pho where they would receive the best initial care in the world, then they would be brought back to the Vietnamese Province Hospital in Quang Ngai City for recuperation and safekeeping as Prisoners of War. We called for the Medevac, telling the province radio team that we could wait until first light - now less than an hour - so that the "Dustoff" pilots would have an easier job of it. The nature of the wounds would allow that wait for two of them, while the third enemy soldier had passed away as we were on the radio. The point should be made here that we were handling these wounded just the way we would have for friendlies - whether Vietnamese or American. Once an enemy soldier cross the river from the island. They had staged about halfway between the island and the 711 camp until the planned attack time of about 2 a.m. A local sapper team was supposed to breech the wire before the attack. Not unusual, but it should be noted that an attacking force at a company-sized outpost should be over 300 infantry troops with lots of supporting mortar and rocket fire. The rule of thumb according to military science was 3-to-1 offensive forces when attacking a fortified defensive position. This small group of 100 with its organic mortar, rocket and rocket-propelled-grenade (RPG) capability would need help. Our prisoners finally solved our puzzle. It seems that the attack by 100 men on our position at 711 company's camp was only a diversionary tactic! The main attack force of almost 300 NVA, joined by as many local VC as they could muster, was supposed to attack the District compound shortly after the attack on 711 company had begun. The enemy had correctly assumed that any fire support available would be monopolized by me at 711 while the remainder of our team back at District would have to convince fire support providers to give them some help to protect a compound that hadn't had a serious ground attack attempted in several months and to divert their fire away from our remote camp already under attack. The other fact was that the total infantry defense force that guarded our District compound was less than 100 of the Popular Force soldiers whose PF Platoons had been detailed to provide security for the District

Chief and the six or seven Americans who lived there. Needless to say, the enemy's plan had to be scrapped when their main attack force realized that the diversionary attack on 711's camp had been thwarted by the successful ambush by the Montagnard patrol. This small team of "savages" , as the South Vietnamese referred to them, had stopped a major coordinated and well-conceived enemy attack in our district. This had been another one of those close calls that our team seemed to make a habit of getting involved in.

After the Medevac was complete, we saddled up with most of 711 company to move out once again to the position just across the river from the Hourglass. This time we were prepared to move across the river as elements of the 2nd division moved in force onto the island from the west/northwest. Meanwhile the junk base was prepared to be an augmented blocking force to cut off the 83rd battalion's escape by way of the South China Sea or at the mouth of the Tra Bong River to the north. We still had the artillery firing in random rounds on the Hourglass when we reached our staging position. Then a strange thing happened. The District Chief radioed out to Hai that he was not going to arrive as planned by chopper because he had not yet gotten the word that the 2nd ARVN Division commander had approved their part of the attack. The problem now was that if they weren't already in place it would take all day for their troops to get in position. I could see that the most important part of this operation was going sour due to the old problem of coordination between South Vietnamese commanders. As a unit or a mission got larger the politics took over. Also, while we had seen some real improvement in the individual unit leadership capabilities, they still didn't trust each other enough to succeed in coordinated operations. Well, it became obvious that we would not be landing on the Hourglass this day. We also knew that we had lost any possibility of surprise as any of the enemy force that was back on the island would have been aware of our movement and staging right across the river. I decided that it would be smart to bring in some other kind of fire support to keep up the pressure and also to disguise our attack plan in the enemy's eyes -

just in case we might come back tomorrow. We couldn't get any helicopter gunships, which would have been the simplest way to work over the island again. We were about to resort to more concentrated artillery fire while we pondered our options when a call came in from Province operations. It seems that a South Vietnamese spotter pilot was looking for a place to practice bringing in air strikes and he had a pair of A-37 "Jungle Jets",flown also by South Vietnamese pilots, ready to bomb. I thought this was a great idea! Even better, it would be a chance to have the Vietnamese ground commander direct the air strikes by Vietnamese jet pilots working through a South Vietnamese spotter plane!! This would be a feather in the cap for the "Vietnamization" program !! No American intervention!!

As the spotter (the FAC-for Forward Air Controller) arrived over us he called me on my radio and in perfect English began to work with me to bring in the strike. I interrupted him quickly and tried to get him to work on the radio with my counterpart on the ground - none other than Captain Hai. The pilot refused to work with Hai. He didn't trust a Montagnard. We tried to hand off to one of the PF Platoon leaders, a young lieutenant whom we were training, but the FAC would not work with anyone but me. At the same time Hai was trying to tell me something through Kinh's marginal translation. I got the idea. He did not want South Vietnamese Air Force flunkies running an air strike anywhere near him. He didn't trust them and was afraid they would miss the target and kill all the friendlies. I finally talked him into letting them drop one strike on the center of the Hourglass just to keep up appearances. We had to have some kind of a show of force or this whole day would look like a keystone cops operation. Plus the enemy would smell a rat. We actually let the Vietnamese air strikes continue for over 3 hours. They got lots of practice and we looked like we were serious about this thing - not to mention keeping the 83rd on their toes. We waved goodbye to the air force, got through the usual lunch and siesta and returned early to the 711 camp. I was really frustrated! We had just witnessed a prime example of the thing that might make it totally impossible for the Americans to ever turn this whole war over to the South Vietnamese. In one day we had seen the failure of the Regular Army to cooperate with the District and Regional forces (not to mention the poor Navy guys at the junk base) in carrying out an agreed-to and pre-planned combined operation as important as this one; followed by the fiasco of neither the Air Force nor the ground forces trusting each other enough to work together for an all-indigenous air strike. Vietnamization didn't look so successful right now.

Back at the camp we found that another special visitor had come to spend the night with us. He was the Navy Lieutenant whose role was called Naval Intelligence Liaison Officer (NILO) so we called him NILO all the time. While he resided in the Province Capital, he was always trying to spend time in the "boonies" with people like us. He had heard that we were finishing up a visit out here and that we had some action going on the coast that he may want to help us with. Of course he was welcome to join us. He was a pretty good guy and had been out on a patrol with me and Dai Uy' Hai before so he felt comfortable inviting himself out. Later that night he told us that he had an idea. The USS New Jersey, largest battleship in the world now, was about 20 miles off our coast out in the South China Sea and had nothing to do that night. After hearing our story about the Hourglass, he suggested that he could get the New Jersey to fire its 16-inch guns on the island for us. Why not? We had never had naval gunfire before. I knew the New Jersey had lots of firepower. Its big guns each fired a projectile the size of a Volkswagen as they always said. This meant the equivalent of a 2000-pound bomb from each gun as often as you wanted it. The guns were supposed to be extremely accurate , too, even from 20 miles. So the NILO said he would get them to fire later on. He promised us a thrill ! We were not to be disappointed.

NILO and I had some rice wine with Dai Uy' Hai and then checked the perimeter. Hai had told me that the word was that the 2nd

ARVN had now completely reneged on their promise to attack the island with us and he had been ordered not to try it by himself. Did this mean that the 83rd battalion would be allowed to just go on living on that island without punishment? We knew the answer here in Vietnam was : "if we don't get it done now , there's always later". Tomorrow we were scheduled to leave Hai's camp and return to the our team house at the District compound. Hai wanted us to wait til the afternoon so that he could host a special farewell lunch for us. We gratefully accepted and bid him goodnight. Nilo and I went back to the hooch, but not before a stroll around the compound. He was fascinated by the people, their activities, and the things I told him about the Montagnards, comparing them for him to the majority of South Vietnamese. I was able to get my point across as he watched them, but just barely. I could imagine how difficult it would be to explain all this to someone who had never been here and experienced this before. In later life I learned that it wasn't just difficult - it was impossible!

We sat around the hooch and b.s.'d for awhile and then started our radio watch routine. I happened to be on watch first so I didn't get the awakening of my life like some others soon would. The NILO stayed up with me, and after about a half hour he borrowed one of our radios and began talking on it. In a few minutes he asked me : was I ready? Ready for what? I had completely forgotten our discussion about the New Jersey and the plan to fire on the Hourglass. Concerned that Hai had also forgotten, I headed for his hooch to see if someone would wake him up. We didn't have to. I was led to the top of the wall on the easternmost side of his fort where we found him sitting on top of the wall. He greeted me and pointed out in the direction of the coast. Now I knew he was waiting patiently for the fireworks to begin - he hadn't forgotten.

We sat silently for a few minutes until we saw a distant flash of lightning-like light on the eastern horizon, then a few more flashes, followed by the unmistakable sound of maybe a dozen guns going off, but it was more like a low rolling thunder. The NILO joined us in our perch in an instant and was counting down seconds. Then he hunkered down and we followed suit, keeping our eyes peeled. Just then the largest explosion I have ever heard shook the entire district. Even though the impact on the island was 3 kilometers away I was scared! Would it ever stop? It was like being caught outside in a thunderstorm when the bolt of lightning hits so close it blinds you and the following thunder deafens you for a moment. Most impressive was the almost earthquake-like result. The ground did literally shudder continuously and the fort started to crumble small pieces off its side. All this was the result of 12 rounds fired from the USS New Jersey on a site just 3000 meters from our vantage point and I really didn't want it to happen again. As the earth settled down again people started to come out from their hooches to find out what had happened. They were in a state of shock. This was incredible. Doc and Kinh came running over to where we were and just looked at a grinning NILO. Dai Uy' Hai then explained to Kinh that we should be told that he had also seen enough. He pointed up to the sky and said - in English for the first time - "B-52".

He was saying that the wrath of a broadside from the New Jersey could only be compared to an "arc-light" air strike from carpet-bombing B-52 bombers. He should know. He had come from the mountains where most of the B-52 strikes in the South had been aimed. It was said that B-52 strikes were the only thing that the VC and regular NVA troops coming down the Ho Chi Minh Trail or hiding in the jungle-covered mountains were really afraid of. The power of the New Jersey had reminded Hai of that environment and he wanted no more. He smiled and shook hands with the NILO and me and Doc and hopped off the top of the wall. He set out to visit each bunker on his perimeter - probably to try to explain what had just happened to each of his troops on guard. I felt bad for a moment - embarrassed for us American kids playing with our toys of destruction in front of a people who had seen nothing but death and destruction for over a generation. I didn't know it at the time, but still another generation of Montagnards would come and go before the fighting would end for them.

Next morning we saddled up again at first light to head back to the coast and the small fishing village where we had gotten all the correct information before. From there we could quickly move up to our riverside position across from the Hourglass if necessary. On arrival at the ville, the Hamlet Chief greeted us with much more enthusiasm than before. He was really glad to see us and to tell us the good news. Word was that the 83rd battalion had left the island fortress and slipped past the junk Navy all the way back up to Son My. This meant that they were not a present threat to our district, even though they had gotten away. I wouldn't say they had gotten away without a scratch. After all, their master plan to attack 711 company's camp and the District compound simultaneously had been foiled by our neat little ambush and we did manage to record a body count of 8 and 2 prisoners taken. Also, the 83rd's time on the island couldn't have been all that much fun with all the firepower we had brought in over 2-3 days - capped off by the awesome power of the USS New Jersey last night. Our disappointment was that we had not disabled the battalion with a decisive battle while they were isolated on that island. We even failed to catch them in a routine movement back to their home district. On top of that, we never set foot on the island to assess any damage we had done with all the support fires - now we couldn't tell our support friends about any results. My sorrow was that all of this mainly resulted from the lack of trust between the different service factions working for the government so that a coordinated operation became a real problem for them. As stated before, this did not bode well for the future.

*　　*　　*　　*　　*　　*

We left the fishing village before lunch and quickly made it back to the 711 camp by about 12:30 - just in time for lunch. This time Dai

Uy' Hai and the Village chief had outdone themselves. A special "going-away" lunch was ready to go except for the main course. He was still being prepared. I could see one of the cooks busily scorching the black fur off of a once-friendly and playful dog about the size of a cocker spaniel. I had seen this playful pet many times this week and he would have the honor of being the entree' in a multiple-course meal for the American Advisers. After several appetizers - right now duck feet,etc. seemed normal - and a warm beer or two we were served small chunks of a braised meat that tasted a little like tough pork. The dog meat needed a heavy dipping in nuoc maum - that very strong "fish sauce" that was the staple for seasoning everything in Vietnam - to make it more palatable. After all, knowing what it was would kill the meat's flavor instantly. It was bad enough for me, but Doc was having a terrible time. He may have gotten one bite down, but I know he kept most of what he did pick up in his mouth for later disposal. With the completion of the meal and warm handshakes around, we packed quickly while waiting for the province chopper to come pick us up. Dai Uy' Hai and his most trusted Lieutenant again went out to guide the chopper in as if they were professional Pathfinders. We took off without further ceremony except for salutes, more handshakes, and kind invitations to come back again for a longer stay and promises that next time we'll get them good!

*   *   *   *   *   *

We looked forward to getting back to our compound and a hot shower from our sun-heated tank system that was high-tech compared to bathing in the river or in the rain, which we had gotten used to this week. The Huey lifted slightly, nosed forward in a southeasterly direction to get lift from the slight breeze, then rose in a sharp banking turn toward the coast and around to the west toward the District compound at the center of our district. As we banked I had a clear look at the Hourglass and its seemingly untouched beauty. Some day we just had to get on that island! We would definitely come back soon to visit with the Montagnards, but for now it would be back to operations with the indigenous South Vietnamese platoons and companies. Hopefully we would have small accomplishments every day to celebrate and to make our little team feel that it was making progress - maybe even doing its part to help our South Vietnamese friends win this war to keep their country.

CHAPTER EIGHT

July passed quickly. As the days without rain extended themselves, the "Dry Season" was just about upon us. Now the rice farmers would begin shifting available water from many rice paddies to a few so as to allow a harvest of some kind during the next few dry months. Soon some of the paddies would be bone dry and cracking in the unbearable sun. Huge water buffalo would still be used to keep the soil plowed up as much as possible. These giant working beasts were about the most fearsome animals I had ever encountered. These water buffalo (or African Cape Buffalo) easily weighed 2 tons each and were ugly and could be pretty mean. A charging rhinoceros could not be any more threatening. We would often be moving by some working farmers on an operation, watching a couple of very small kids work the water buffalo - and scolding them if they got out of line. All of a sudden we would see the giant rear up its head and snort. We were discovered by our scent as different, and the strange American smell did not make the water buffalo any too friendly. Sometimes he would charge our formation, looking for the foreigners, but we would be saved by tiny little kids who beat up on the beast until he gave up the charge. Neither we nor the Vietnamese local forces we worked with would dare to shoot a water buffalo for two reasons. First of all, they were the most valuable possession that any farmer could own - the government could not routinely destroy this most valuable farm worker. Secondly, I thought, it probably wouldn't do any good to open up on one of these hulking monsters. All you would have is a madder, wounded water buffalo on your hands. Interestingly enough, after a few weeks of these terrifying encounters with the water buffaloes, the problem seemed to diminish. We figured out that as each new American began to smell like the locals by eating their food, the less the scent of an American was discernible by any animal.

Toward the end of July I would be getting promoted to 1st Lieutenant (*Trung Uy*) - just in time to take over the MAT Team. Ron would be rotating back to the U.S. by early August. But there would be one more operation we would both be going on before he left. This one came out of necessity and dedication to a principle more than good sense, but we did it anyway. The experience came close to being the last of any kind for both of us.

We got the hushed word of the operation directly from *Thieu Ta' (Major Hoa)*, who told us that the 2nd ARVN (Army of the Republic of Vietnam) Division would be running a major sweep operation across the northeastern part of our district in two days. They believed they would flush out many dispersed elements of a North Vietnamese company-sized unit and drive them west from the coast towards QL-1. Our job was to set up a blocking force to catch the stragglers as they ran. It sounded easy, but part of the plan was for us to move out to set up this blocking force at 3 a.m. This was something you just didn't do! You never moved around that late at night. To do so would invite certain disaster. Despite Ron's protests, we were told that if we wouldn't go along, they would try it anyway. Ron and I agreed that we had to go along to help with fire support for the inevitable contact the column would make with the NVA. Actually, it also amounted to a question of honor. If we didn't go, we might lose face - be thought of as cowards! We also agreed that since it was almost sheer suicide that we would not assign anyone else - we would be the minimum two advisers and would take Tu with us as interpreter. By all rights, Ron should never have gone on this operation. He was way too "short" - about 20 days left. But who else would go? We readied our gear, then sat down to write the "last letters home" in which we would both "subtly" say farewell to home without letting on how frightened we really were. Yes, frightened. I'll admit that - and anyone who wouldn't is a liar!

ALWAYS!

SCARED ,
OR APPREHENSIVE

By the time night came, we were still hoping that this operation would be called off like so many of the joint operations with the ARVN had been. No such luck. Tu was sent around to wake us up at 2 a.m. - as if I had been sleeping - so that we could join up with about 80 Popular Forces soldiers led by the little 2nd Lieutenant whom I had become quite confident in. (To this day,and to my sorrow, I can't remember his name, though). As we walked out of the team house a whole gang of PRU's (Province Recon Unit) thugs gathered around us. They would be our bodyguards - sent specifically by *Thieu Ta'* to protect us. Usually you could tell how much enemy contact was expected by the number of PRU's that Hoa assigned to the advisers. If there were 4, it meant maybe no contact. If it were 6, then contact of some kind was expected. If there were 8, sure contact with a strong force, and so on. For the first time since I had been here, the PRU contingent sent to protect us numbered 12 - the biggest group I had seen. This didn't serve to calm me down much, although we knew these men would fight to the last to avoid losing an adviser.

As we prepared to leave the compound I reflected on what my fear was really based on. I actually feared capture more that I did anything else. Getting wounded meant going home; get killed and you didn't worry about it any more; but getting captured by the VC meant a fate worse than death. *BADLY SHOT UP!*

We left the compound gates behind, sauntered mob-like down the Hiway about 50 meters, and then the point element pushed across the road and through the bushes toward a familiar village, one that we had eaten lunch in just a few days before. The troops still moved in single file, with the command element about half-way back. The two advisers and our interpreter were a part of the command group - the little Lieutenant walked just in front of me with his radio operator next to him. I carried our team radio and Ron and Tu were right behind me. As usual, there was no noise discipline in this mob - the only quiet people were the PRU/bodyguards who - for now - brought up the rear of the column.

We were now only about 600 meters from our own Headquarters Compound - ambling along a narrow trail between the rice paddies that led to the little "friendly" ville. By day this would be a simple operation, but by night it could be ----

--- The night exploded in a hail of very close-in fire! Tracers, mostly green ones, were flying all over the place - on line and then wildly glancing off something and bouncing skyward. It was like being caught in the middle of a firing range! A steady blast of automatic weapons and machine gun fire kept up for no more than 15 or 20 seconds, but it was enough. We had been ambushed - at night!! Chaos ruled!

The instant reaction was to fall just off the trail on the side opposite the ambush. As Ron and I did this and hit the hardening paddy mud, two bodies fell on the trail and gasped their last breaths right in front of my face. It was the little Lieutenant and his radio operator. They were among the many who died instantly in the short but extremely violent ambush and we had been right next to them when it sprung! Later on we would learn that we had lost half of the PF troops - either killed or wounded - in that few seconds in the killing zone. The rest of the troops, with a sergeant in charge, had fallen back to the half-dry rice paddy on the same side of the trail as we were. Another sergeant low-crawled over to retrieve the Lieutenant's radio, then slithered back to his men. We were strung out - now on line with the tail end pointing toward the District HQ. My instant thought was of how long could we count on these troops staying here or would they run back to the district compound. I think some of them had tried to run but the PRU's had stopped them at gunpoint and then moved to gather around us. Ron was desparately calling the artillery people to get some illumination rounds up in the pitch black night. Before the first illum rounds went off a small burst of fire at the front of the column scared the hell out of me, but I noticed it to be all red tracers. The friendlies used red tracer rounds while the bad guys usually had green. This wasn't the rule or anything, but it was normally a safe bet that red tracers meant that friendlies were doing the firing. In this case some of the PF's either saw something and opened up in panic or were just so frustrated that they let go into open space.

It had now been about 2 minutes since they sprung the ambush, and there were no signs of additional enemy moves yet. Surely if this were an organized ambush these people would want to move on us and mop up. Surely they knew how effective the first blast of firepower had been. We were half wiped out! The first illumination round from the artillery fire base popped open and it's bright, drifting parachute flare lit up the trail dramatically. It was littered with bodies - some dead, some wounded but motionless, and some crawling slowly. It was then that I realized that this particular rice paddy no longer smelled like human waste. Now the sweet, sickening smell of blood permeated the air around us. The smell of fresh death was everywhere. All the survivors stayed hunkered down, using the trail as a berm of protection against the inevitable charge by the enemy across the killing zone. It never came. My thoughts turned to the possible flanking movement. The next illum round helped us to see behind us across a broad expanse of rice paddy. No sign of any movement to the side or rear. Perhaps this had been a hasty ambush set up by a squad of North Vietnamese who were scrounging in the village. They might have heard us coming, set up quickly, let go all the ammunition they had, and run away. They knew that the only way to break up an ambush is to charge it, and if the desperate PF's decided to charge, these few communist soldiers probably didn't want to be anywhere around.

So, in a total of about 15 seconds, a handful of opportunistic bad guys had virtually destroyed the better part of 3 PF Platoons, killing one officer and killing or wounding at least half of the troops. We still didn't know what would happen next. It wasn't even 3:30 yet - over 2 hours till first light - and the district HQ could not risk sending anyone out to relieve us or to render medical assistance. After about an hour one of the PF sergeants got up the nerve to organize the troops so that slightly wounded soldiers could try to move severely wounded back to the district compound. What did they have to lose? Besides, by this time the bad guys were long gone. What remained of our group, some still bloody from their own or others' wounds, could hold out here until first light when a relief force surely would come the 600 meters to help us. We stayed hunkered down in that paddy and fired artillery illumination until the sun came up. I had never in my life been so relieved at watching that huge red ball climb up into the sky! The longest night of my life was over. We could see around us. It was safe! Death would leave us alone for another day. But the grim reaper had taken his toll of our Vietnamese comrades already. We would feel just as much pain over these losses as we would have if they had been American boys. I was growing very fond of these people, and now I was losing friends. I know there were Americans in Vietnam who regarded the Vietnamese as less than human, but I wish they could have had the opportunity that I had to get close to them.

*　　*　　*　　*　　*　　*　　*

As sunlight flooded the area, I could see that the devastation in human terms was even greater than I could have imagined. At least 20 bodies were laid out in line now and were mercifully wrapped in white cloth provided by the local civilians. As a relief column of RF troops arrived, I noticed that *Thieu Ta'* had come with them and was silently paying his respects at the sides of the dead PFsoldiers. Suddenly he spun on his heel and marched determinedly into the small village. You could see the anger in his swagger. In a few moments he returned, followed by 3 PRU's who dragged the Hamlet Chief behind him. The Hamlet Chief wore the customary white dress shirt, but I could see drops of blood all over the front of it and I noticed his nose was bloodied. He had been pistol-whipped by the District Chief for his failure to warn us of the presence of NVA soldiers in this otherwise peaceful Hamlet. Then I saw - to my shock - that the Hamlet Chief had a bloody rag tied around his right forearm where a hand should be. The story was then complete. The enemy had used their favorite form of terrorism - cut off the elected official's hand - as a warning to ensure that he wouldn't talk. Then, because he didn't, our own District Chief had punished him. He was understandably in deep shock. As a follow-up note, the next time I visited this little hamlet, there was a brand new chief there. Who could blame the previous chief for giving up?

Last of all, what had ever happened to the ARVN Division regulars that should have swept their way to our area by now?? Well, it seems that the District Chief had received a radio message just as he had moved out of the compound with the relief forces. He had been told then that the ARVN troops had been ordered to stand down. No operation this early morning. The General in charge had decided that it was a bad day to work - maybe tomorrow. It quickly reminded me of the time that we had been in need of artillery and that the ARVN artillery battery would not shoot because the General was sleeping and they did not want to wake him up! So, due to laziness on the part of the ARVN leadership and the more important systemic problem of coordinating Vietnamese forces, this operation had been a non-event. But, wait a minute!! I had lost 20 friends killed and as many wounded and had come close to getting my own butt shot off! This was not a non-event to me! But, unfortunately,in the scheme of things, I guess the most important night in my life was not so important after all. It sure was important to the families of those who fell alongside of us. Someday, I hoped, we would avenge their loss.

*   *   *   *   *   *

Ron and I moved slowly back to the District with the escort of our PRU bodyguards who had stood so bravely with us. Once we were deposited in the safety of our compound, the PRU's started to filter out of the compound to who-knows-where. I ran over to shake each of their hands with a two-handed grasp. No words were necessary here - just the looks of mutual respect. I would see these guys many more times in the next few months.

We sat quietly with a beer. Neither one of us spoke. We just communicated what we both were feeling. What a stupid thing for us to take a chance on late-night movement! What a waste of good men on an operation that never developed! Why would Ron go out on a fiasco like this? The whole operation had disaster written all over it from the first time we had heard about it. Why didn't we dig in our heels and not let the operation go at all. We knew better!! Why! Why! Right then I vowed not to let anything cloud my best judgement in the future. From now on I would stand my ground when I saw us being drawn into a foolish operation. Well, at least that was what I vowed to do.

There was one more piece of business to take care of before we left this operation behind us. Ron went down in our bunker to make a radio call on the "secure" system. This was a coded radio system that could be decoded automatically back at the Province headquarters and at the MACV advisers compound for the team that advised the 2nd ARVN Division. Voice communications were scrambled at our end and unscrambled at the receiving end, and of course the answer would be handled in reverse. In essence, you were talking over the radio almost normally, but you could say anything you wanted !! And Ron did. He finally got the Senior Advisor to the 2nd Division to come to the radio and then proceeded to read him the riot act. How could they let the Division Commander get away with what he did? And if he couldn't sway the General to live up to his promised operation plan, why couldn't the advisory team have warned us in time and cancelled our suicide night movement?? The Major on the other end really didn't have much to say. What could he say to make it right? Ron closed the conversation abruptly because he was about to push it a little too far. He finally told the Major to keep his sorry troops out of our district. After Ron finished he acted a little embarrassed. After all, he knew what little control the advisory team probably had - think how much we had. But he would never forgive them for not telling us the operation was off before we moved out into disaster! I knew then that I would have a hard time ever working with the ARVN's or their advisers again. This was a lick on them and they'd have a hard time living it down. This wouldn't be one of those mutual admiration situations between our two teams.

*　　　*　　　*　　　*　　　*　　　*

So, by late July,1969, Ron had officially stacked arms and I was virtually in charge of the team. I couldn't blame him a bit. He now was down to 15 and a wake-up before heading home and he had been through enough. There were not too many other officers' slots in Vietnam where you stayed out in the field for the whole 12 months. Sooner or later you had to have a break. Ron would not go out on any more operations. The last one had been his grand finale'. Even if he had wanted to go out again, I would have talked him out of it. In about 8 months, I hoped, I would be short and out of the field too. Everyone had their turn. Some went to the rear. On a MAT Team you just hunkered down a little more and took fewer chances. Then one day you would leave for home. Just think. From this third world environment back to the real world in a period of a couple of days for out-processing. What a shock that would be. Right now, after only 4 months in-country, I found it hard to remember the image of a typical suburban neighborhood and all the trappings. How hard would it be to handle "re-entry" into normal life? Someday we would all face that challenge. Or at least we hoped to - 365 days from the day we entered this fantasy-land.

After our most recent experience I actually had some doubt if all of our team, and I, could make it to that day.

The casual observer might think that mere survival was the only goal in Vietnam. Well, at times - like during a night ambush where your team is the "ambushee" - survival is all there is! Yes, there were times when the mission and long-term goals were set aside - but just temporarily - and the objective would be to get through a situation in one piece. Some Vietnam veterans have indicated that survival was always the only goal. I don't see how anyone could say that. Most of the vets I know will say that no matter how bad things got, they still felt they had a job to do and did it. The after-action reports of a thousand firefights will back up those statements. I will always feel that those of us in the field as advisers had a chance to feel accomplishments - however small - from time to time, while an infantry platoon leader in an American unit would have a totally different outlook and attitude. Their only measure of success was the kill ratio or the "body count" of enemy killed. War was a pretty grim business all around , and I had gotten a pretty strong taste of it.

CHAPTER NINE

By 28 July I had been in-country for 4 months and, coincidentally, my first year as a commissioned officer was completed. It was time for the automatic promotion from 2nd Lieutenant to 1st Lieutenant. The promotion was almost symbolic in nature because it was automatic, but it felt good to suddenly be considered an experienced officer rather than a green one. Along with my orders for promotion came orders awarding me (and several others) the Combat Infantryman's Badge (the C.I.B.). I had wasted no time in qualifying for this coveted prize. At the time, the qualifications were that you had to be an infantryman serving in an infantry slot in a combat zone for at least three months. The catch was that on top of this you had to have been involved in direct ground combat with a hostile force on 3 separate occasions while on infantry operations. Simply stated, you had to be in at least three real firefights - or "shot-at-and-missed" at close range. I had chalked up those three qualifiers very quickly.

The C.I.B. has since become more important to me than any other award or decoration. This award is frankly, what separates the combat soldier from everyone else. In Vietnam, the total number of Americans who served was over 2.5 million. One in five actually served in combat for a living, and only half of those were Army infantrymen. Half again would not serve in direct qualifying slots, so even though they should have, they might not get the C.I.B. Subtract again those who, sadly, never came back - and the total number of guys walking around with a C.I.B. from Vietnam is probably under 100,000. It makes me proud to be a part of that group. Also, when I go as a guest to the Special Forces convention with all those Green Berets (those airborne bigots) the fact that I hold the C.I.B. makes me welcome even if I *am* just a "leg" - the paratrooper's constant derogatory slur for all non-airborne Army types. When they find out I was in combat just like they were I get a lot more acceptance.

Well, the team decided to have a blowout promotion party for me. They picked a Saturday afternoon and invited all the Province military and civilian people they could think of. They had all heard about the party we had thrown for *Thieu Ta* Hoa's promotion and would probably all show up for mine. It may again sound crazy, but we would spare no effort to create a memorable event - even out here in the "boonies". There would still be security until early evening for those returning to *Quang Ngai City*, and a few would probably stay over at our little compound. There would be a cook-out and lots of beer and wine to drink. Of course the invitees would include American and Vietnamese officers and key senior enlisted men from the Province and all of the team and our Vietnamese officer friends in our District.

By late Saturday morning the compound was alive with the bustle of preparations. An old parachute was hoisted over the entire American compound as a shade canopy. Someone had built a barbecue grill out of 55 gallon drums cut in half the long way and somehow had procured a ton of charcoal. When I saw the dozens of charcoal bags, I just shook my head in wonderment. Where do people find this stuff in a war zone? There were also four extra 55-gallon drums set up as coolers for the beer. One of the engineers" 5- ton trucks would deliver all the ice we could use later. Nobody asked where it came from, but the driver would be instantly added to the invitation list. We guessed the ice was stolen but that the truck wasn't. Around 2:30 (after the traditional siesta) the party would start. All sorts of vehicles started arriving. Several helicopters would come and go, dropping off their passengers on our new, fancy chopper pad with the white rabbit head painted on pierced steel planks (psp). The District Chief had detailed a platoon of Popular Forces to provide constant security at the chopper pad and around the hiway entrance to our compound. Within an hour the party was going strong under the parachute canopy, with charcoal-broiled steaks(scrounged from the Navy guys at Chu Lai), beer, and all the trimmings. There must have been over a hundred extra people on our compound at once during late afternoon. The crowd included quite a few attractive Vietnamese women who worked at the various U.S. and Vietnamese province offices. They were all dressed in the traditional *Ao Di'* , pronounced "ow zaye" in the Saigon Dialect. This dress consisted of long black silk pants and usually a white silk top with long, tight-fitting sleeves and long, flowing ankle-length skirt slit up to the waist on both sides. These made very graceful traditional costumes. In addition to the traditional white over black, some of them wore more colorful combinations of silk. I often thought the colorful ones might be the more expensive while the white and black were cheaper and more for the plain women. They were always worn by the high school and college girls in the Province town. Anyway, the presence of these women and the addition of some loud Motown music (remember, this was the sixties) made this more like a party.

At the appropriate time, a short ceremony would bestow upon me my new rank. In the traditional manner, the Province Senior Adviser - the colonel I hadn't seen since my first arrival here - pinned a silver bar over the cloth gold bar on the collar of my fatigue shirt. Then, following in like fashion, *Thieu Ta* Hoa removed my Vietnamese insignia for 2nd Lieutenant (*Thieu Uy'*), a single black metal lotus blossom, and replaced it on the front of my shirt below the first button with the insignia for a *Trung Uy'*. This was a set of two lotus blossoms, signifying that I was now a First Lieutenant. I would wear this insignia proudly for the rest of my tour and I still have it today as another prized possession. I often wear it at ceremonies and am instantly recognized and befriended by Vietnamese in America who are so happy to see someone who served closely with their military people. Maybe this kind of

American understands why they want their country back - even today.

The last part of the ceremony consisted of the opening of dozens of bottles of champagne. They were passed around, and everyone who approached to give me a congratulatory handshake would then want to toast with me. Even these small sips would add up - one at a time for me and one each for them. I was outnumbered! Along with each toast the person would pour a small amount of champagne over my new rank - another tradition. *Thieu Ta* was the first Vietnamese to greet me and he poured champagne over my Vietnamese rank as well, starting a new tradition. Needless to say, after going through about 50 of these rituals, I was soaked in champagne and getting rather tipsy. Fortunately the party settled back to normal again, but now the champagne flowed everywhere. The sixties music got louder and lots of dancing broke out. It was a great party until sunset came. The compound started to empty out rapidly at that point. Most of our visitors wanted to get back to the relative safety of the Province capital. By dark most of the visitors - and all the ladies - were gone.

It was then time for a quieter time and another "ceremony". This time a huge urn of home made Rice Wine was dragged by the Vietnamese to the center of our compound. I could guess what was coming next. I thought everyone would have to take a long sip of this potent stuff through the one long straw that stuck out of the 3-foot high urn. I had guessed almost right. Actually, as the guest of honor, I had to take a hefty sip with every one of the Vietnamese officers and senior sergeants in our headquarters. So each one of them walked up, shook my hand, and, after bending over to take a swig off the straw, ceremoniously offerred the straw to me for "my turn". After about 15 "my turns" I had finished the round of Vietnamese and was still standing, but it wasn't over yet. Now each of the Americans on the District and MAT teams wanted to get into the act. OK, eight more sips wouldn't hurt. Unfortunately, I was getting very drunk when the Vietnamese wanted to go another round. I had to politely excuse myself. This was the only time I would turn down anything offered me by my Vietnamese friends, but they understood why. I headed back to my hooch and crashed. It's a good thing I was completely off duty and that nothing happened that night, because I didn't wake up till almost noon the next day - and then I wished I hadn't. What a hangover! The rest of the team knew what I felt like, and they whispered around me for the rest of that day and night, knowing I would react to any loud noise - like someone's voice. They had also played a nasty trick on me during the night. I woke up with a bedmate. Someone had neatly tucked our pet pig into bed with me and, I would learn later, had taken pictures of me and the pig sleeping together. I guess they forgot to remove the pig after the pictures - probably laughing too hard. So there I was in bed with Mr. Snort. I started to laugh, but it made my head hurt. I was silently thankful that I would only get promoted once over here. If some General had dropped in just then to give me a field promotion to Captain, I would probably have turned it down just to avoid the party!

*　　　*　　　*　　　*　　　*　　　*　　　*

Two weeks later it was time for another party. It was Ron's going away party. He had finally reached his DEROS (Date of Estimated Return Over Seas) date and was ready to go home - "Back to the World" as it was commonly called. Ron didn't want an elaborate DEROS party, just the team and some of the Vietnamese officers would be just fine for him. Most of us were releived that we wouldn't face another blowout like the promotion party.

On the day before Ron's departure the District Chief held a formal flag-raising ceremony in the compound. All the troops that normally manned the compound - about 100 of them - turned out looking sharp as the flag was raised to the strains of the National Anthem of the Republic of South Vietnam played on a tape recorder hooked up to a loudspeaker system. Then Hoa pinned a medal on Ron's uniform. He had been awarded the Vietnamese Cross of Gallantry with Bronze Star by the Province Chief (at Hoa's recommendation) for his duty as a combat adviser. I thought this was very fitting and that it was one way that the Vietnamese could show their appreciation to Americans who had fought alongside them. I did learn years later that there were American units that received, almost automatically, the Cross but not with the Bronze Star device. The one Ron received was specially awarded by the people he worked with and not by some bureaucratic channel.

That night we held a small, quiet party for Ron, including the Vietnamese officers. We had gotten a plaque made for him with crossed U.S. and South Vietnamese flags and a brass plate with a suitable engraved citation on it. We toasted Ron to a great future, he made a small speech, and so did Ken as District Senior Adviser and Major Hoa followed him. A few more toasts followed. One of them was offered by one of the Sergeant's on the District Team, who wished Ron a good trip home and that we all would be joining him there soon. There was an awkward silence. Sure, all of the Americans, if they survived their year, would be returning home someday, but what did that mean to Hoa and his fellow Vietnamese. We'd serve our year and fly away, leaving them to continue the fight for God-only-knew how long. It was a sobering moment. Ken very diplomatically broke the silence with a toast to our Vietnamese friends and Ron added : " ..and to their country".

Then Hoa smiled and said something like – "who knows but maybe we all really will end up in the U.S. some day". What a prophetic comment!!

The next day we drove Ron to Quang Ngai City to catch the Air America puddle-jumper to begin his long trip home. At the airport, Ken broke out another bottle of champagne and each of us was handed a tiny plastic cup. A quick toast and Ron was gone. Hoa turned to me before the plane even got off the ground and congratulated me for now having officially become the Team Leader of Mobile Advisory Team I-1. He reminded me that my radio call sign would now be MIKE-ONE-ONE, then asked me if I would ride back to the compound with him in his jeep. He would let his driver sit in the back, he would drive, and I would ride in the right seat. Ken winked at me as I retrieved my weapon from his Scout vehicle as if to let me know that he knew that Hoa liked me and that this gesture of driving me home was part of that. A new phase of my tour in Vietnam was beginning.

*   *   *   *   *   *

Within a week of Ron's DEROS, I got a message that a new 2nd Lieutenant had arrived at Province HQ and that he would be assigned to my Team as assistant team leader - my replacement was here - and we could pick him up the next day. Doc and I went in to the city and brought home a somewhat nervous 2nd lieutenant I'll call Dave. On the ride back to Tu Nghia I learned that Dave was also from North Carolina and he had followed about the same path I had in getting here. After graduating from one of the Universities in our home state, he joined the Army on the "College Option Plan', did his 16 weeks of basic and advanced individual training and then the 23 weeks of Officer Candidate School (OCS) at Fort Benning, GA, - "Home of the Infantry". Then, after six months of pushing basic trainees in the States, Dave got orders to Vietnam and an assignment to MACV as an adviser. He had left a young wife at home with no kids just like I had. Dave seemed like a solid citizen who would fit right in. The way he talked you could tell he just wanted to do something to contribute over here. Like a lot of us, he wanted to make the most of this experience in his life.

We arrived back at the district compound just before noon, and from there Dave's indoctrination into the environment went almost exactly as mine had four months ago. Why not? It seemed to have worked for me so far. I wanted to give Dave just the same kind of solid footing that Ron had started me off with. Later, I would be able to let him branch out and learn more of his own style as he developed it. One thing I would do differently than Ron was to spend more time with Dave on the culture and psyche of the Vietnamese so he wouldn't be surprised. There were lots of things that were not covered very well in the Advisers' School that we had both gone through for the first two weeks in-country back in Saigon. Boy, that seemed like long ago and far away to me now!

I was happy to have our team back up to full complement now, with Dave as assistant team leader, Doc as medic, Sergeant Lew for light weapons adviser, and Sergeant El as heavy weapons man. And the good news was that we would operate as a unit for 8 months before I would rotate home! I thought this was the best team in country and would keep it as active in training and civic action projects as we were in day-to-day combat operations. I wanted to spend more time out with the Regional Force Companies in their outposts and their areas than we had in the past. With stepped up pro-active projects came the necessity of having everyone staying very active and not just hanging around the compound waiting for something to happen. We had a lot we wanted to accomplish and not much time to get it done! One thing I wanted to reinforce to my team was that their ideas were extremely important to our operations and that we would all discuss them - and the projects that the ideas might spawn - among ourselves and with Ken and the District Chief. And we would do all this planning as a unit. It was the only way I could imagine that a 5-man team could be successful. I believe that my approach made each person's job more interesting and rewarding and probably made the time go much faster too. I know it made us more effective and it made the Vietnamese officials sit up and take notice. We were very visible! I guess we were visible to the bad guys - the local Viet Cong Infrastructure (VCI), too, because they sure tried hard to counter us. When I learned that they knew me by name I knew we were getting to them.

*   *   *   *   *   *

About a week after Dave joined the team, he had the opportunity to go out on his first operation with me and *Thieu Ta* Hoa. We were to take 4 Popular Force Platoons about 4 kilometers to the northeast to investigate a place we called "The Rockpile" - a rumored haven for what was left of a local Viet Cong guerilla unit. The Rockpile was really just a large rock formation that shot up out of the now-dry rice paddies close to the major river that flowed from Quang Ngai City to the sea. Theoretically, this position could have commanded the waterway, but this rag-tag group of guerillas didn't really have the means to do much damage. They were also closely watched by the 107 Regional Force Company that manned a small outpost alongside the river road. Our mission today was supposed to have been to attack the Rockpile, but word was already out that there were too many booby-traps and other fortifications there. Here began another exercise in conservative warfare - to say the least.

We made our way to the friendly outpost in about 2 hours and joined up with the 107 company, a fairly decent-looking group. Their triangular outpost looked functional and well-kept. All this time I was wondering why we hadn't had that much contact with this company until now. I got my answer. The company had traditionally been more subordinate to the Province Chief as the first line of defense for his own hide in Quang Ngai City, so Hoa didn't pay much attention. The 107 company also provided road security along the road that ran parallel to the river from the City out to that Navy junk base we had visited before. They were more of a palace guard for the bigwigs in the Province Capital. As soon as we arrived, the troops started to move out toward the Rockpile as if in search of a good fight. But everything stopped when we got to about 500 meters from the enemy camp. Hoa suggested that we soften the place up with some artillery fire, which seemed like a good idea at the time, so I called up the boys at LZ Snoopy and had them pound away for about 15 minutes. Just when I thought that the troops would be ready to start some kind of infantry maneuver, one of the JAKE FACS showed up over us. This spotter pilot had heard there was something going on and flew on over to see if we had any work for him and his jet fighter friends. It was a nice gesture, but it sure altered any plan we had.

I knew that *Thieu Ta* would want to take advantage of the American fire power now with air strikes, so without trying to change his mind, I told JAKE 4-2 to go ahead and drop whatever he had close by right on the rocky area. Five minutes later a trio of F-100 Super Sabre jets with U.S. Marine markings came up on station. I must admit that it was fun to watch them work with JAKE 4-2 in complete control and the jets screaming by for pass after pass, dropping multiple 250-pound bombs as they pulled out of their dives. When they were done, JAKE made an inspection pass and immediately drew small arms fire. As he swooped down over the site he cut his engines and we could hear the chatter of AK-47's on full automatic. They were shooting at JAKE, who quickly powered up and tore out of harm's way temporarily. We estimated that there were maybe 6 to 10 bad guys in there, probably with good covering spider holes among the rocks to hide in as a defense against the artillery and air strikes. JAKE 4-2 and I discussed it for a minute, then he got off my frequency to find out where he could get more resources. I knew what would be coming now. Napalm!

The best way to get these dug-in enemy was not to blast them out with high explosives, but you could either burn them out, or suffocate them, or scare the daylights out of them with the burning jelly-gas from above. JAKE 4-2 came back in a minute with the news that another set of fast movers was inbound heavy with Napalm canisters - just what he wanted. These local yokels had tried to pop him out of the sky and he was going to make them pay for that. The jets soon came along at about 20,000 feet, but after JAKE gave them a marking rocket with its white smoke right on top of the place he had drawn fire from, one of them dove in and dropped one drum of Napalm right on the Rockpile. That was apparently all it would take! In a few seconds I could make out the image of 3 raggy-looking men coming across the dry rice paddy from the Rockpile with their hands held high and waving a white rag. While I expected our troops to open up on them, they held remarkable discipline and allowed these now-unarmed guerillas to get all the way to within 20 meters. They were then told to stop.

The enemy soldiers dropped the rest of their gear while our troops moved in on them. One of them wanted to "*Chieu Hoi*", which was an amnesty program (translated "open arms") that allowed an enemy soldier to walk in on his own and surrender. This guy must have been joking. The *Chieu Hoi* program didn't work if you were captured in battle! He would be an ordinary POW. They were quickly tied with arms tight behind their backs and roughly marched right past us as if they were so many trophies of the conquest. I noticed that one of these guys was at least six feet tall. Was he Vietnamese or maybe Communist Chinese (Chinese were often much taller than other Asians) ? Too late to find out, these prisoners were whisked away under mild protest. I wondered, as always, what would happen to them. Perhaps I just turned my head, though. The South Vietnamese had not cornered the market on human rights and we knew it. They were, however, head and shoulders above the North Vietnamese communists on that issue. This has been proven true in spades since the eventual communist takeover of all of Vietnam.

Now that there was silence from the direction of the Rockpile, I once again expected to see an infantry maneuver on the stronghold. To my delight, the troops did move forward and swept over the enemy position. We followed with the command group and eventually discovered the 5 dug-in enemy bodies - 2 burned beyond recognition and 3 seemingly untouched but turned blue from asphyxiation. The Napalm had done its job in both killing ways. Once again I thanked my lucky stars that we had this weapon and they didn't. This was horrible stuff !

Just before we left the area, I called up JAKE 4-2 and reported 3 prisoners and 5 enemy KIA, jokingly calling 2 of them "crispy critters". It was always important to report success to the people that gave us such vital support. A body count was magic and earned us even more support. Body counts meant success, pride and esprit de corps and often earned other plaudits, extra time off,etc., to the fire support troops. To us it meant progress - winning ! Sounds morbid now, but that's part of war - including the jokes. With the help of all the might of the U.S. Air Force and Marines, we had rid this God-forsaken Rockpile of "Victor Charles" - the Viet Cong - the communist threat to a freedom-loving South Vietnam - our allies (and - our dependents). My (our) job - was to guarantee them their independence !!! Welcome to Vietnam, Dave. Your turn to run this rag-tag outfit will come and when it does - I'll be so short
----

CHAPTER TEN

A few weeks into August the dry season was in full swing.
Operations got even more brutal, with dust fouling up the air
breathed by humans as well as by the ever-important helicopters.
Things got a little quiet for a few weeks, with the exception of the
customary mortar attacks - token as they might have been - on our
district compound and American team house. Usually starting at 2
or 3 a.m., these mortar barrages became so routine that I once was
awakened - not by the exploding round's impact, but by the "thunk"
of the first round being dropped down the tube. The "incoming
olympics" continued, with my racing times to the bunker winning
hands down. Each time this happened, we would call for
illumination - requested and cleared by the District Chief, Major
Hoa, - and would fire two or three rounds of the artillery-borne
flares. The bad news was that these artillery illum rounds would
drop a heavy canister after deploying the flare on its parachute for
its slow descent. The impact of these empty canisters, when fired
for max illuminating effect on our perimeter, would fall directly on
the nearby overpopulated refugee camp. Occasionally the canister
impact - approved with political and military clearance by the
District Chief - would cause injury or death in the refugee camp.
Routinely, the next day would bring claims for money from the
camp leader and weeping and wailing from the family of the

WE USed HAND FLAres + LOCAL
MOrTAR illUMINATION FIRST

unfortunate random victim. This was truly as painful as anything we
did here, but we learned to treat it as an unwelcome necessity.

I always hated to go near the refugee camps for several reasons,
not the least of which was the constant reminders of the terror that
our own weapons had caused the residents. In providing protection
for our compound, we dropped a lot of those heavy illum canisters
on this huge camp. Other things that bothered me about the camp
included the knowledge that the people had been uprooted and
didn't want to be here and were thus vulnerable to the constant
politicking by the Viet Cong Infrastructure (VCI) that travelled freely
in these camps. Last , of course, was the rotten feeling you would
get just by witnessing the depressing living conditions here. It was
really sad. We did what we could to scrounge materials to give to
the government so that they could maintain the hooches, but a lot
of it would go the route of corruption and would never be used in a
refugee camp. I was told that once there were a hundred bags of
cement donated by one of the U.S.A.I.D. offices that wound up
being used to reinforce the Province Chief's personal bunker
instead of to build a small school for the refugees. These were the
stories that frustrated us, but they also became the most publicized
ones that then turned into the cliché's and generalizations that I still
hear today from the misinformed. That really sets me off, too! All of
the Vietnamese leaders were not corrupt - but some of them were.
They viewed themselves as taking advantage of their position
deservedly because of the great sacrifices it took to be in a
leadership position here. I guess they thought they had a little
largess coming.

In August I had my first real encounter with the mysterious
Buddhist Monks of Vietnam. These guys were the ones that ignited
the passions of the American people (and themselves) when, in
1963, they engaged in public "self-immolation" - a new term coined
in the bizarre "sixties" - to show devout protest against the Catholic
President Diem (zim). On several occasions in those days the

American people were "treated" to dinner-time family room entertainment on the national news-and-talking-head programs - complete with graphic visions of a monk on a Saigon street corner dousing himself in gasoline and setting himself on fire while crowds of bystanders stared in shocked disbelief. These displays had eventually destroyed the Republic's government and brought on the coup-generated death - assassination - of President Diem in November of '63. The incidents stuck in my mind as I entered the South Vietnamese culture as an adviser on borrowed time, trying to understand the intricacies of Vietnam. My first and always reaction would be to assume that these monks were anti-government or at least enough under suspicion to be treated with alertness. The Monks had revolted several times against whatever South Vietnamese government was in power at the time, and they often demonstrated against the current President Thieu, calling him a "puppet" of the Americans, etc. This always made us suspicious that the monks were basically agents of the communists. We didn't feel this way about all the Buddhists - that would be 70% of the country - just these sneaky monks.

So, one stifling hot August day we were out on an operation with two platoons of Popular Forces (PF's) and had met with some sporadic contact with a few scattered enemy troops that had annoyingly kept us occupied for several hours - much to my frustration. During one of the exchanges of fire across a well-traveled dirt trail, the firing from the enemy side of the trail abruptly ceased for no apparent reason. Just as I was trying to figure out what was going on, Tu, my interpreter on this operation, pointed out that there were three figures approaching down the trail. Our troops remained locked-and-loaded but did not fire at the three Buddhist Monks that calmly sauntered down this trail, their orange robes flapping in the breeze, shaved heads shining in the sunlight, and bare feet leaving tracks in a muddy trail that featured a mixture of blood and dirt. The casual appearance of these monks so startled us that we just stared as they continued on their way down the trail. Even the local civilians, as often as they had been near the middle of a firefight, would never have been this nonchalant! The monks must have known not to be afraid of the Viet Cong or of us. Could that be because they played both ends against the middle? Tu tried to tell me that they were "off limits" because they were "holy men". I wasn't so sure about that. For that moment I wondered about Tu's honesty as well. Could you really trust anybody over here? I watched the monks all the way to a small Pagoda about 300 meters down the trail, where they went inside - presumably to pray. Why did the VC stop shooting to let these people pass? They wouldn't have done that for any other South Vietnamese - not even women or children.

 As the monks disappeared inside the masonry building, my attention was quickly snapped back to the business at hand by the crack of AK-47 bullets over my head - the bad guys were shooting at us again. Lieutenant Hahn - in charge of the operation today - came over and, through Tu's interpreting, told me he wanted artillery fire to help get this little skirmish over with. Before Tu could translate, I already understood what Hahn wanted and I agreed with him. Maybe we could clean this up, getting the enemy on the run, before lunchtime. Then we could enjoy our lunch and siesta. While I got the artillery people on my radio to call in the fire mission, Hahn called back to get clearance from the District Chief or his duty officer - a routine but necessary matter - as I would have to relay the political and military clearance to fire to the artillery battery officer - with my initials as the responsible American on the ground. Clearance accomplished, we started firing a few high-explosive rounds about a minute later. Then, in a pause, we noticed that there was still small arms fire coming back at us but that it had moved further down the edge of the trail. So, we "walked" the artillery in that direction. Before we knew it, we had come very close to where the Pagoda stood. I looked at Hahn, who smiled and said "ban! ban!", which means shoot - shoot!   I radioed the artillery fire base to keep it up. In a few seconds we saw an artillery round explode right on top of the Pagoda. It was damaged severely, to include losing its roof and one wall. Now, we didn't know if the monks had left or not. We didn't have time to check it out, but were pretty sure that they had left safely when they heard the very first artillery shells explode at fairly close range. We never heard later of any monks being missing, but didn't really try that hard to figure it out. I did have a feeling that, for one reason or the other, I wouldn't see any monks brazenly hanging around when I was out on my next operation. So much for the Buddhist Monks for the time being.

*   *   *   *   *   *

By the end of the month, the dry season was almost complete. We could look forward to the beginnings of the rainy season - the monsoon. In our area (I Corp) it would run September through almost the end of November, with the middle six weeks consisting of total rain, fog, and flooding to the degree that air support and some ground movement would become dangerous - if not impossible. This could make it tough if the enemy chose to launch any major offensives in our area at that time. Our edge in technology would be greatly reduced. But, I'm convinced that the bad guys didn't want to fight in the mud much more than we did. They probably missed a good chance to catch us in a weaker moment during monsoon, as they carried out only a few small actions in our district..

Just before the rainy season was to begin, I had the opportunity to go on another night Medevac. This wouldn't be my first but it would end up being my most exciting. This time we were all in the District compound one night, playing poker and killing time. Around midnight one of Major Hoa's aides came running over to our teamhouse, excitedly urging me to come over to Hoa's communications bunker with him. When I got there, Hoa explained in his near-perfect English that out near the coast a squad of his Popular Forces had sprung an ambush successfully against a dozen North Vietnamese Army regulars, but that one of the friendlies was severely wounded - shot in the head. He asked for a Medevac helicopter to see if the man could be extracted and hospitalized in time to save his life. I glanced at the map, and after assurances that this was for real and that there were over 30 PF's on site to provide security for the chopper and its crew, I agreed to call for an American Medevac. The trick to this was that since there again was not an American on the ground at the PZ (Pickup Zone), the chopper would come here to pick one of us up and take us out to the site for the pickup operation. This was a matter of security and identification, but it also allowed the Medevac crew to "bend" the rules to support the "Little People" as they were called in radio transmissions. (If it were an American down, the word would be that "Uniform Sierra" - U.S. - needed help).

We got an instant response from the American Medevac people. They were great! Before I could think about it, Dustoff 1-6 was inbound with an ETA (Estimated Time of Arrival) of 15 minutes. There was no question that I would do this one myself, taking only Kinh, an interpreter, with me. A squad of PF's provided security out to our chopper pad - it was outside the wire and across the highway - and set up a perimeter on the far side. Dave and Rich went out to the pad with me - no American would ever go out there without another American along - and they brought a radio for contacting the Dustoff pilots as they approached. The call came soon, asking for a signal. Dust-off 1-6 was now feet-wet (just off the coast) and ready to turn west to our location. I turned on the mini-strobe beacon light and the little pocket light started to blink so brightly that I had to hold it way over my head to avoid the blinding flash. Dustoff 1-6 spotted it immediately and headed right for us. Three minutes later, with no lights at all, the big Huey flared down to touch its skids to the pierced-steel-planking of our pad and we scrambled aboard in seconds, allowing the bird to take off quickly. Inside, the crew chief in the open-air passenger compartment handed me an aviators helmet so I could talk to the pilots and direct them to the pickup zone. They knew the map coordinates, but wanted to get my inputs and also wanted to make sure that I had instructed the ground forces how to handle this extraction. Using hand signals I got the crew chief to give Kinh another helmet to get him in on the conversation. Then, by pushing a button on his headset, Kinh could talk over the radio to the platoon leader on the ground, instructing them to form a large perimeter and to find a way to signal us (and to simultaneously warn us of the signal by radio) to ensure we were landing in exactly the right spot. The last instruction was to make sure we minimized the chopper's ground time - it's most vulnerable time - by fast action loading the casualty.

The pilots seemed reasonably comfortable as we approached the site near the coast. We could just make out a torch being waved by somebody in the general direction of the PZ, so the pilot started to corkscrew down for a landing. Just as we got about 20 feet off the ground a huge and very bright light bloomed right in front of us. Somebody on the ground - trying to help - had lit off one of those giant airborne "Spooky" flares I had scrounged off the Air Force weeks ago. These flares had about a million candlepower and now, instead of drifting down from a plane on a parachute, this one was on the ground, in full flower of its intense light, right in front of the pilot's eyes. The only possible reaction for the blinded pilot was to pull up radically. After a few well-chosen words, the pilot asked if I could get those people to turn off the sun!

The flare disappeared momentarily, and the pilot - still somewhat dazed but determined to make this pickup - started his descent. This time we landed on a rice paddy dike with a lot less trouble. I could look across the next section of chunky dry paddy and see a gaggle of people all waving their arms and jumping up and down but not bringing the wounded man to us - and I knew they had him there. Meanwhile here we sat - the helicopter and 4 of my American comrades (2 pilots, the crew chief and a medic) plus Kinh and myself - pinned to the ground in a vulnerable position that every bad guy within 5 klicks could figure out, and the ground troops were not helping us get out of here. Through the helmet intercom, the crew chief yelled at me, promising me that this bird was taking off in 30 seconds - casualty or no casualty on board! To top this off, I caught a glimpse of some green tracer fire careening over the chopper and off into the air in my view. This meant that there were enemy soldiers still out there and they were firing at somebody - probably the troops that we hoped were really out there protecting our backsides on some kind of loose perimeter. All of this was of course happening in a matter of a few seconds, and I could see things easily coming apart if somebody didn't do something. This was my party so it was up to me to take some kind of action.

In the heat of a situation, most people react without a lot of deep thought. There is in most of us a special sense of what needs to be done and what will work. So we don't have to analyze optional action, potential outcomes, long-term effects, and probabilities of success. Sometimes if we did all this analysis the answer would be - no way! This was one of those situations that I now hate to think about, because in hindsight any analysis would come out with a very poor prognosis and maybe a no-go decision that would have had long-lasting negative effect on the image of our team's efforts.

So, without much thought at all, I jumped out of the idling helicopter and started running - or trying to run - across the 50 meters or more of dry, cracked, plowed up rice paddy. In my haste, I tripped and fell flat on my face twice before reaching the other side and the people who gathered around the wounded soldier. The first time I fell, it dawned on me that I had left my M-16 rifle in the chopper. It's strange what we think of and when, but here I was unarmed and out running alone in the boonies - at night! Which of a myriad of bad things might happen next? But such split-second thoughts go away as fast as they come. On reaching the casualty, I then found myself in almost a tug-of-war with a young woman - obviously his wife or sister - who was afraid to let her loved one be taken away by this strange foreigner, to be flown to who-knows-where on this giant flying machine Would she ever see him again? The platoon leader had apparently been trying to convince her to let the others carry him to the waiting chopper with no success but, now that I was here he got a little stronger in his persuasion and finally she let go. I tried to be as gentle as possible in carrying this poor victim back across the chunked-up paddy while making the trip as quickly as I could. Fortunately, I didn't fall with my burden, but the progress seemed agonizingly slow. And, as in any race with time - or death - you are most frightened as the "finish line" draws closer. When I had gotten within 10 feet of the dustoff, I could see green - now red - tracers going everywhere. Those bad guys were trying with all they had to get to this bird sitting on the ground, but apparently our little PF platoon was doing a good job of holding them at bay - but could they just hold off for maybe 1 more minute? If so, we'd be out of here and on our way to safety!

At last we were carefully loading the wounded soldier on the chopper and I found myself half crawling and half being dragged on board. The pilot had already revved up the turbine engine and gave us a hell of a jolt as he took off and immediately banked hard away from the main firefight. The medic was already working on the head wound and within seconds told the pilot that this man was critical and needed to get to the surgical hospital at Duc Pho. There would be no drop-off at our team house tonight. Kinh and I would fly all the way to Duc Pho without complaint - this man's life may be saved by saving that 5 minutes.

Following the national highway down to the giant American brigade base camp at Duc Pho took less than 10 minutes. As we approached this version of civilization American-style in the middle of nowhere, I saw a long airstrip, bright lights, and dozens of plywood hootches and other semi-permanent buildings. One of them had a chopper pad with a big red cross painted on the metal planking. This would be the evac hospital where Medevac birds would bring in the casualties of hundreds of firefights. The pad looked big enough to land a bunch of helicopters at the same time.

We landed near the emergency entrance and were immediately met by four nurses with a stretcher. In the ambient light I was shocked at the appearance of these four "round-eyed" young women - American women - in their army fatigues, but there was too much important work being done here to allow staring at this unusual sight for long. The patient - the Vietnamese soldier was now a patient instead of a casualty - was whisked inside the hospital hooch while the chopper lifted off again to find another pad for overnight parking. Yes, we were going to spend the night here. Why should the pilots risk another night flight to get us back to our compound when they could haul us back home first thing in the morning. They probably thought we would enjoy one night in the luxury of a rear area, but clearly Kinh was uncomfortable - and so was I, for that matter. The cultural switch in me was beginning to show. I actually felt safer among my Vietnamese friends than I did at an American base camp!

We followed the flight crew back to the hospital building. We all wanted to inquire about the condition of our Vietnamese patient. As we entered the emergency treatment area I was taken aback at the scene in front of me. There on a gurney lay our PF soldier, being worked over by two doctors and two nurses in the open room. My heart was in my throat as I found myself staring at the poor soldier's head - part of which was missing - with brain exposed for all to see. One of the doctors turned his eyes to me and I could see the compassion in them. He could only shake his head as if to indicate helplessness. The medic grabbed my arm and led me out. He told me that if our friend lived he would probably be severely brain damaged. After all we had been through, had we still not done enough? The pilot sensed my despair and assured me that we had done all we could but that we might lose this one.

It just didn't seem natural, but Kinh and I accepted the empty bunks assigned and sacked out. I slept lightly as usual. In about an hour my try at dozing was interrupted by several loud explosions. Kinh and I were outside the hooch in a flash and in the bunker across the way just as quickly. To our embarrassment there was only one other person in here with us. The G.I. was on radio watch and actually was startled when I ran in yelling "incoming". He laughed at first, but straightened up when he noticed my darkened rank insignia. He explained that what we had heard was outgoing artillery fire. The brigade base camp included a battery (6 guns) of 8 inch Howitzers - the really big guns. They were firing in support of someone out there who needed help. I went back above ground and was happy to hear the loud sounds of merciful help for those in trouble. But I didn't sleep any more that night.

Next morning we were ready to get back home, but first I wanted to find out what had happened to our patient over the night. Almost as expected, the nurse on duty informed me that he had not made it. He had received the best care possible, but nothing could have saved him. I insisted on claiming the body so that he could be returned to his village and family. We had already had one of these soldiers' bodies get lost in the shuffle and I wasn't going to let that happen again. We grabbbed a cup of coffee in the mess hall and watched as a heavy body bag was delivered by golf cart to the helicopter that belonged to Dust-off 1-6. The flight crew came by, grabbed their coffee, and then trudged off to their waiting bird. We followed solemnly.

At 0800 on a lazy Sunday, Dustoff 1-6 radioed our compound - advising the team that he was 10 minutes out with 3 passengers aboard. One of them would require a vehicle for transport from the pad to safety. This was our fallen comrade. Just as this adventure had started, I watched from the pad as the chopper took off and rolled to the south. I called Dust-off 1-6 one more time, thanking him for all his help. He replied in the usual macho way - indicating "no problem" and "we'll get the next one". That was all we needed to say to each other. On to the next experience - good or bad ! I would have many of both kinds in my year in Vietnam

CHAPTER ELEVEN

Suddenly we knew it was September 1. You could tell because the Province chopper came in with our pay and mail and another set of computer reports to be filled out. The mail was the only thing we wanted. Pay didn't mean anything much - 90% of my big Lieutenant's salary went home in the form of an allotment. I think I kept about $50 in cash each month - $10 for the community beer supply, and the rest for poker games or 10 cent drinks at the MACV compound in Quang Ngai City. We were paid in MPC (Military Payment Certificates), the "monopoly money" we were supposed to spend at U.S. facilities or exchange at the official rate for Vietnamese Piasters (118 P for the dollar) to be spent in Vietnamese markets, etc. I usually took half my cash in Piasters so I could pay my share of our housemaids salary (about $5 per month each) and buy occasionally in the villages. We were not supposed to let the Vietnamese have MPC or worse - U.S. "greenback dollars". We weren't even supposed to have those! A couple of times during my tour an instant currency exchange took place as a surprise to the Vietnamese. The idea was to change the old MPC for the new version so that any Vietnamese caught with "old" scrip would find it useless. This would always cause panic among the more well-to-do Vietnamese who had amassed quantities of the Military Pay Certificates. An American Finance Officer would show up in a helicopter out of the blue and exchange any MPC we had for the new style. (I often wondered how it was so easy for characters like this to get a chopper when we always had to beg for them.) It just seemed that the U.S. went to a lot of trouble to keep valid scrip out of the hands of the Vietnamese, but in spite of all the controls there was lots of U.S. currency floating around in their economy. Unfortunately there were many Americans involved in this and other black markets in Vietnam. Many were caught and punished but many more were never found out. Seems the "ugly American" was hard at work in the black markets.

This first day of September, almost like clockwork, also brought the rainy season. That morning was the last time we would see the sun for three months! At the height of the monsoon season we would see temperatures go as low as 60 degrees and would feel like we were freezing to death. Funny how we had grown accustomed to the heat and now felt cold in mild weather. Everything is relative, of course. This also would be a dreary, depressing time. Rain, fog or mist was always in the air. At times we couldn't get helicopter support - but somehow the Province Finance and paperwork gurus would always get one, arriving dry, fresh and smelling like a headquarters overstuffed sofa. Upside-down again! What really made the rainy season unique was that the enemy action slowed to a crawl. You would think that our difficulties in getting aerial support would leave us wide open to stepped-up enemy action. Our edge was diminished greatly by the rainy season, yet the enemy didn't seem to take advantage of it - at least not too often.

There were some days during the rainy season that was relief enough from the heavy rain to carry on training. Dave, my assistant team leader, had gotten the idea from the Captain who commanded the artillery battery at LZ Snoopy that we should bring all our Vietnamese officers and sergeants to the fire base to learn how the artillery battery worked. This would give them not only an appreciation of what was going on every time they requested artillery fire support, but the experience would stick with them as a motivation to be correct on every call. These artillery guys worked their butts off and didn't need to be jerked around by some infantry officer who didn't know what he was doing. They were also very conscious about being accurate, of course. They loved their work and would keep things going as long as they were given feedback - results. This was good for morale and it was their only form of gratification for their hard work. They would hump 150-pound shells and turn 10-ton guns all day long if you told them they were making a difference. We spent the day on Snoopy - also known as Nui Dep , which was Vietnamese for "beautiful mountain". This beautiful mountain could bring fire and brimstone on the unseen enemy at any time - it was sure beautiful to us when we got in a scrape. At the end of the day I told the assembled members of this battery that they were definitely making a difference in our little war! They may not always get an enemy body count out of it but they should be aware that they always saved our butts. They most assuredly had a huge impact on the day-to-day war between our local forces and the bad guys that threatened the survival of our lowly District on a day-to-day basis.

This first training mission that Dave managed was very successful and helped to build his image and rapport with the officers, including *Thieu Ta* Hoa. The Major liked Dave and seemed increasingly appreciative of the overall support he was getting from our MAT team. We were lucky to have collected a good group of guys since I had arrived. Ken made note of this in my Officer's Efficiency Report - the highest evaluation I ever got. I supposed that if I ever changed my mind and decided to make a career of the Army, my record in combat would speak well for itself. Although I knew I was doing a good job, I also was thankful for the great team the Army had given me to work with. How could we go wrong?

The rest of the rainy season is a blur to me. I do remember that I made one trip to Danang for a 3-day "R&R" (rest & recuperation). My real purpose was to visit with my best friend in the Army, Glenn, who had been my roommate in Officer Candidate School at Fort Benning. We had learned of each others' Vietnam duty locations through our wives' letters. Glenn probably wished that he had another assignment - like out in the field with me. Considering his plight, I couldn't blame him. It seems that he was the son of a funeral home owner and had studied to be a mortician himself. It was obvious that he would take over the family business back in Georgia some day. After being commissioned an Infantry Officer with me, he had been assigned to what the Army called "Graves Registration". Later, in Vietnam, he was assigned to run the Danang Mortuary. Every American who died in the northern two military regions - or corps - of South Vietnam would find his way through Glenn's facility. They would be embalmed and prepared for return to the states and to their families. His had to be the most depressing job in-country at the time.

Glenn and I planned to meet at the officer's club in the 1st Logistics Command base - known as the First Log - through which all supplies for I Corps and II Corps passed . Yes, there was an Officers' Club and it was quite plush in its location in an old French villa. Again I was amazed at the luxury some of the people in the rear enjoyed. When I saw Glenn, I was taken aback. He looked very old. To him, I looked real skinny but in good spirits. He was just the opposite - fat and unhappy. After a few hours' discussion and more than a few drinks I had learned what Hell was like for my friend. He felt helpless because he wasn't in the middle of the action, and he had to see every one of the American boys who passed through his department - "tagged and bagged". Then he confessed his biggest fear - that of finding one of his friends in his daily inventory. He told me he wouldn't know what to do if a body came through one day with my dog-tag between the teeth. In my gallows humor - grown coarser every day in war - I flippantly told him to make sure that I looked my best and that - like the cowboys of old - make sure it looked like I had died with my boots on. It took a long time, but Glenn finally got the humor and smiled - however weakly. I knew he was really depressed. I suggested we appropriate a jeep and go downtown to the Marine Club that I had visited once before. It was almost in civilian country and featured gambling and all sorts of normally outlawed entertainment. We spent the night there. Next day I said goodbye to Glenn, promising him he would never find a body-bag with my name on it on his shift. He gripped my hand as hard as I think I had ever felt before and told me I'd better be right. Years later Glenn and his wife came to visit us. He and I headed out to the local bar for old times sake. He couldn't resist reminding me that years ago his greatest fear in Vietnam was to discover that I was one of his customers in the Danang Mortuary. I allowed as how I was glad I never needed his services. We drank to that - several times !! This experience taught me to be thankful. No matter how tough you have it, the next guy may have it worse. In reflecting on this, I am often reminded of the famous quote : " I wept because I had no shoes, and then I met a man who had no feet."

My return to Tu Nghia after Danang brought a welcome sense of comfort at being "home" again. Soon after that we found ourselves in the midst of what would pass for the "Fall Offensive" - a rather meager show of force by the North Vietnamese Army in our general area - but return to the routine of daily operations and occasional contact was welcome. The NVA had slowly, under the cover of low ceilings and dismal flying conditions for the good guys, worked their way down fron the mountains to the coastal districts of I Corps. Platoon-sized units would annoy the local security forces and our District was no exception. This was the time when I found out that the enemy knew me by name and actually had a price on *yes* my head. Truthfully, this was a bit flattering. How many 24-year-old Americans can say that they had a price of 10,000 on their heads? Of course the 10,000 was in Piasters and represented just less than $100. I thought I should be worth a lot more than that until I was reminded that $100 represented over a year's salary to most Vietnamese workers! I was proud - in a strange, macabre way.

During the Fall Offensive I had another one of those chilling experiences that I will never forget - one of the mental images that still occasionally haunts me in the hours of darkness. On one particularly eerie operation in the rain, we had made contact with a small force of NVA when - during a lull in the action - I received a call on my radio frequency which made my blood run cold. A sinister voice came over my radio frequency in Vietnamese. As I held the radio hand set to my ear I heard the Vietnamese-speaking voice tell me in no uncertain terms that they would kill me. The voice used my name! It spoke slowly enough so that I could understand almost every word. I was listening to his propaganda when Major Hoa ripped the handset away from me and began to yell in Vietnamese. He called the NVA radio man every name in the book. Hoa patted me on the back when it appeared that his threats had worked. I was still a little stunned at this experience, and I thought about it many times after that. I now realized that the VC knew our every move. Example: the night ambush that they had sprung on us back in July had to be set up by their knowledge that we would be moving troops at 3 in the morning. Otherwise they knew we never moved at night. Someone had told them our plan! Someone probably told them all of our plans.

Another chance encounter with an American I had known at Ft. Benning came during one of our infrequent joint operations with the Americal division, whose AO (Area of Operations) was the western mountains of our district and the adjacent district of Nghia Hahn - a known enemy stronghold. The battalion of the Americal was set up on a fire base called LZ 411 - named for the elevation of the hill it had been built on. The joint operation was supposed to involve a platoon of the Americal and one of our Popular Forces (PF) platoons, but when the early morning time came to helicopter out to the rendezvous site, we could only get one chopper. So -

improvising as usual - we loaded 14 of the PF's, two advisers (Sergeant El and myself) and one interpreter on the lone Huey at first light and headed west. We were lucky that this chopper was fairly new and strong because we certainly had it over-loaded! A Huey D-model was supposed to carry only 8-10 G.I.'s in combat gear. Of course the Vietnamese soldiers were much smaller than Americans and carried next to nothing in the way of gear. We still just barely made it off the ground! For some of our PF's, this was the first ride in any kind of aircraft. To make them feel more comfortable, I brazenly perched on the floor at the door opening with my feet out on the landing skid, smiling back at our "little people" and forward at the pilots like some kind of John Wayne or something. In reality, I was just about as nervous as they were. To be honest, I had once been a white-knuckle flier. My first flight had been the run from Ft.Dix, New Jersey, to Charleston - at age 23!! I was no seasoned flier here either, but I loved to fly in the Hueys. Besides, I had to make it look good for the little people. 15 minutes later we landed in a small clearing that had already been secured by the grunts of the Americal. As soon as the chopper had blown its way out of the LZ (landing zone), a very young 2nd Lieutenant of Infantry ran up to me and saluted (I could have killed him just for saluting me out here!). Right away I recognized this platoon leader as one of the Officer Candidates in the last class at Ft.Benning that I had been a Tactical Officer for. I remembered that this guy had not been in my platoon but had been a loser that we had tried to get washed out of the program. Apparently after I had left he had survived and graduated and was declared an Officer and a gentleman by a program that had become more tolerant of marginal performers as the war dragged on and as the need for 2nd Lieutenants had increased - mostly due to "attrition". (Attrition was a euphemism for getting "zapped" - killed!) We "old-timers" all liked to think that we had gone through the "old program" at OCS and were therefore much better than anyone who had come after us. In the case of this guy, it was true - he was a real loser. I was instantly leery about this operation.

So, we walked in the sun for a couple of hours, then went into a village for a routine inspection. The Americal boys stayed in the background as our Vietnamese troops handled the interrogation of suspect villagers. I was almost surprised - but glad - at the background role the Americans played. A short time later I would find out what made them so shy about dealing with indigenous civilians.

After the uneventful village search it was time for lunch and "siesta". The American G.I. s were at first shocked at our "stop-the-war-it's-time-for-a-break" siesta habit, but soon they followed suit. With minimal security our combined force took siesta until 2:30. In spite of the steady, light annoying drizzle we relaxed and enjoyed our brief respite from the war. At 2:30 the troops began to stir and the young LT. agreed that this operation was over and that he should move his unit back to their base camp - on foot of course. My entourage would wait for the chopper(s) to come pick us up.

The platoon moved out on its 1-klick(kilometer) hump to LZ 411 while we collected our gear and made ready for a helicopter extraction. About an hour later I heard the distant "wop-wop" of Huey blades popping the air and simultaneously got a call that 2 choppers were inbound to pick us up. As the din of the Hueys increased we popped yellow smoke to identify our position. About that time a strange thing happened. Out from behind a bamboo thicket wandered an American soldier from the platoon that was now long gone. The young soldier was rubbing his eyes - he had obviously overslept siesta and his platoon's departure! I was stunned! What was the cardinal rule of any unit leader? "KNOW WHERE YOUR PEOPLE ARE!" Count them! The American platoon leader - the loser - and this soldier's squad leader had screwed up royally! They had left one of their men behind!! What if we had not been there and he had been left completely alone in Indian country?? Well, I was beside myself! The young soldier - he couldn't have been over 19 - was afraid that he was in for it, but I re-assured him that the problem belonged to those in his chain of command and that I would take care of it and would get him back to safety. As the 2 Hueys landed, we split the troops and loaded in a hurry. Chopper drivers didn't want to sit on the ground for long. They felt like fish out of water when they did. I ordered one chopper load to go back to our district compound with most of the PF's. The other one had an interim stop to make at a certain Americal Division fire base and carried a cargo that would cause someone in that unit to be in deep trouble.

Our Huey made its way west to LZ 411 and eventually landed on the dirt right outside the battalion commander's hooch. The LT. Colonel happened to be inside and came storming out to find out why this chopper full of rag-tags had landed in his front yard. I calmly walked the young G.I. over to the colonel and explained that his platoon leader had left him out in the boonies and that I was happy to return him. You could see the colonel's blood pressure rising as through clenched teeth he got the unit leader's name out of the shivering soldier. It only took a glance to his aide to signal a summons for the incompetent 2nd LT. whose platoon would be back at the firebase by now. With that assurance that the jerk who never should have gotten a commission in "my" Army was about to get relieved (fired), I turned on my heel and hopped back on my chopper. Somehow, I felt a measure of satisfaction in the knowledge that an incompetent officer was about to get his butt reamed and would probably get relieved of his command - never to put soldiers in jeopardy again. When his tour was over he would probably just go home, muster out of my Army, and resume civilian life without further punishment, but he would never know the pride I feel at having done my job well in combat. Actually I felt here in a combat zone - as much as I had at Ft. Benning - that it was my responsibility to help identify the weak people. As my chopper took off from LZ411 I gave the battalion commander a friendly wave - sort of a half-salute. He was still fuming, but he probably knew that I had done him a service by helping to identify a poor officer before he got people killed. As if by coincidence, I was about to experience another intriguing aspect of my tour in Vietnam when the journalists started swarming like locusts to investigate the actions of yet another questionably qualified junior Americal Division officer named William Calley.

In the fall of '69 the activity of the U.S. press corps increased markedly. They, along with their foreign colleagues, smelled blood and would not give up the feeding frenzy until they had a conviction to go along with their suspicions. They were on the trail of a major scandal! We started getting lots of visits from writers - both famous and obscure, all intent on getting a scoop on the evil actions of some American troops that had supposedly taken place nearby in the spring of '68! The story unfolded with the leading questions of the hungry press in a barrage against the people in our district - just five miles away from a ville that would become famous by its name - "My Lai". The press had uncovered a potential bonanza of liberal shock-value "journalism" which would soon indict the platoon and company commanders who were the closest to what really happened in the village of My Lai - known as "pinkville" to the American troops. Most of the typically uninformed press thought that "pinkville" was given its name because the residents were "almost red" - communist - but in reality the troops called it that because the ville was colored pink on all the maps we had - including the tactical map in my pocket.

According to reports, the platoon of soldiers from the Americal Division had been tasked with the mission of wiping out any communist resistance in the village and were told to use whatever force was necessary to accomplish that mission. One would have to know the history of this civilian area before passing judgment, although those that opposed the war for selfish reasons of their own (cowardice in most cases) managed to embrace the "atrocities" of My Lai as their own personal cross - without caring about the extenuating circumstances or about the realities of the war effort itself.

My own personal knowledge of My Lai - a small hamlet across the river in the district to our north - consisted of Vietnamese folklore about the area and reports of the multitude of failed American forays into the decidedly communist area. The enemy ownership of the whole village of Son My, of which My Lai was a part, wasn't important to the hot-shot liberal "journalists" of the day. Their only interest seemed to be in proliferating the myth of the "ugly American" in Southeast Asia. Reporter after reporter (including some "great" ones) descended on the province and even our district headquarters looking for a Vietnamese that would be willing to denounce the Americans on taped TV.

With a little help from me, our district officials managed to avoid this interrogation. What good would it do for officials of a different district to speculate on the bait the journalists would throw out with their endless leading questions. Interestingly enough, when we tried to tell the "journalists" the facts about that area, they didn't want to hear it. There would be no sensational story if they listened to the facts from us or our Counterparts. Anything the locals had heard was just surface info - this wasn't hard news . We continued to endure the endless probing by various news media eager for a controversial report, but nothing worth printing or showing on the 6 o'clock CBS news would come out. Eventually the reporters abandoned the search for facts and just used their own imagination to write the story of My Lai. Years later, looking back, I have concluded that what happened at My Lai was understandable but must have been carried to an extreme that made the Army unit's actions unforgivable.

The way the story unfolded over the months and years after my return, it is obvious that Lt. Calley's platoon moved into the village with the knowledge and fear that everyone there was VC or at least VC sympathizers. The residents of My Lai had been repeatedly coaxed and ordered to come into secured areas of the province with no voluntary results. The area had been the site of as many booby-trap casualties and terrorist acts against American Marines and members of the Army's Americal Division for over 5 years as any place in the whole country. Many Americal units had been involved in search and clear missions that year with no enemy contact but constant casualties from snipers, mines, or booby-traps. In 1965 the story went that the Marines had come ashore and, again without seeing the enemy, had taken 50% casualties. Even our own situation maps in 1969 showed the 38th Main Force (VC) Battalion with its headquarters located in My Lai (4), right where Lt. Calley was to go in.

The story line on My Lai was that Calley's men moved in, lined up "innocent" civilians, and shot all of them in a ditch - over 200 women and children. They apparently met no armed resistance, but proceeded to torch the village anyway. A helicopter pilot and some of Calley's own men reported the killing frenzy. Eventually, needing a scapegoat, the Army court-martialed Calley, found him guilty and ran him out of the Army as unfit. While we were in Vietnam none of this came out in any news, but by the time I was back in the world 6 months later it was all over the TV news and in the papers. Calley was doomed to be the scapegoat and would be left out in the open by all his superior officers, including his immediate company commander, who should be known as the poorest "leader" in the history of the military - what a cop-out! Company Commanders were so close to the platoons of their units - or should have been - that anything that happened had to be known and condoned by the Company boss. That officer apparently refused to shoulder any of the blame and let it all fall on his platoon leader, Lt. Calley. Ever since that incident, the reputation of all OCS officers has been tarnished with unfair generalizations and lumping in of all OCS officers with Calley and my "friend" from LZ411. Even today, I read the totally uninformed "analyses" about the Army's leadership in Vietnam and am appalled at the blame placed on the general category of OCS graduates - said to be "inferior" to those from West Point and even ROTC officers. These writers are totally uninformed and don't seem to care, but it enrages me to see this kind of hogwash printed as if it were fact - more importantly that this new generation reads it and becomes additional victims of the same uninformed and inaccurate "journalism". In truth, Army officers - regardless of the source of their commission - served extremely well in Vietnam. But there were mistakes made by comparatively weaker officers from any of the groups. Mistakes like those of Calley and the young Americal Lt. who left his lone soldier behind with us that day. Selfishly, but proudly, I happen to think that OCS officers had to work harder for their commissions - most already had the college degree under their belt - and served closer to their men than either West Pointers or ROTC graduates. Some of the literature now says that OCS gave commissions to "those of lower intelligence, breeding, and economic levels". The 137 college graduates I finished OCS with would surely take issue with that ridiculous and unfair "analysis".

Back in Tu Nghia the attention from the press died out as swiftly as it had built up. Guess we just weren't good for an exciting and damning story. Our routine settled back into the monsoon doldrums for a while - but just a short while.

One rainy October night my friend the NILO (Naval Intelligence Liaison Officer) showed up unexpectedly in a helicopter and asked if he could spend the night in "the field" - in our team house. I welcomed him with a beer and we sat up just talking with Ken, our District Senior Advisor, for a while. About midnight I was in the bunker - my turn for radio watch - when a messenger came running over from *Thieu Ta* Hoa's hooch with the news that one of our patrols had sprung an ambush on a small group of "bad guys" as they made their way off the beach after landing in a small craft of some sort. Hoa wanted some artillery fired right away at a certain set of coordinates. It seemed that the bad guys were putting up one hell of a fight! Seconds later my Navy friend came diving into the bunker so fast that I thought there was a mortar attack or something. The NILO had that deer-in-the-headlights look as he asked me if I had any enemy contact reported by any of our Vietnamese troops near the beach. I told him that it had just been reported and that I was just about to call the artillery boys at LZ Snoopy for some fire support for our troops. I grabbed the radio handset to begin my transmission to Snoopy while the NILO checked my map markings of the target location against his folded up tactical map. Just as the artillery guys answered my initial call, the NILO grabbed my arm and said - "don't shoot yet". He then - rather sheepishly like most intelligence guys acted when they had to admit something - told me that the "bad guys" that my troops were in contact with might be one of his SEAL teams made up of an American Navy SEAL adviser and a team of third country nationals (could be almost any nationality of mercenaries). While I put the artillery fire mission "on hold", the NILO went back to the team house to use his secure radio to double check. Sure enough, scant minutes later he returned to the bunker. By this time one of Hoa's lieutenants was in with me trying to find out what the problem with the artillery support might be. You could tell that our people out there were getting real nervous without the big guns to help them out of this jam.

My Navy friend then came clean with his story. It seemed that the SEALs had told him of their training test tonight but he was instructed not to tell anyone - even me - about the plan. The test was simple. These third country nationals - mostly Filipino - would graduate from SEAL school if they passed it. If they didn't - well, the worst that could happen would be to get killed taking the test. Their test was to infiltrate at least 500 meters inland from their landing on the beach, then report to their American adviser back on the boat and then safely ex-filtrate the way they had come - without detection. And they were going to pull this stunt in *my district* !! Without telling me !

NILO explained that to tell us about it in advance would have ruined the authenticity of the test. What's more he added fuel to the fire by - somewhat arrogantly - saying that he never thought any of our district troops would be effective enough to spot his SEALs - let alone ambush them. To add insult to injury, he was now worried that the fight would progress to the point that the "superior" SEALs would have to kick our troops' butts and then leave. Needless to say, I was pretty ticked off but maintained enough composure to calmly suggest that we both get messages out to our respective troops to disengage this fight - that we were both on the same side !! It worked and the SEAL team worked its way back to the water and made off in a rubber boat in a hurry!

Now the only problem was explaining this stunt perpetrated by the crazy American intelligence community to *Thieu Ta* Hoa. Oddly enough, when the NILO and I quietly explained it to him, he burst out laughing. He then told of a couple of cases of this tomfoolery by the "spooks" that he had encountered in the past. We all had a beer and a good laugh. What a strange place - Vietnam. Never a dull moment here in the district. What a bizarre little war !! What a way to play soldier.

CHAPTER TWELVE

Our District team took on a new member sometime in October of '69. Another young 2nd Lt. - this one a Military Intelligence Officer - was assigned to manage the advisory effort to the Phuong Huong program, better known in U.S. circles as the "Phenix Program". This very young black Lt. was so new to Vietnam that he became the butt of all the jokes about "newguy" etc. This was only fair. Each of us had taken our turn at his dubious role. But Lt. Diocc - I'll call him that because of his official title as District Intelligence Officer for Command and Control - was especially vulnerable because he had a great sense of humor and really liked to be the center of attention.

The "DIOCC" was funded by the CIA and ran the program that called for systematic identification and capture of members of the Viet Cong Infrastructure (VCI), the shadow government that worked completely underground while waiting for a military victory by the Viet Cong guerillas and their North Vietnamese backers. DIOCC paid large sums of U.S. dollars - yes, greenbacks - to informants for information about the VCI in our district. He also would have primary use of the Province Recon Units (PRU's) who normally just provided bodyguard duty for us. The PRU's were sent out to try and capture ("arrest") VCI operatives at night. Often the DIOCC went with them - by himself! I thought he was crazy for going without another American, but he liked the independent and mysterious nature of his job. Many times the target for arrest would resist and would end up dead. Nowhere did it say that they had to go to trial.

DIOCC liked to play poker and always managed to start a game late at night. The games were often interrupted by a few mortar rounds from the bad guys or by an emergency snatch operation that the DIOCC would have to go out on. It was interesting to watch this seemingly young newguy grow up in a big hurry. The Phenix Program was apparently very successful in our district, but we weren't privy to many of the details. That's how the CIA worked. There has been a lot said and written in later years about the Phenix Program - most of it negative and highly sensationalized. The do-gooders who hated the war effort and always wanted to blame everything that was bad on America had a field day when they found out about Phenix. It was labeled as a murder program. It wasn't. Most of the targets in our district survived the snatch operation (arrest) and were turned over to the South Vietnamese for interrogation and incarceration. Only a few who resisted arrest violently were killed. We knew that these traitors did not receive kid-glove treatment in their interrogation and imprisonment, but would anyone like to compare their treatment to the gross atrocities perpetrated by their kind on innocent civilians in the name of liberation? At least that's the way I interpreted it.

One night a bunch of us were involved in a particularly late poker game in DIOCC's hooch when we heard a terrible racket coming from behind the team house area and from the general direction of the Engineers' compound on a hill about 3 klicks(kilometers) south of us on National Highway 1. About the same time Dave came out of the bunker (he had the radio watch from midnight to 2) and yelled that the Engineers were under a ground attack. They had called on the radio to let us know that they had been hit by sappers (bombing experts) and had spotted NVA infantry on their night vision devices - lots of them. They had called for gunships and told us to just stand by in case they needed any help from us.

The Engineer compound was pretty well fortified on its hill. They had several 50 calibre machines guns and lots of well designed wire and mine barricades. The sappers would try to breach these defense lines without detection and blow open a spot for the infantry to attack en masse. This time the Engineers had detected the sapper activity before they could complete their mission, but they were definitely in the wire and had made some breeches. The attack would be on in a few minutes. Many of the sappers had given their lives for the enemy's cause.

A strange thing happened then. Most of the Americans in our compound made their way around the line of team houses to the back (external) side of our compound. We all found vantage points between the team house and our defending bunkers to watch the show. Like neighbors at a holiday block party we settled in to watch the fireworks from ringside seats. Some of the guys brought lawn chairs - all of us brought a beer. This could be fun - watching the war from a safe distance. And we were about to watch innovative American firepower in action without our hearts in our throats this time. We were in no danger now - we thought.

About the time we settled in I noticed the running lights of a rather large aircraft coming into orbit at about a thousand feet over the Engineers' hill. The ceiling was a little higher than usual in spite of the rainy season, and only a very light drizzle marred a perfect, cool night. While I was trying to identify the aircraft the hill erupted in another "mad minute" of maximum fire from every fighting position. The Engineers must have sensed the ground attack!

Included in the mad minute was a barrage of 50 calibre machine gun fire. Some of them fired in our general direction, and for an alarming moment we heard the loud "thunk" of several of these large bullets sailing over our heads. They didn't crack like most small arms fire when they went by. They were so big and relatively slow that the half-inch diameter rounds just thudded overhead. We hunkered down a little to avoid being hit. Even at this range a 50 cal round was nothing to play around with. It would make you get your head down in a hurry.

The mad minute stopped just as a huge illumination device lit up below the fixed-wing aircraft I had spotted. Someone pointed out that it was "Spooky" starting its work - something I hadn't seen before. The Engineers were blessed to be getting the support of an AC-130 Spooky flareship. Spooky not only dropped those brilliant, million candle-power flares (like the ones I had scrounged earlier), but also was armed with 3 "mini-guns". These electrically controlled multi-barrel machine guns could fire 6000 rounds per minute and, with 3 of them firing, could obliterate a grid square (1000 meters on a side) in a couple of minutes. Any troops in the open would be obliterated, too.

Under the false daylight created by the continuous flares, the Air Force C-130 crew was able to see the NVA regulars advancing toward the hill and opened up with their mini-guns. On every machine-gun belt every sixth round is a tracer round. The red phosphorous glow of these rounds shows just where the gun is impacting. With the incredibly rapid firing rate of these mini-guns, the trace was a solid ribbon of red fire racing towards earth. It was a sight to behold. I was able to get some available-light slides with my 35-mm camera of this ballet of the Spooky. As the big aircraft circled, the ribbons of fire followed it like searchlights. The fire was heading down though, like fire from a dragon's mouth. For this reason, some of the earlier Air Force air-to-ground gunships had been called "Puff the Magic Dragon" (after the Peter Paul and Mary hit of the era).

Eventually Spooky stopped firing at the area surrounding the hill and reverted to flare-dropping only. It was time for the helicopter gunships now on station to mop up around the closer-in wire perimeter under the bright lights from the flareship. Another beauty of a picture, and I caught it with my 35! The choppers raked the perimeter for several minutes, and then it was over. The enemy had obviously had it for the night and retreated. This time they barely had time to drag their dead and wounded with them. The guns worked their way farther and farther away from the hill as if herding the bad guys on their retreat. Once again I was extremely glad that these were our weapons and not those of the bad guys. I couldn't imagine what it would be like to try to fight an enemy that had so many tools of devastation as we had. They must have been the most motivated - or stupid - soldiers in the world. We would learn that motivation was the correct description for the North Vietnamese.

The next day we rushed down by road to the Engineer compound to see what the results were. They had already policed up the few enemy bodies they could find and had about 20 of them laid out at the gate to their compound. Most of them were obviously the sappers who had been caught in the wire early in the attack. But still, with all that destruction and its rapid application, why weren't there more dead enemy soldiers found. The answer was that they would always try to drag off all their dead and wounded. Most Americans gave mysterious legendary status to this enemy habit. Some still think they did it to frustrate the body-count hungry Americans and to affect their enemy's morale. But think about it. What do Americans or any other fighting group want to do? They always want to recover their dead for proper burial and their wounded for treatment. It's part of the morale issue. A soldier who thinks he will be abandoned will not fight as hard. Also, with the

Vietnamese intense desire to be buried in the place of their birth, it is easy to understand why the communist Vietnamese were so intent on clearing the battle area as they retreated. They didn't always accomplish it entirely, but they had come close this time. There could well have been 5 times more casualties than the Engineers now had evidence of.

I don't know how, but the Engineers reported that they had been attacked by a battalion-sized enemy force, which would have been over 500 people. My concern was the obvious. In order to form such an attack, the NVA would have had to move large units and numbers of soldiers clear across our district during the late night hours for this 2 A.M. attack. This would mean that they made the trek right through all the observation and ambush patrols that we were supposed to have out there every night. How could they have done that? Was it possible that our patrols were that ineffective - or were they almost non-existent. Did they go to sleep on watch all over the district or did they really not deploy the way we thought they did. Major Hoa, who had ridden with me to see the aftermath of the attack, appeared to be puzzling over the same dilemma although he didn't say much. The Engineers didn't think about it. They probably assumed that our security forces were not for real anyway. I was embarrassed. I could imagine how Hoa felt.

Late that afternoon I heard some yelling coming from Thieu Ta's office. It went on for about a half hour and then about 20 soldiers scattered out of his office and disappeared on bicycles and motor scooters out of the compound. Ken walked up to me and commented on this little meeting that Hoa had called for his Popular Force (PF) platoon leaders. He had basically chewed them out in no uncertain terms. The next day I saw a memo which Kinh, my interpreter, translated as a directive from the District Chief to all PF platoon leaders. The gist of the directive was that they would in fact post 50 percent of their troops on active observation and ambush patrols every night. If caught violating this directive or allowing their troops to avoid it, the offending PF platoon leader "must go to jail". Major Hoa did not intend to let this sort of thing happen again - or else!

The next thought that crossed my mind was the obvious - what if the enemy had decided to attack our District compound instead of the Engineers? Our old minefield and the 100 PF's that stood watch on the perimeter might have some trouble if the attacking force was as big as the one that was suspected of assaulting the Engineers. I had a chance to add something to our defensive strength if I could get another directive from *Thieu Ta*. If we could divert all civilian traffic far enough away from the compound for a short time, I would work with our artillery friends at LZ Snoopy to plan and register Final Defensive Fires that could be stored in the fire direction center's computer and fired immediately if we called in the code names for the targets we wanted to hit. This was something I had done at the Regional Force outposts and had promised myself to do here at the District but had never gotten around to it. It was time to make time for this little tactical move.

Hoa agreed and we decided to do the defensive fires registering during siesta the next day - Sunday. Nobody would be allowed to come within 600 meters of our perimeter between noon and 2:30 pm. This meant the highway outside our gate would have to be closed for at least a half hour sometime in that period, too. We didn't want to take any chances with civilian casualties in this situation. We would actually be firing artillery and adjusting it where it would be most effective and we didn't want anybody getting in the way.

As I climbed with radio and field glasses to the top of the old chimney on the District Chief's house - highest observation point in the compound, I noted the terrain around us from a unique vantage point. Three sides were practically all open rice paddy with a few cart trails and a hooch or two within 500 meters. To the east was the highway with fairly thick woods on the other side due east. Northeast across Highway 1 was more rice paddy and the huge refugee camp. I could see our fancy new chopper pad with the playboy insignia on it just across the newly paved road. The young Aspirant (almost a second lieutenant) and Kinh came up to join me. We put together a mind's-eye plan of about where we wanted our pre-planned artillery targets to provide an instant rain of death on top of any bad guys who tried to overrun our compound. Hanh followed the process on his map and nodded his agreement. Then it was time to get to work. We had only a couple of hours to work with.

I got the fire base up on the radio and we were ready. What we needed was a ring of pre-programmed targets around us and at varying ranges. The inner-most targets might end up being 50 meters or so from the compound's bunker line. If the bad guys ever got that close in strength, the term "final" was appropriate to describe these defensive concentrations. It goes without saying that the last target we would plan would be much closer, though. Anyway, we started by picking out a very identifiable point where two trails intersected to the west of us and carefully plotted that point on our map. Calling in the 6-digit map coordinates to Snoopy, I asked for "willie-pete 200-up", which meant I wanted the first marking round of burning white phosphorous to explode 200 feet over the trail intersection. This made it easy to see and allowed margin for error on the first try. A minute of so later the round was on the way. It exploded high over the intersection, which I liked. Just to confirm, we asked for "willie-pete on the deck" - a marking round on the ground. The impact looked good so we asked the artillery boys to record that as DEFCON-1 (defensive concentration # 1). If we ever wanted that target fired on in a hurry all we would have to do is call in DEFCON-1 and we'd have maximum artillery on it within seconds.

The next target would be done the same way. It's initial position would be in reference to DEFCON-1. I called in "left 200, drop200-willie pete 200 up", which meant from DEFCON-1 come 200 meters to my left and 200 meters closer to me (they knew where I was, of course) and fire the marking round 200 feet up in the air. The second marking round was almost over a lone grass hooch that really shouldn't have been out there in our defensive zone anyway. Hanh (through Kinh) told me that it was abandoned and would be better off down anyway, thereby removing a concealing item for an approaching enemy to use. I agreed with him. I told the artillery guys to go ahead and drop one on the deck. They did - right on the grass roof - and started a great fire with the white-hot phosphorous! To our surprise, two old women came scurrying out of this "abandoned" hooch and high-tailed it off to the tree line farther west of us. We would never find out what that was all about but I have often wondered. They were probably spotters, watching everything that went on all day in the compound - particularly the American side - and reporting all they saw to the Viet Cong. They probably knew more about our patterns of activity than we did.

This brings up an interesting aside. One of the important things we learned in Vietnam is to never set up patterns of any kind of activity, even if it was your eating times or any other seemingly mundane, routine things. The VC made it their business to look for trends or patterns in everything we did so they could take advantage of our predictability. For example, let's say that they decided they wanted to kidnap one or two of us and they observed that every other day at the same time , two of us would drive to Quang Ngai city - about 5 miles on a seemingly safe, now paved road. It would be so easy to have a snatch team ready to grab us with impunity while our guard was down. Our safest bet was to be completely unpredictable. Even so, it was inevitable that any spies that could watch us long enough - particularly in the relative safety of our own compound - would eventually pick up some useful information. I was glad we had destroyed the old hooch "by accident".

We continued the process of registering these defensive concentration all around our perimeter, actually firing as close to our wire as 100 meters. The 50 meter targets were left to the computers to compute, and the final target - ground zero in the middle of our compound - was recorded with a totally different target name. This would be used if we got overrun and were abandoning the compound. The thought that gave me worse chills than that was that we might be forced to fire inside our own perimeter if overrun while still occupying it - right on top of ourselves and the enemy at once! Bunker or no bunker, we would have only the slimmest chances of surviving that kind of necessary action. I shook off the thought at the time but I've thought about it many times since.

Our mission completed, the word went out that all was clear. Now the compound and its surroundings would get back to normal. The highway was as busy as usual with people going to and from market, soldiers on a free afternoon riding jeeps, motor scooters, and bikes to the big city - Quang Ngai City and its 25,000 people - and lots of real military traffic. While most of the military traffic around here was Vietnamese, there were always the Engineer vehicles going back and forth to the grading and paving job that was now progressing further north every day - almost to Chu Lai and the Americal Division Base Camp. As the highway became paved, security operations were a little easier. Sweeping the road every day for mines was still up to the Engineers, but now they only had to check the edges of the road, making the clearing much faster. Now they'd be able to declare the road from our area all the way to Quang Ngai by 8 a.m. every day.

After completing the defensive fires project, Dave and I decided to drive into Quang Ngai City and the ARVN / MACV compound. There we could pick up a couple of items at the tiny American PX store that was run for the several small groups of civilian and military people that worked in this province capital. My guess is that there may have been about 150 Americans in the city, but most of them were civilians from agencies with acronym names like USAID, JUSPAO, CORDS & others. I'm not sure what all of them did and which ones were funded by CIA, etc, but they were mostly involved in helping the province in its nation-building efforts. The military included our province team, the adviser team to the 2nd ARVN army division, and a few people who supported air operations out of the city's airfield, even a few Air Force and Air America pilots from time-to-time.

The ARVN compound even had a small Officers' Club for the Americans to drink and relax at. It was nothing more than a plywood hooch with a bar and a few tables - and air conditioning !!! Beer was 10 cents, while mixed drinks were a whopping 25 cents! The bartender kept everyone well-supplied with fresh hot popcorn, but that was about it. Of course 60's music played at all times. Dave and I made it a point to stop in for a beer this afternoon to see who was here to trade war stories with. There were a couple of the American advisers entertaining three Austrailian officers who apparently were temporarily a part of their team. I knew one of the Americans, but we weren't exactly friends. This young captain happened to be on the 2nd ARVN team when they let us walk into the night ambush back in July and Ron had read him the riot act for that. The incident was history now, but I never could get to like this guy - just tolerated him (for a while). The Australians and their hosts must have been there a while because they were getting louder and occasionally broke into their rendition of "Waltzing Mathilda", the famous Australian drinking song.

Dave and I were about to leave after a couple of beers and all the singing we could tolerate when an Air Force captain in a flight suit came in by himself. He looked like he had been ridden hard and put away wet, as they say. Must have had a rough day. He sat one stool away at the bar and waved a sort of salute, which I acknowledged by telling the bartender to put a drink for him on my tab. I was pretty sure that he wasn't an office type and had probably spent his day in harm's way helping out grunts like us. He could have a drink on me any time. We introduced ourselves and it became obvious that we already knew each other. He was JAKE-40, one of the FAC(Forward Air Control) pilots who had so adroitly supported us with the air strikes he directed while risking his life in the small spotter plane time after time. He remembered me instantly as MIKE-11 (my radio call sign), broke into a huge grin, and slapped me on the back like a long-lost friend. We reminisced by telling Dave stories about each other in past firefights and air strikes. Each story got more vocal, animated, and probably exaggerated as we each tried to heap more praise on the other guy. Here we go again. It's just a pattern. Men who have shared combat experiences want to talk about them and almost always want to give credit to the other guy who had it tougher or took more risks or did more clever things during the fight. It just becomes part of the camaraderie - the brotherhood of war - that I now know is universal. Now JAKE-40 wanted to buy a round for the house just because he was so happy to meet me. We had traded stories for an hour when Dave politely reminded me that it would be dark soon and we should be heading back to Tu Nghia ASAP. We didn't want to get caught in the dark! JAKE-40 said he was just here for emergency repairs and could normally be found at the Chu Lai base camp. I promised to look him up if I was ever there. Then he asked me if I would like to go on one of his missions sometime. This was something I hadn't thought of, but now was excited at the idea of seeing things from the back seat of his little 2-engine prop plane while he swooped all over the place directing jet fighters on their air strikes for some group of friendlies that has gotten themselves into a fight. It could be hair-raising but lots of fun, too. I told JAKE-40 that I'd love to tag along sometime. Maybe if I went to Chu Lai on a scrounging mission, I could join up with him for a flight. A week later I heard through the province grape vine that JAKE-40 had gone down hard while returning from one of his "routine" missions. Apparently he crash-landed, almost saving the aircraft but not himself. The story went that there was just too much stress on that old plane and it finally gave up, mechanically.

I was really saddened to hear about JAKE-40's fate. After all, I had just gotten to meet him face-to-face but the relationship we had built in many radio conversations in the middle of battle was that of close friends - and now he was gone. My mind's eye pictured a swashbuckling barnstorming flier complete with the leather aviator's hat and scarf flapping out the window of his low, slow aircraft. That's kind of how I had once pictured all of the JAKE FAC's before I met Jake-40 in person. That's probably the mental picture I'll always retain. I wished that I had made just one flight with him but was selfishly thinking : "what if I had been on board when he bought the farm?" I suppose that's normal. I hope so. The next opportunity I had to call in an air strike and work with one of the other JAKE FAC's, many of whom I had also worked with before, I made it a point to encourage him to "put in a good strike for JAKE-40". The sentimental thought was appreciated and shared.

OURS WAS "ALOFT" A LT. NAMED PEDRAZINI I PUT HIM IN FOR A DFC (Distinguished Flying Cross) FOR HIS DARING AT LONG THANH WHEN THE ENEMY TRIED TO OVERRUN OUR DISTRICT HQ

CHAPTER THIRTEEN

All the Americans in Vietnam were not "Ugly Americans" as the re-writers of history would have you believe. American influence in Vietnam was everywhere, but it was manifested in many different ways and in both negative and positive veins. Apologists for and members of the anti-war crowd still try to make the case that we were always the "Ugly Americans", just like in the famous book. In fact even today there are people who actually believe, based on what they read, that America was the aggressor - the colonialist power - out to take over all of Vietnam. These are the same misguided fools who say that Ho Chi Minh was really only a nationalist - not a puppet of international communism - who just wanted independence from the American "imperialists"! Of course there were incidents where lack of understanding of the Vietnamese, their culture, and their war led some Americans to be extremely insensitive, rude and sometimes cruel. I am still appalled when I meet so many other vets who display a total lack of knowledge of and respect for the people they were fighting to save a country for. They were there and didn't understand! They bravely risked their lives every day and still didn't understand! How could millions of other Americans who weren't even there begin to see the truth about Vietnam? Most then got and are still getting their information from slanted news broadcasts, slanted books and, now, terribly slanted and cliché-ridden movies. How could they possibly know the truth?? It was never reported.

Perhaps a view of the American influence from the Vietnamese perspective - 1960's vintage - would be helpful. The view would be different depending on whether the Vietnamese expressing it were city dwellers or the typical hard-working rural farming family. My experience - a year of living in a rural, unsafe, oft-contested district - is with the latter. Most of the local people I came in contact with were very much in awe of Americans and their impressions of the American largess and omnipotence kept their curiosity at a high level. At times it felt uncomfortable to be the object of staring and whispers in a small village we visited, where some of the people had never seen a six-foot, blonde, fair-skinned European-American before. While there would be only 2 or 3 American advises in a large group of Vietnamese soldiers, we got most of the attention. They were fascinated, but were even more awe-struck when they could get a glimpse of Doc or Sergeant El or the DIOCC, who were black. When you add the physical differences to our language and demeanor, we were really a conversation piece. In most villages, the civilians would gather and stare at us, then begin whispering and giggling right in front of us. Actually the giggling was a very good sign that this was a friendly village. The adult women would encourage their young children to make contact with us - mostly hoping for a handout, unfortunately, which we would normally provide instantly. The kids were unbelievably cute, but almost always quite dirty. The smallest would wear no pants at all. This would avoid any personal accidents, as whenever and wherever nature called, they would oblige - anywhere. They didn't even have to pull down their pants! How practical - if unsanitary. Naturally, we felt very sorry for these children, innocent victims of an ideological conflict - and a shooting war - that they may never escape alive. Anything we could do, we would. One of the most important things was the MedCAPs - Medical Civic Action Patrols - that Doc, on our team, and the local *bac si'* (medic) would perform, bringing modern medical care to these fairly primitive locales. Most of the assistance was in the form of advice on personal hygiene and public sanitation, although many of the civilians received shots and other medications. Hopefully the local *bac si* would be able to sustain the things that Doc had initiated.

Most of the rural Vietnamese paid less attention to the Americans after the initial curiosity until the effects of our presence, often a firefight with the VC, and the ensuing firepower from above were felt. It soon became easy to detect the bad guys' presence or influence in any village in our district by observing the actions of the local populace. If they went about their daily work and commerce normally - in spite of our appearance of a threat - we could guess that there were no significant enemy activities to worry about and no fear of a clash breaking out between the two warring factions. If , on the other hand, our visit to a remote village with about 100 PF (Popular Forces) soldiers elicited looks of fear on the people's faces instead of the friendly giggles, we were probably there just a little too late. In most of these instances the enemy had already been there recently, performing their usual propaganda, scrounging, and terror acts. Sometimes they were still close at hand. If they were, the civilians would give it away by quickly disappearing. They didn't want to get caught in the cross-fire of what would soon be a battle. It got to the point that observation of the people and their attitudes was the best barometer of what kind of a day we were in for. I soon learned that these tell-tale signs of enemy proximity were easy to pick up - it was like observing the birds for similar signs of an approaching predator. As a result, I learned that the villagers didn't dislike us, but that they were afraid of what could happen to them and their homes when we encountered an enemy unit in their presence. They were well aware of the concept and reality of what is called "collateral damage". The immense firepower that we commanded at the end of our radio hand-set could do lots of damage and if the bad guys stayed near inhabited areas - a favorite ploy - there would indeed be collateral damage. One of the more sarcastic depictions of American involvement in Vietnam was a quote used by one of the most anti-war writers describing a briefing by a U.S. Army official : "in order to save the village, we had to destroy it". Well, sometimes we did! Does that make us the Ugly Americans?

It would be dishonest not to admit that at times I was embarrassed - even angry - at the behavior of some of the regular American soldiers from the big units who might pass through our District. Often there would be convoys of troops or supplies that moved up and down the National Highway right past our compound. Typically these convoys would come blasting through at break-neck speed - partially out of fear, I guess - but also partially out of arrogance. Lots of the Americans felt superior to the Vietnamese. After all, we were "fighting their war for them" and we paid for everything. In truth, the very highway these convoys raced down was being paved by the good old U.S. of A, but we were still the invited guests of the Republic of South Vietnam. If these rowdy troops couldn't respect that, they could at least have a little compassion for the people they were frightening to death and often forcing right off the road. Unfortunately, the regular U.S. unit leaders didn't emphasize this with their people.

Unfortunately, this behavior continued until one day we got a call that there was trouble brewing between "the allies" just two miles up the road toward Quang Ngai City. Seems some American troops had crashed into one of the Lambretta "buses" that served as mass transit in Vietnam. There was a standoff under way that could get ugly very fast, so Dave and I hopped into "Tramp" - our run-down, seldom-used jeep - along with Sergeant Tu. We would need an interpreter, if not an international arbitrator!

The term "standoff" was an inadequate descriptor of the scene we encountered just north of the La Ha bridge. The American contingent consisted of a jeep and a loaded 2 1/2 ton Army truck - the ubiquitous "deuce-and-a-half". About ten G.I.'s were circled around their stopped vehicles with M-16 rifles at the ready while a very young 2nd Lieutenant - an Engineer type - was sitting in his jeep shouting frantically on his vehicle-mounted radio. I already heard over its loudspeaker a voice at the other end asking : "how many of them are there?". While I hoped this was in response to the convoy commander's call for a medevac for injured civilians - I knew there had to be somebody hurt in this mess - I also feared that the question was in response to a call for armed help to fight off the "gooks" , or some other such derogatory term usually used by the "grunts". My approach to the commander's jeep was met with a look of relief. I guess he could figure out by the way Dave and I looked - a little shabby and pretty ticked off - that we were the local advisers. He no doubt thought we would get him off the hook.

Like the local sheriff I had to ask : "What's going on here?" , or something just about as unimaginative. It was obvious that the jeep in the lead had run right into the back of the loaded Lambretta. Now, "loaded Lambretta" may not mean much to the average person without a description of these mini - buses and how they were used. A Lambretta was basically a motor scooter with a larger, open-air passenger compartment stuck on the back of it. The passenger (and freight) compartment was probably just a little smaller than that of a mini-van of today, but one could not imagine - without first-hand experience - how much these people would cram into one of these rickety vehicles! I've seen a Lambretta with a dozen people crammed inside a compartment that should have seated 6 in semi-comfort - along with their belongings, market baskets, and various animals. I saw one Lambretta driver try to get a full-grown water buffalo and his handler into his shaky vehicle. It had almost worked!

The accident scene was an ugly one. We could identify 3 people that were in serious condition - maybe critical - and 4 others that could use some kind of medical attention. My assessment of the young Lieutenant's earlier radio call turned out to be painfully accurate. He hadn't called for a medevac since none of his people were hurt. After all, why would he call in an American medevac for just Vietnamese anyway? No, he had been calling for possible re-enforcements in case he had to fight his way out of this "gook" traffic jam. I got on my radio and called back to the District compound for Doc and one of the District officers to get out here on the double. We needed first aid and political stability in a hurry. Rich was on radio watch and asked if I needed a medevac. He had read my mind, as usual, before I could get the next words out. (Rich was an outstanding asset to our District team and we would all miss him when he went back to "The World" in a couple of weeks!) About 10 minutes later Doc and *Thieu Ta'* Hoa himself drove up. Their arrival was followed momentarily by a call from "Dustoff 1-5" and, almost simultaneously, the now-so-familiar and heart-warming sound of a Huey "popping the air" with its giant rotor blades. (That unmistakable sound is one of those sensory stimuli that I will never lose. Even today, if a now-rare Huey is anywhere out there, I'll hear it and will just stare skyward until it leaves earshot. I read once where a Vietnam vet couldn't cut his grass because the sound of the lawn mower reminded him so much of a Huey that he would stop in his tracks, stare up into the sky, and even tear up at the memories that this stimuli had evoked. Certain sounds and smells affect us that way, whether we'll admit it or not.

****

Thieu Ta' Hoa took charge of the scene immediately. He was amazing as usual. He backed up the civilians, including the hamlet chief who was leading the angry tirade against the Americans and explained to them how his American friends had made a mistake and were now going to show them how much they regarded the Vietnamese people by bringing in a "my by wop-wop" (helicopter) to whisk the injured off to an American hospital for the best medical care in the world. While Hoa spoke and I eavesdropped in Vietnamese, Doc acted as "triage officer" and sorted out the ones that he could help and the ones that needed the medevac. It looked like there were 2 of the civilians that Doc wanted to fly out of there. As soon as Dust-off 1-5 landed we had more trouble. A tug-of-war started between Doc and some civilians who were evidently related to the 2 casualties who were the center of the tugging contest. They were afraid to let their people be taken away by the big American machine. They didn't trust us again. At the same time the young Lieutenant was yelling to "get them out of here before they die"! He obviously guessed there would be even more trouble if anyone died on the scene - sounded like he wanted to sweep this one under the rug, though.

Eventually cooler heads prevailed, but not before *Thieu Ta* Hoa had to intervene and take charge of everything. He convinced Doc and Dustoff 1-5 that it would be better to fly these people to the Province hospital in Quang Ngai City - just a couple of miles away - than to take them all the way to the 91st Evac hospital at the base camp at Chu Lai. He then told the relatives what the plan was and told them to go on to the city to meet their loved ones at the hospital. This worked, but only because they trusted their District Chief.

After the Dust-off lifted off in a cloud of dust, hats and other debris, Hoa turned to the task of getting people to go on about their business so that the American convoy could move on in safety. This took some doing, as several people, mostly older men and women, shook their fists at the American vehicles while yelling things I had a hard time understanding, but I knew it wasn't pretty. After about 15 minutes, the American troops were fed up enough to force their way out. One senior Sergeant yelled out to the Lieutenant that they should just bust their way out and "to hell with these .... people". I calmly walked over to him and set things straight. They weren't going anywhere until my District Chief made things right and he had better cool it or one of us would have him brought up on charges of something or other. As it was, they were lucky if this incident didn't draw a formal complaint from the Province government that he was a guest of. The sergeant heeded my advice. Soon what was an ugly incident in American/Vietnamese relations calmed down and the convoy was allowed to slowly pull out. Hoa had done a good job of cooling the people off. At the same time he reassured them that *his* Americans - we advisers - were different from the Americans they had just encountered and were here to help. He also promised them that he and I would check up on the casualties at the province hospital and report back to them, while reminding them that even though it was Americans who caused the wreck, it was also Americans that called for and flew the medevac that probably saved the lives of their friends. It worked. Hoa was a diplomat as well as a warrior.

If this nasty encounter in our little district was any indicator of what could be going on around the whole of South Vietnam, I would be very worried about the image of Americans in the eyes of the Vietnamese in the much more populated areas. At this point in the war the American presence had been at the 500,000 level for about 2 years and at least 250,000 for the two years prior to that. In a country that had only 15 million people (with a million of its younger men under arms), the percentage of American military and their own military was very high. I guess the American soldier was quite noticeable here. Given these conditions, how could we avoid ugly encounters when we did very little to educate most of the troops about the country, its people, and its culture?

As I mentioned the Vietnamese military, a little about how they were perceived by their own rural civilians is appropriate. One way to depict this dynamic of military, government, and the people is to relate an example of a "cordon-and-search" operation in one of our more remote villages. One example that stands out with me was an all-day operation that included most of the elements of the interplay between the people and their government up-close and personal.

As I recall, the objective of this operation was a good-sized ville toward the northeastern part of our district and very close to the coast. It would be my first visit to this particular ville, which was the main one in the village of Hung Nhon Nam. (A village was a political entity consisting of many hamlets, which would each have a few "villes" - actual groupings of people and their hooches.) This ville was home for the Village Chief , a one-room grade school, and a small marketplace. There may have been as many as 150 people living here, but that's just a guess. The ville was also near a small river which fed into the Song Phu Tho, a larger river - about 50 meters across - that led right to the South China Sea and the barrier islands at the edge of our district. These islands were a favorite spot for the bad guys to use as landing and staging areas when they infiltrated our district by sampan. They used the smaller rivers at night to work their way inland, as most of the people they would target would be near these rather narrow rivers that wound through the eastern half of the district.

This area was actually very beautiful - a tropical paradise with all the coconut palms and banana trees you would ever want to see. There were the usual bamboo thickets and other general shade trees everywhere - some of them looked like hardwoods from back in North Carolina. This area, while pleasant to look at, afforded a great deal of concealment for anybody who wanted to hide - like the VC. This was the only thing that detracted from a pleasant environment. As a matter of fact, most of Vietnam was beautiful. It was just the war that gave it an ugly tint.

In this setting, a remote ville so close to the areas frequented by the enemy, we set out to perform a cordon-and-search operation. Two Regional Forces companies - nearly 200 soldiers - would arrive from their outposts just at first light and set up a cordon around the ville. This would seal up the area and prevent anyone from leaving, but also was a defensive cordon for the ville itself. As the people awoke, small patrols would carefully check out the area inside the cordon. Once they were satisfied that the area was relatively secure, they reported in to the District Chief by radio. It was time for our entourage to join in the operation. The helicopter we had laid on for this morning would be on our pad by 0930 (9:30 a.m.) to pick up Hoa, his Phenix program leader and an assistant, the DIOCC - our new adviser lieutenant - , myself, Kinh the interpreter, Doc, Ken the District Senior Advisor, and 8 PRU's (Province Recon Unit troops). The PRU's were undoubtedly there as bodyguards for this chopper-load of important people (at least important in our own District) but they would also help with the interrogation of villagers as part of the Phenix program work. Because of the loading factor and my own reluctance to have this many key people on one Huey, we decided to split our group into two trips. The Huey pilots were happy to do it, as it was only a 10-minute ride each way. They were actually probably relieved that we weren't in our usual mode of grossly over-loading a chopper every chance we got! I was frankly more concerned about getting one chopper shot down with all these key officers than I was the loading issue. I don't even remember who went on which load, but within an hour we were all inside the cordon and ready to begin the meat of the operation.

The first order of business was to assemble every living soul in front of the schoolhouse, and within minutes the entire population was seated obediently facing the District Chief, who spoke from the steps of the school like a southern senator at a Fourth of July picnic. I had never seen so many conical straw hats in one place! Hoa spoke for 30 minutes and I understood about half of what he was saying. It was apparently general propaganda about the South

Vietnamese government and its programs of Rural Development (funded by Uncle Sam - not Uncle Ho!). He also promised to rebuild the school which had sustained major damage from a terrorist attack about a month earlier. He then explained what would happen next.

All the women, who comprised most of the adults, would gather under a large shade tree for about an hour's worth of educational speaking by one of the Phenix people, while what men there were (all of them old) would be interrogated by the PRU's and another Phenix operative. The children, appropriately gathered inside the school, where the good Doc (my American *bac si*) would do his MEDCAP magic. Hoa would supervise the overall operation, while Kinh explained what was being said at each sub-meeting to Ken and me. Often Kinh would get called inside the school - now a doctor's office - to translate something that Doc just couldn't handle. All this would go on for about an hour, until it was time for lunch and then siesta - yes, even in the middle of an elaborate operation. All stop until 2:30! We ate with the troops this time - no fancy lunch prepared by the villagers. They weren't too happy right now. All this was interrupting their various jobs.

I took this opportunity to reflect on what was going on here. A whole group of residents of our district were being detained from their daily work while their government - the good guys - interrogated and lectured them. The people had no choice in the matter because of the absolute power of the district chief and, of course, the presence of armed troops still forming a ring around their village. No wonder the women at the lecture grumbled under their breath, the old men being interrogated were fearful, and the kids were frightened - at first - to have this big American doctor checking them out from head to toe. In reality, there was no threat here, but it was a hassle for the villagers. They had work to do and were being kept from it.

During the siesta time Hoa briefed Ken and me a little. He emphasized that this was a necessary evil and that he would try to make it as painless as possible for his people. He reminded us that he had promised to rebuild the schoolhouse and asked if Ken and I could help - to which we immediately agreed. Then he formally introduced us to the Hamlet Chief, who had just arrived after hearing that this operation was going on. He was the only person allowed passage through the cordon. After the usual greetings, we learned from the Hamlet chief that the V.C.I. (VC Infrastructure) cadre had run about the same kind of operation here just two nights earlier. They had done the same thing we were doing ! The difference was that the VC did their work through more threat and intimidation these days, while - at least in our district - these things were done with the least amount of bullying as possible. This should have given us an edge over the communist cadres, but regardless the villagers were really tired of this tug-of-war using them as the rope. Yes, both sides were trying to "win the hearts and minds of the people". We just used different methods and our side did it in the daytime while the bad guys had to sneak around under cover of darkness.

I keep emphasizing the benevolent dictator we had for a District Chief and how gentle he really was with the civilians. This may not have been the case in all districts (and there were 200 -odd districts). Also, we knew that some regular army (ARVN) units were notorious for treating the civilians with disrespect when they traveled through populated areas. For example, Hoa had a standing rule that none of his troops would ever steal food from civilians. They would always pay for a duck or a chicken when they stopped to take lunch. Regular army troops had a habit of just taking what they wanted as if they were privileged characters. Just an example.

After siesta, the 3 meetings continued for about another hour. During the process, one of the old men was arrested. He was suspected of being VCI - a local communist operative at night while a normal farmer by day. There was some protest from a few people, primarily his wife who reached the wailing stages before it was all over, but I think most of the other villagers knew he was guilty and didn't put up much of a fuss. The DIOCC adviser and his counterparts would take care of this guy. I didn't want to know any more - just that he was no longer able to work this area for the communists.

About 1600 (4 pm) all were reconvened back in front of the schoolhouse for a final talk by Major Hoa. Remember that he was now acting more as the political leader - District Chief - than as military commander. It may have been confusing but what else would one expect in a situation of martial law? Hoa tried to explain why this operation was done and that his most important concern was to protect these very people so that they could continue to work their fields and rice paddies in as much safety as possible. He tried to convince them that the arrest of one of their number would serve to help them in the long run. A few of the old men nodded their heads in agreement. Hoa then urged each villager to be on the lookout for any other such suspicious characters and to report any harassment they received from the VC immediately to their Hamlet Chief. He then pointed to us and said that his American advisers would help him to win the battles that might ensue and to drive out the communists. He added that we helped him in civic projects also, like the MEDCAP that Doc had just completed and that we had promised him to help in the schoolhouse rebuilding project. If we weren't already committed to playing sugar daddy on this one, we just became that way. Hoa closed by explaining that he and his troops and his advisers would now move out to sweep all around the Hamlet and then back to the District Headquarters. This would ensure an area clear of any enemy - for a short time anyway. The villagers gave obliging applause as Hoa completed his short speech, then watched in silence as we saddled up and moved out. The only exceptions were the kids, who came up to the Americans smiling and laughing as if they hadn't a care in the world. Doc was now of course the most popular, but each of us had to pose for pictures, but the cameras were ours. I had long since learned that most Vietnamese loved to pose for pictures even if they never saw the results. I'm lucky enough to have many slides of those beautiful, but sometimes pitiful, faces. They are some of my favorites amongst the hundreds of slides that someday I'll sort out and look at again.

With this operation over and just the sweeping drive back to the district compound ahead of us in the waning afternoon and evening, I again reflected on this day's experience. From the beauty and the delicious fresh fruit bounty of this area to the stark reality of the day-to-day and night-to-night psychological battle for the hearts and minds of the people, we ran the gamut of experiences in our little war for control of the district that our Vietnamese friends lived in. Yes, the government could look just as heavy-handed as the communist forces at times, but if we and our counterparts did it right, we hoped to gain a significant advantage. Sometimes this would be measured by the smallest of achievements, like the absence of a bridge-blowing for more than a week. Other times, just the greetings and happy faces of the people in a previously scary village would give us a measure of our success. Unlike other young army officers whose assignments may be as platoon leaders slogging it out for survival in the field or as rear echelon guys who never saw battle, we could measure some success or progress almost every day. Sure there was frustration, but any indicators we could count toward winning the hearts and minds were celebrated and gave us the drive and motivation to continue trying.

Those Americans who came to Vietnam alone and as replacements for other young guys in large units or at the huge rear area U.S. installations had a different outlook. They were here to do a job and to survive 365 days and go home. They often could see no progress at all, just the daily grind with only the frustrations and the horrors - or the rear echelon boredom and distance from the action. And this was by far the lot of the overwhelming majority of Americans here in Vietnam. Given the lack of indoctrination and the independent nature of their existence, they seldom encountered the indigenous troops or civilians in a positive light. It's understandable that this environment would not give most of the troops the same experience we as advisers had. It didn't excuse all their actions but might explain some of the more negative behavior.

I think the civilians felt the same way we advisers did about their day-to-day existence. It wasn't just survival they were looking for, it was progress! If they could do it without selling out their very souls to the American strangers - do it on their own - they were much happier. The Vietnamese were not lazy parasites on the American hide as many Americans visualized. In spite of being night or day targets for propaganda and re-education - along with control - these villagers were trying to make their way in the struggle for life, liberty and the pursuit of happiness - in that order !! Sometimes they did it with our help, and sometimes they did it in spite of big brother United States. Unfortunately, later on when the chips were down, our country's abandonment of the South Vietnamese people cost them everything - even their very country!

CHAPTER FOURTEEN

The time soon came for us to live up to the promise we had recently made. We would help rebuild the school in the ville where we had just finished the cordon-and-search operation. We already had the commitment from old Charlie at USAID for fifty bags of cement for the exterior walls. Now we needed lots of plywood and other lumber for the interior and to shore up the roof. The answer to this requirement became obvious. It was time to head for Chu Lai and the Americal Division to scrounge up the building materials as well as to find any other treasures that our trading and scrounging ability might bring. We also needed lots of supplies for our team house - including ammunition that we couldn't get through channels. I would go on the scrounging run for my first time with the experts - Doc and Johnny. This might be fun!

Before we took off, there were a few trinkets - trading materials - we needed to get together for the REMF's (Rear Echelon "people") at the Division Base Camp. These people loved to get battle souvenirs to take home and impress their neighbors with - even though most of them had never seen a shot fired in anger. These were the people that re-told the wildest "war stories" and made the most of the souvenirs they had once they got back to "The World". That's OK, they had jobs to do here and, for the most part, they did them very well. Why should real field people begrudge them the embellishment they poured on every story they told. Incidentally, most field soldiers tell few war stories. Most of us tell the funny or ironic stories - not those that tell the listener how bad war really is. We know that there is no way to describe it for those that have never experienced the terror - and the rush - of combat. So, with the REMF's in mind, Doc and Johnny gathered two SKS rifles - standard enemy issue - and a half dozen Viet Cong flags for trading material. The flags were authentic in design if not in origin. They had been sewn together by our housemaids, then shot through to create bullet holes seemingly incurred in battle. A little duck blood and dirt added more credibility. What a wall-hanging these would make for guys from the rear to show their neighbors when they got home. Here's hoping they all made it home - souvenirs and all.

Our mini-convoy was ready to take off by 0930. Doc and Johnny manned the district 3/4 ton truck while Sergeant El and I rode in "Tramp" - our jeep - with a small trailer in tow. The 35-mile trip to Chu Lai would be smooth on newly paved Highway 1, which paralleled an abandoned railroad track that led from My Tho in the Delta region to Hanoi itself - probably 600 miles. There probably had not been a train on these tracks since 1940!

The old rail line made me pretty nervous. It was on the west side of the highway and usually it stayed about 100-200 meters away from the roadbed. But sometimes the track came much closer and, with its steep banks that raised it above monsoon water level, presented an excellent hiding place for a sniper or an ambush team. Every time the road drew close to the tracks I flinched and raised my guard. Sergeant El didn't like it either. His side - the driver's side - was closer than mine was. Doc was driving the 3/4 -ton in front of us and was moving pretty fast. I could sense what was going on in his mind at the time. We were all by now spiritually close enough to be of one mind most of the time. By the time we reached the outskirts of Chu Lai, the town, we had built up our tiny convoy's speed to the break-neck level. Now here we were flying through a small Vietnamese town just like we thought only the "ugly" Americans did. Guess we were scared just like they were. So, it was obvious that no matter how long we lived in Vietnam, we never lost the edge and became careless. Fear is a good thing - keeps you on your toes. National cemeteries are filled with those who lost that edge - got careless out here. None of my team wanted to join them.

We found the main gate to the Americal Division base on the right side of Highway 1 easily. It was well-marked, so much so that it looked like the entrance to a theme park back in the World - well, maybe it would be a fun place for us today. Our two ragged vehicles careened around the winding road up to the main base area. We should have had a map to get around, it was so big. I remembered seeing the sprawling base from the air on my first flight from Danang down to Quang Ngai City about 8 months ago. Fortunately this was Johnny's umpteenth visit and he knew his way around pretty well.

Our first stop was at a supply depot - what else?! The Sergeant in charge there seemed to recognize Johnny and Doc and much discussion took place - followed by exchange of one SKS rifle and 2 "VC" flags for a free pass to a huge walk-in refrigeration unit full of fresh food that we could take our pick of. While we went about our business - practically looting the place - we suddenly became aware of a huge stack of green rubber bags stacked up on several pallets about 10 high. Everything stopped at once. Four of us silently stared at the stacks of body bags being kept cool while waiting for transport to the mortuary in Danang - my friend Glenn's place. There must have been 30 of them. These weren't just tagged rubber bags. They were filled with dead American human beings, each of whom had parents, wives, and even children who waited at home for their return. Now they would return in aluminum coffins to their loved ones. This was about all we wanted out of this reefer. Our little troop tore out of there as if we had encountered the devil himself. But not before we had loaded lots of potatoes and vegetables and even some frozen chicken from the secret freezer section. There was a giant ice machine outside, which we robbed to keep the chicken cold in large plastic food containers (also scrounged of course) on the way home.

Next stop was the EOD - Explosive Ordnance Disposal - team where the offer of another pair of "authentic" VC battle flags earned Sergeant El and me a browsing trip to the unit's old ammo dump where we could have anything we wanted. Doc and Johnny headed off to get the building materials we needed from the Seabees - the Navy's construction division and some of the best people here. All the stuff at the EOD dump was scheduled for disposal - meaning it would be blown up - because it had reached the end of its officially recommended shelf life without being used. We gathered dozens of invaluable Claymore command-detonated mines and a whole case of the blasting caps needed to make them work. There were cases of hand grenades and even some 2.5 inch helicopter rockets whose explosive warheads might be of some use.

I noticed another stack of those huge "Spooky" flares like the one that had almost blinded us and our medevac pilot late one night. I decided to pass on those. After we picked over the best stuff like kids in a candy store there was still room in our trailer. We decided to load up a bunch of old mortar rounds. Sergeant El assured me they would be OK and that Phu - the compound mortar man - could make successful use of them.

Our trailer full, Sergeant El and I headed for the rendezvous point near the "Americal Beach". We parked "Tramp" near the main G.I.

beach and walked out near the sand itself. There we saw a most incredible sight. It looked like Myrtle Beach - well, almost - with hundreds of sunbathing G.I.'s with their portable radios, suntan lotion, and beer - lots of it. I noticed that there was one particularly thick clump of guys and soon figured out why. There were a few American women - "roundeyes" - in the mob and everyone was gawking at them. As I walked closer I recognized two of them as nurses from the 27th Surge (Surgical Hospital) that I had met when bringing in two Vietnamese civilians that we had injured with "friendly fire" a few weeks before. Somehow I couldn't connect the revelry here on the beach with the serious business these men and women conducted when on duty. On second thought, why wouldn't they want their scarce free time to be as far removed from daily work life as possible. Especially the nurses had to be forgiven for this. They deserved a break.

One other strange sight here at the beach was the prowling Huey helicopter gunships that I noticed flying at low level up and down the beach and occasionally firing their mini-guns at something in the water. I soon learned that they were on shark patrol, protecting the troops swimming here. How ironic. After weeks at the time of slogging through the boonies hunting, and being hunted by, human game, these G.I.'s were just taking a break. Above their heads the same gunships that protected them from bad humans now flew cover for them against the oldest predator in the world. I'm sure there was some gallows humor attached to this phenomenon, but I never got a chance to find out.

It was getting about time for us to move out, but before leaving Chu Lai I wanted to quickly pay a visit to the headquarters of the Jake Facs (Forward Air Controllers) - the group that had supported us in so many firefights with the jet air strikes they directed. I wanted to give them a special gift of two VC flags - one to hang in memory of Jake-40, my friend who had died trying to save his rickety spotter plane a few weeks earlier.

Johnny and Doc caught up with us soon. Their truck was now overloaded with stacks of plywood and heavy lumber - not to mention a large iced-down tub filled with large flat boxes. Doc pointed triumphantly at the boxes and said: "Lobster,Sir!" He had traded 2 quarts of Johnny Walker Red Label scotch whiskey to some cooks on a Navy ship that was docked in the small port facility. It seems that the Navy guys couldn't get access to booze, but they sure had the food. Lobster, of all things! We could only hope that the ice packing would preserve the frozen shellfish delight for the trip back to our compound. There we had an old freezer that was powered by that large diesel generator that was a godsend to us.

After our quick stop at the Air Force compound it was time to head back to Tu Nghia. We definitely had to get home before darkness fell for security reasons, but our hurry also had to do with the frozen food jackpot we had hit. How long could it last. True, in the waning days of the rainy season the temperatures were not as brutal as usual. Maybe about 80 degrees with lots of humidity. Hot enough to quickly melt ice and the food it protected. So,satisfied with our days work, we headed out of the base camp for the hour's ride home. As we passed the main gate, the gate guards just smiled, waved us on and looked away. They knew the rag-tag advisers had made a haul, but that it was probably mostly on the up-and-up, at least according to the supply "rules" that were normal in Vietnam. Oh, I'm sure there were a few places in the rear where paperwork rules were strictly followed. I remembered actually signing a hand receipt for my M-16 and other gear upon arrival in Saigon 8 months before, but that had been the last paperwork I had noticed.

 The trip back down QL1 was uneventful enough, but the uneasiness was there as always. On top of the obvious possibilities of sniper fire, ambush, or collision with any one of a hundred different kinds of indigenous vehicles, this time there was the risk of spontaneous detonation of any of the electrical blasting caps now being jostled around in the trailer that followed me and Sergeant El at a distance of 3 feet. One mishap - one bad bounce - and the whole trailer-load of explosives would go up in a spectacular blast. There would be little left of us and our jeep but a grease spot. Once again, the anticipation of the worst eventuality kept us on our toes but also kept the pucker factor at a high level. Fortunately we made it without incident - and well before nightfall. The rest of the compound gathered around us on our return. They wanted to see if we had brought home the bacon. It was like Dad returning home from an adventure and all the kids gathering around to see what souvenirs he had brought for them. The housemaids were excited about all the food, most of the troops pored over the ammo and other explosives, and Ken marveled at the building materials. As District Senior Adviser, Ken's main focus, as always, was the nation-building part of our mission. He was very anxious to get started on the school repair project. Everyone pitched in to get things unloaded and secured in the American section of the compound. Funny, in spite of all our close relationships with our counterparts in the Vietnamese hierarchy, we never were able to trust the masses of Vietnamese troops to break their habit of snitching everything they could carry away. It was almost a way of life, with no malice aforethought, that if you left anything unguarded you were inviting pilfering. The culprit was not responsible for your negligence or maybe even his actions. That was just the culture, sad as it was. Everything was OK if you kept things secured, and there were no hard feelings or inferred insults because of your extra precautions fueled by the fear of having everything stolen. Keeping watch on your valued possessions - all of your possessions - was just good business.

Ken and *Thieu Ta* Hoa were anxious to get to work on the school, so we agreed to get started next day if we could find a way to transport all the materials out to the ville that needed them. Say no more! One call to Province was all it took to put the next day's Province chopper at our disposal for two morning hours. I had hit it lucky this time! The chopper was available! We would be able to airlift all the scrounged materials out to the site in the ville along with a few men each trip to start the unloading and building process. Two local Popular Forces platoons provided security on site. Hoa, Ken and I went out with the last load. Then we sent the chopper back to Quang Ngai City to pick up the cement from the USAID compound warehouse and drop it off at our site. Now the challenge was to finish construction in one day. Somehow we did it! Everyone, even the old village women who had no children worked to re-create this house of learning for the young people of Vietnam. The skilled labor - actually artistry - was provided by a four old carpenters who were really ingenious in their use of primitive tools and other field expedient methods. Even the PF's pitched in with the grunt work of mixing cement, etc. I was moved to imagine this scene being repeated all over the country every day. Unfortunately, there were just as many hamlets that would lose their institutions of rice-roots government and education tonight, or the next night, or some night soon at the hands of the Viet Cong - the communists who would deprive the people of their rights, their self-rule and everything they wanted - including the very education of their children. In this one little ville - for now - we had taken a step toward thwarting the communists from reaching their sinister goals.

Well, this bit of nation-building at the rice-roots level gave us some of that satisfaction that I've talked about - at least until two months later when the same school got severely damaged again. The cycle would begin all over. Ironically, this time the cause of most of the damage to our school building could be pinned on one of the 250-pound bombs that we had our Air Force drop in the middle of a firefight in the area The one bomb was a little off-target but not by much. A platoon of enemy soldiers had dug in close enough to the ville to use it as protection against even more Allied firepower. This was a favorite enemy trick. As usual, what had been the scene of some good work for the civilians had become a battleground again, thanks to the persistent attacks by the VIet Cong on what we thought were relatively secure villages. This is the part that would make you crazy! Just when you thought you had made two steps forward, you had to take at least one step back.

After the school-building operation was over we walked back to the compound with the two PF platoons in an uneventful movement - almost a "smoke-and-joke" walk in the sun. Once again I dwelled on a mystery. How come sometimes we could move un-challenged across the entire district like we did today, and other times we couldn't move one kilometer without being challenged violently by the bad guys. It was as if they dictated the rules of engagement, but it was more like an understanding between the government and the communists - but that they didn't follow it like the good guys did.

I was dog tired and retired to the team house early. It would be my turn for radio watch at 0200, and I would probably stay on it until first light. What good would it do to go back to bed when my three-hour watch was over at 0500. I'd just stay up and let someone else off the hook this morning, knowing the favor would be returned some other dark night. Unfortunately the couple of early hours of sleep I hoped for was interrupted by another of those harassing mortar attacks. I was awakened in the team house by the sound of the first round sliding down the mortar tube at distance of 600 meters. Yes, even before the "thunk" of the round's firing upward and out of the tube both Dave and I were on our way to the bunker. Eight rounds later, two of which did make it inside the district compound but without major damage, we declared an all-clear and wandered back to sleeping areas. The first thing I noticed when I glanced onto the sandbagged top of the framing over my bunk was the glow of two red eyes. Instant recognition said it was a rat - a mighty big one judging by the space between the two red eyes. Then I figured out why the rat was standing his ground above my bed. He had chewed his way into the canvas bag containing LRRP (Long Range Recon Patrol) rations - mostly dehydrated foods - that I had brought back from Chu Lai. This huge intruder - about the size of a large cat - wasn't going anywhere until I gave him clear passage out of a wide-open doorway, encouraged by the wild flashing of my flashlight. I would have shot the ugly varmint, but he was closer to my .45 calibre automatic sidearm than I was as it hung on its shoulder holster on the frame over my bunk. Anyway, now I was wide awake and trudged down to the bunker - with my .45 this time - to take over radio watch early. Why not. I was wide awake by now - thanks to our friend the nightly mortar man and the unfriendly rat.

Oddly enough, a rat decided to pay me a visit later down in the bunker. While I was reading - and laughing out loud at - a well-used copy of "Catch-22", the totally irreverent military satire, my now-exceptional peripheral vision caught sight of a huge rat walking the tightrope on a radio cable over my shoulder. Before I could lock-and-load for a good shot with my .45, he jumped to the top shelf over the makeshift radio console, which was stacked with boxes of candy bars gleaned from the "SP" packs that we occasionally were issued - kind of a CARE package from Uncle Sam. I couldn't shoot the intruder now because he was in front of a case of hand grenades. With all the other explosives we had stashed in this bunker, I wasn't about to take a chance on blowing up some triggering device that could bring us to Armageddon. While the rat went about his business of tearing into the candy bar wrappers, I calmly slithered out of the bunker, returning with a D-handled shovel. All I could do was stun the beast with a full-force blow and shovel him out to the moat that surrounded our defensive lines. Then, having conquered the enemy, I probably swaggered back to my post on radio watch and to my book.

These weren't the only rats we encountered in our home-away-from-home (12,000 miles, to be exact). They virtually ruled the moat around us, and if anything edible was left out, in they would come to scrounge. The fear of a vicious rat pack forced us to keep our pet dog and cat in cages at night. Once the district team brought home a pet pot-bellied pig, but it had to stay in a cage most of the time to protect it from rat intruders. One night the pig had been let loose by accident and two of us had to use our .45's to shoot up a pack of attacking rats to save the little pig. With a .45 nobody can hit much, but we did manage to blow away a couple of the horrible creatures before they scrambled back to their lair in the mysterious moat. There wasn't much left of the rats we hit. A .45 does a lot of damage if it does hit something.

There were other, less threatening creatures around our team house. Most entertaining were the gecko lizards. I've heard some of the troops had a different name for them, as the sound they uttered sounded more like an abusive expletive than the word "Gecko", which gave them their name. The lizards were our friends, as they had voracious appetites and ate every bug in sight. A night of entertainment often included watching the lizards climb sure-footedly up the team house wall to attack a moth or other insect. We would bet on our favorite lizard, hoping ours would get the moth first or which one would take the highest total bugs, or which would climb the greatest height to grab a snack. All the while, we would be treated to the familiar greeting : "Gecko! Gecko!" Obviously, it didn't take much to entertain us, did it? Well, considering the fact that we had electricity (most of the time) provided by our 30 kw diesel generator, we were lucky enough to have light, a refrigerator and a freezer in the team kitchen, and radios and tape decks for musical entertainment. Ken had a professional tape deck and reels of music of all kinds. We would often gather in his hooch - mostly the officers - to listen to music, B.S., and watch the lizard races. There would be a poker game most nights in the kitchen, and I would often participate. In fact, we played so much poker that after a year most of us had just about broken even. The law of averages dictated that. I never got that good at poker, but it was fun - especially with play money - our military pay certificates. MPC wasn't real - and who cared anyway. You could get killed tomorrow.

Most of the team would stay up till well after midnight when we were in the compound, unless we had an early morning operation the next day. Then we'd sleep lightly, anticipating the 2 am mortar attack, then really go to sleep until first light - about 0530 usually. That was the routine when we were in. When the MAT team stayed out in one of our Regional Forces outposts we played it by ear. Back in the district compound the nightly radio watch was more alert and active when part of our team was out in the boonies for the night. This little fort was command central for everything that happened in the district. Of course it's counterpart across the compound was where Major Hoa ran the real business of his district, while ours was more of a "shadow" operation. But, oddly enough, there were times when I would briefly forget that I wasn't the District Chief. This could happen when I was talking to an outsider and usually defending the reputation of our little militia forces. I felt like they were my troops then - my people. Sometimes I still feel that way. Even today, a derogatory comment about the South Vietnamese and their citizen-soldiers sends me into an angry, defensive mood. Maybe they will always be mine - my troops, my people.

CHAPTER FIFTEEN

One of the unique features of the American soldier's tour of duty in Vietnam was "R&R". Each of us was provided with a 7-day Rest-and-Recuperation trip out of Vietnam at government expense. There were several choices like Australia, Hong Kong, Bangkok, etc, where most of the single guys would go for a week of hard drinking and hunting for women and souvenirs. Australia seemed to be the favorite, as it was populated with "round-eyes" who reminded them of Americans. For many of the married guys - I would guess a large majority - there was a trip to Hawaii where you could meet your wife for a seven-day vacation! Right in the middle of a war! The airlines, with persuasion by the government and a desire for some positive publicity, made extremely reasonable fares available for the wives to fly to Honolulu for this reunion. The best and most famous beachfront hotels in Honolulu gave special R&R rates to visiting couples. All sorts of tourist businesses gave R&R discounts - considerable ones - to add to the special treatment we would receive. Although I didn't know it at the time, this would be the only time that we who waged war in Southeast Asia would be given anything special as a kindness for our sacrifice - until the '90's. But that's getting ahead of the story.

I opted for the Hawaii trip and, with carefully coordinated planning through the mail, we planned Thanksgiving week, 1969, for our reunion. This would prove to be a rather prophetic choice of weeks. As the date for my flights grew closer, I found myself taking fewer chances - a phenomenon that I would again experience when it was time to rotate back to the states. When you're "short" - whether it was before an R&R trip or for final rotation back to the world - you would maintain what was called a "low profile", taking extra care. It was sort of like holding your breath at the end of a race, hoping you can make it to the end without your opponent catching up. The difference was that in war the opponent was the grim reaper in a race with fate - death itself.

The Saturday before Thanksgiving Dave and Doc drove me to the Quang Ngai City airfield for the Air America hitch-hike ride to Danang and the Pan Am flight that waited to take 250 of us to Hawaii - all to meet our wives for the first time in 6-8 months. Needless to say, the mood of these passengers , all dressed in "Class A" khaki's - some borrowed, some scrounged, and some saved from the trip months ago into Vietnam - was up-beat at a minimum. I had saved my khaki's and had the housemaids wash and iron them before I left Tu Nghia. Strangely, the jovial mood on the R&R flight covered the real thoughts that I know everyone had. While this felt like a freedom flight, the freedom from danger would only be temporary - 7 days in the real world and then back to the war. Just another of the bizarre trappings of the Vietnam war! On this flight I imagined going through the same routine for my final departure from the war zone four months from now. Surely these same thoughts and dreams coursed through the minds of every guy on this and all the other R&R flights. Even though this was a false "freedom flight", we would make the most of it. After all, we could be dead soon. As I would find out in just seven days, this cavalier attitude was just a front for the fear of reality.

BIRd

Those of us who went to Hawaii were pretty well behaved, but the stories of those who ventured to Hong Kong or Sydney became legend. I'm sure that the attitude of most of the hell-raising G.I.'s on R&R was : "So what are they going to do - send me to Vietnam?". Actually, this became the clarion call for all of us. Every time we felt the pressure of the bureaucracy hovering over us for breaking "regs", we would say "What are they going to do - send me to Vietnam?" Many years later, when we're among friends, the phrase often comes up again - followed by the knowing laughs of those of us who are brothers united by a common experience - the "Vietnam experience", as it is now so remotely referred to.

*　　　*　　　*　　　*　　　*　　　*

We spent a wonderful week in Hawaii - taking advantage of the myriad of specially discounted activities, but mostly just enjoying the overwhelmingly friendly - often sympathetic - attitudes of those who served us in restaurants, bars, and stores. Even though I dressed in civilian clothes (loose-fitting because of my startling weight loss) , it must have been easy to spot me as a soldier on R&R. Just in case, we had been issued special identification cards at Fort Derussey upon our reunion, but they weren't really needed. It was obvious to the merchants who we were. And they all treated us like visiting royalty! For a tourist trap, Hawaii was OK in my book.

We had Thanksgiving dinner together at our hotel - the beautiful Illikai right on Waikiki Beach. It was the house buffet with real turkey and all the trimmings. We really had something to be thankful for. It might not have been guilt I felt for enjoying this luxury, but I thought of many others who were missing this kind of an opportunity because they were fighting today, and those who may never see another Thanksgiving or any other holiday. Mostly, I thought of my South Vietnamese friends, most of whom, I thought, would never have the opportunity that we Americans could look forward to when we got back to "The World", as we called home. I was there this week! Hawaii was part of "The World"! Many of the South Vietnamese that we were trying to help build a country would have no concept of any kind of an occasion to give thanks for good fortune. Perhaps I actually did feel a little bit guilty after all. What was a wonderful Thanksgiving for me was just another day of war and struggle for my friends. My mixed feelings from that Thanksgiving day in 1969 are usually re-lived each Thanksgiving.

The dream week passed all too quickly. Before we knew it, it was midnight of Day 7 and time to say good-bye again. (All planes out of Hawaii seemed to leave at midnight.) This was when it hit me the hardest. Now that we both knew what my role in Vietnam was all about, we both experienced simultaneous feelings of hope and fear. This last four months could be the worst of my tour from this standpoint. Many years later, I have told many people that R&R - as wonderful as it was - made parting again more painful than ever before. The removal from the battlefield and now the re-introduction to it might be the most painful thing I endured that whole year. Fortunately, my sharing of this concept with others many years later has found much commonality of emotions - I know I'm not the only one. As with many other emotions now shared, the R&R reunion paradox now seems normal to me. On the other side of emotions, I was actually anxious to get back to work in the district. There was so much to do and so little time to do it! Incredibly - in spite of the desire to get home - I actually became concerned that it would all be over too soon....... too soon for me to accomplish the goals I had set for our team.

*　　　*　　　*　　　*　　　*　　　*

One last R&R experience will always stay with me. It was the return to Danang airfield in that PanAm "Freedom Bird". The troops were rather quiet most of the way, while the very attractive PanAm flight attendants were trying to make everyone feel at home. As the "stretch" DC-8 - it wasn't a "freedom bird" any more - made its "final" approach into the airfield, I swore I detected a crack in the voice of the announcing senior flight attendant. She apparently felt very sad that they were bringing us back to the war. Who knows, she may have also lost someone very close to her in Vietnam. In later years it became obvious that most American families had lost someone or knew someone that did.

Just as the wheels touched the 12,000-foot runway the big jet suddenly roared back up to takeoff speed and left the ground again. Instead of fear, you could sense the humor as a loud cheer went up from the passengers. Guys were yelling: "we're going back to Hawaii!" and such. As we circled for another approach, the pilot came on and told us that we had to do that "touch-and-go" because a pair of F-4 Phantom fighter jets were trying to land after a combat mission right behind us. We didn't want to get in their way, as they had no brakes! Made good sense to me! So we just circled around and, to everyone's simultaneous relief and disappointment, we were back on the ground again in beautiful Vietnam. When I stepped out onto the rollaway stairs it was like déjà vu. The hot blast of humid, putrid smelling air reminded me of my first arrival 8 months before. At the bottom of the ramp a G.I. greeted us with the punch line of an old joke about people in hell : - "ok, break's over....everybody back on your heads." I knew I had much more travelling to do to get back to Tu Nghia, but for all practical purposes I was back in the war again.

*   *   *   *   *

Back in the district I felt at home, and I started running! I wanted to get everything done before I left Vietnam! Keeping busy probably helped me avoid the fear also. This was probably a trait of all advisers that the South Vietnamese were used to by now. Every American adviser would go through this period, I guess. Remember that we could only take vicarious pleasure in the exploits of the troops we advised, but it was satisfaction indeed. We couldn't push too hard, but every time our counterparts were able to get their troops a win on the battlefield, we felt a sense of great pride. Until the next failure, we probably actually got a little smug. We called it confidence -others may call it arrogance. Reality says we usually didn't have enough time to celebrate and develop arrogance over a win before that next failure befell our troops. But now I was in a hurry to make more things happen. I was determined to win this thing in the next 4 months - singlehanded if necessary!

*   *   *   *   *

Shortly after my return from R&R we got into one of the heaviest daytime firefights of my tour. The rainy season was over, and what started out as a routine "walk in the sun" became a fierce battle with what apparently was a reinforced company of tough NVA regular troops. Our small force of 3 PF Platoons - about 100 men - made contact in a nearby village at about 11 a.m. on a beautiful, sun-bathed, 100-degreee day. It wasn't just the size of the North Vietnamese unit that concerned me, but the firepower they possessed, with heavy machine guns and large mortars landing death and destruction all around us! The familiar distinctive "pop-pop" of AK-47 bullets cracking over my shoulder was heavier than I had ever experienced. I can still hear that unmistakable sound of those Russian-made weapons. Of course, they say that you're lucky to hear this sound because the bullet that gets you will make no sound at all - or at least you won't hear it.

One of the Jake FAC's came on station without being summoned. He'd heard on the Province net that we were in a good fight in Tu Nghia and then had monitored my excited calls for lots of artillery. The little two-propeller spotter plane started making lazy circles in the sky over us. Jake 4-2 and I discussed lining up the battlefield for maximum air strikes. As luck would have it, the clock soon struck high noon and everyone went to sleep before we could

BS!

exercise the heavy fighter attack. Strangely enough, the FAC pilot understood this "siesta" phenomenon and went back to base to re-fuel, etc. I knew that this pilot - JAKE 4-2 knew the score. His fallen leader had been a friend of mine, and he had a price to extract for that. The JAKE FAC returned at precisely 2:30, and so did the fury of the enemy. Our PF's could barely hold a perimeter, let alone advance into the fray. We were taking close hits from 82 mm mortars and the PF's were starting to form up for one of their classic retreats! These NVA regulars, about 150 of them, were actually gaining tactical advantage. We dared not even call for medevac helicopters for the many wounded PF's. It would have been far too dangerous for the choppers, and I knew they wouldn't have the gunship support that would be needed to even attempt the dustoff. The PRU's (Province Recon Uits) once again kept me from being left out in the open all by myself, and kept the friendlies from getting into a complete rout again. In the midst of multiple incoming explosions, Sergeant El was hit by a small shrapnel fragment from an 82 mm mortar, but insisted he didn't need a medevac. His wound, thankfully, was the only one my small team would suffer in my year in command here. Fortunately his wound was not life-threatening. The command post, including *Thieu Ta* Hoa and ourselves, remained in place in a clump of large black volcanic-looking boulders while our troops returned fire weakly. Heavy machine-gun fire took its toll, as we had lost about 20 people in the half-hour after siesta had ended. It was time to get the heavy stuff in here. The artillery I had steadily directed was just barely keeping the enemy off of us. These North Vietnamese were tough and determined, and probably could have overrun our unfortified position at any time if they wished. I could only figure out that they weren't sure enough of their ground firepower superiority to try an all-out assault yet. Let's get the air strike going before they figure out that they're winning!

Jake 4-2 made another very low pass just to identify the enemy while I marked my best guess at their location, firing a willie-pete (white phosphorous) round from my M-79 Grenade Launcher in their direction. Jake was able to spot the bad guys and confirmed about a company in strength. Unfortunately for him, the bad guys opened up like a shooting gallery on him when he made his spotting pass. As the old saying goes, however, this only served to tick Jake 4-2 off. The display of American firepower that followed was no less than awesome! To further mark the target for the jets, he fired a couple of air-ground rockets from a no-power dive position. He then brought in multiple sets of fighters with bombs and napalm canisters until we thought the barrage could be lifted. A slow lazy follow-up pass by Jake 4-2 to check the enemy site out was next. To my shock, as Jake pulled up from his observation run, the shooting gallery opened up again. Jake was being fired upon again by what must have been the deafened stragglers from the NVA Company. This was a no-brainer. The U.S. Air Force made one more big run and this time the napalm silenced this group of North Vietnamese for good. This heavy battle, like many others, was eventually squelched by the U.S. Air Force in support of yours truly. We had kicked butt this time and were proud of it! All the credit would go to the PF group leader and my friend the District Chief. The American firepower would be treated as incidental supporting fires. What we wanted to do was to elevate the image of the Popular Forces now carrying the war to the local village level. And we wanted to show that the program of Vietnamization we had embarked upon was working. We may have stretched it a little in the reporting, but I had to think that a year ago, this would have been a disaster resulting in a rout of our forces. We were making progress! Sure we had lots of help, but that's why it was there at our disposal. Progress was progress!!

*   *   *   *   *   *   *

While this pitched battle was going on, and during the lunch break that we had all been accustomed to, I started to feel the need to carry the message of what we were doing to those that needed to know the truth. It was clear that we were able to win this thing - day by day and village by village - if the bureaucrats would let us and as long as the great fire support was available to us. Unfortunately the bureaucrats would rather end the war - no matter what - regardless of the shame that complete withdrawal might bring. By 1971, Nixon's real doctrine of "peace at any price" led to the deaths of several of our long-lost brothers - the POW's/MIA's of Vietnam. The signing of the Paris Peace Accords ignored several hundred of these prisoners and missing Americans. What a disgrace! The cut-off of American money and material, meaning no more bullets and fire support, in 1974 would spell out the fate of those gallant Vietnamese officers like the ones that I had fought alongside. Then the country quickly fell to the communist invaders from the north in 1975. Most of the officers that I had had any contact with would have been killed or sent to "re-education" camps for years on end where many would die from "natural causes" in the worst human conditions possible. We had promised South Vietnam success in 1954 and had doomed them to failure almost two decades later. We didn't lose - we quit!

*   *   *   *   *   *   *   *

Clearly, the air strikes had caused the North Vietnamese to break contact. Across the rice paddy their covered position had backed up against a thicket of bamboo and other woods that stretched far enough to their rear for them to make a hasty retreat, surely carrying their dead and wounded with them. Now, normally we should have had a blocking force in place to cut them off, ambush their retreat, or at least slow them down for another pounding by air support. We had not been able to do this for obvious reasons. In order to encircle their positions the District Chief would have had to muster a large force and then personally lead it through some dangerous unknown conditions to get around behind them. Also, sure as day follows night, the enemy had been smart enough to put out security so that any attempt to move troops around would have resulted in a sure ambush and another firefight that we couldn't

PRE-PLANNING ?

control. To the average infantry tactician it may seem that we violated one of the school solution rules, but that's just the point. It would have been a school solution to try it. Unfortunately, in Vietnam and particularly in the rice-roots war we were fighting here, school solutions didn't always work. We had learned that once a firefight starts, it would be foolish to try fancy movements by our small forces. Once the enemy had the initiative - one of the basic principles of infantry combat - we had to be much more conservative, fighting them off, hunkering down, and calling in the world. The teachings of The Infantry School at Ft. Benning had changed, I hoped, with the lessons learned in Vietnam.

After a quick medevac of 5 seriously wounded PF's by chopper, our troops regrouped and moved across the line of contact while I kept "walking" the artillery in the general direction of the NVA retreat all the way to the coast. It was now after 4 PM. Jake 4-2 was relieved by the new Jake 4-0 who provided spotting cover, but could not see hide nor hair of any enemy on the run. We decided that there would be no more air strikes, but Jake helped to walk the artillery in front of us. On reaching the previous enemy position, we were again awed at the destruction. Lots of scorched earth, bomb craters, and even numerous blood trails. Small parts of bodies and clothing were found, but no complete enemy soldiers' remains were left behind. Counting the pieces was a gruesome way to estimate success, but we concluded we must have inflicted at least 20 percent casualties. They had been bloodied if not defeated. But they were gone, albeit temporarily, from our territory - probably on the Hourglass island, from which they would probably head for the next district north by boat after darkness fell. I made a request for intermittent artillery fire on the Hourglass all night long before we wrapped up for our return to the District compound. We reported to Jake and the artillery folks at LZ Snoopy that we estimated about 30 enemy casualties, but would only be guessing to break down dead from wounded. Our force of less than 100 had taken about the same number of losses. We lost 10 dead and 15 or so were wounded to various degrees. Guess you would say that in the body-count sweepstakes, we just broke even. But we had made another step towards overall security by not faltering under the steady tactical pressure of a well-organized enemy. There had been tense moments, but we had held up pretty well this time.

Our small troop was exhausted and slowly made its way back to the District HQ. Johnny, who had been monitoring and supporting us from the district team's bunker all day, radioed out to ask if we wanted a pick-up, but I elected to turn it down. We would walk out with the troops. The closer we got to home, the lower the level of security precautions became, and we soon turned into a herd of smoking-and-joking buddies. We were all elated with our success and perhaps even in awe of our survival of such an ordeal. (This could have been a fatal mistake - to let our guard down on the way back. Stories of ambushes on a unit's return trip within site of their destination were legend in Vietnam.) The camaraderie was always the thickest right after a major fight and when you could still talk about it - even though most of the PF's could only communicate in rough pidgin-english and we were the same with our Vietnamese. One PF that I recognized from many other operations pointed back behind us and yelled :"Beaucoup VC!, Beaucoup VC!" Well, he was partially right. There had been "beaucoup" of them, but they had been tough North Vietnamese regulars, not Viet Cong guerrillas. Most Vietnamese referred to the enemy generically as "VC". This one guy had started something, as one-after-another most of the rest of the PF's would come up to me and Sergeant El and yell "beaucoup VC!" and then shake our hands. We were now tight comrades-in-arms. We had gotten bloodied together and had thought we won together. All the carryings-on were quite normal. As I have pointed out before, the greatest feeling in the world is to be shot-at-and-missed! We were celebrating!

Back in the compound I slowly came down from this euphoria with a quiet beer, a little shakiness from left-over fear, and newly imagined fear at what could have happened. Ken wanted to hear

ADRENALIN

all about our firefight. So did many of the others. *Thieu Ta* came over to join us in a more serious post mortem than a celebration. I could tell by his warm smile that he felt even closer to me now than before - as I did to him. We were more than just comrades-in-arms, we were brothers We had survived the worst together and were united in the common bond of teamwork and respect.

*   *   *   *   *   *   *

The days seemed to pass quickly - perhaps too quickly - until it was almost Christmas. Part of this holiday season, the strangest one of my life, included a party at the "Embassy House" in the province town - Quang Ngai City - about 10 miles away from our team house. All the American civilians would gather for a rather formal affair that included all their Vietnamese employees and other camp followers - mostly women - and a number of the Vietnamese dignitaries. All officers' attendance was required by the Province Senior Adviser, but we were excused to leave early for any security reasons, a dispensation which we would be sure to take advantage of. The atmosphere at this soiree was stuffy at best. It reminded me of an old movie where - in the middle of a war for survival - the upper crust would hold lavish parties and gossip about the state of the society one rung below theirs. In the case of the "embassy" party, Vietnamese high society as well as Americans were really into this plantation mentality. So we endured the flitting socialites and military and civilian social climbers about as long as we could, then made our excuses and made tracks to get back home before dark. On the way out I couldn't resist the temptation to liberate a fancy leather shoulder holster from the table where everybody - some of us reluctantly - had checked our weapons. I didn't look on this as stealing, as I traded my cheap plastic, made-in-Taiwan holster for the expensive cowhide one. After all, these rear-echelon people didn't need things like this and they deserved to be ripped off once in a while. Needless to say, I didn't hold city warriors in very high regard. It also amazes me that I thought so little of taking something - maybe after all the scrounging and underground supply systems, I didn't give it a second thought. Strange.

So we headed back to Tu Nghia and the "comfort" of the place we had now called home for almost a year, fully expecting to find things just the way they always were. We were surprised by two additions to the District compound. First we couldn't miss the fact that 4 artillery pieces - Vietnamese 105 mm howitzers - had been set up in the yard of our compound. Apparently the holiday truce we had heard about would be punctuated by stepped-up ARVN (South Vietnamese Regular Army) operations. The 2nd ARVN Division artillery had been moved in to support them. On the other side of the compound - in the American section - I spotted an actual manger scene that one of the guys had had shipped in by his family so that we could celebrate Christmas together. Here again was the irony. Under the big guns of war we would try to hold some kind of a Christmas ceremony. Some of the Vietnamese - several of the Catholic officers like Major Hoa - would join in with us tomorrow in celebrating Christmas here so far away from our homes and families. We would probably not exchange gifts, but would just commemorate the real meaning of Christmas - peace on earth. There had indeed been a truce declared in honor of Christmas, but nobody believed the North Vietnamese would follow it to the letter. *I WAS ON AN AMBUSH CHRISTMAS*
~ AN AMBUSH IS A DEFENSIVE OPERATION

Doc and Johnny had gone to Chu Lai to do some more scrounging and had come back with the prize - a whole real turkey for our Christmas dinner. Ken had told them he wanted a real turkey - no turkey breast or turkey parts or "processed" turkey. The District Senior Adviser was duly impressed with the fine job our two senior scroungers had done. But no cranberry sauce?? Just kidding, because someone's family had sent him a small canned turkey and two cans of cranberry sauce! We were set. A little rice and gravy would make the meal complete, and we knew we had access to rice. Thanks to the generator on the compound, we could cook the turkey in our "kitchen" quite nicely. Christmas dinner was beginning to take on the trappings of a home-cooked meal. Once again I was impressed with the creativity in this small outpost of America.

Now it was Christmas Eve. Shortly after dark all the Americans gathered in the little courtyard of our sector of the compound. One of the guys had received a tape recording with Christmas music on it. When "Silent Night" came on someone started to sing the words quietly. Soon everyone had joined in. Each of us probably formed his own mental picture of what it would be like to be home with family at this time. It became a rather emotional moment and there wasn't a dry eye in the group. When the song was over we started shaking hands and telling each other "Merry Christmas".
Something caught my eye at the gate. It was *Thieu Ta* Hoa, his wife, and their two small children. As our host in Vietnam, Hoa wanted to join us at this moment, but he waited politely outside the gate until our touching song and handshakes were done. I quickly escorted the family inside. To my recollection, this was maybe the only time other than my promotion party months ago that Hoa's wife had come to our compound. Her visit on this occasion meant a lot. Now someone broke out a bottle of great Scotch and poured a swallow in each person's paper cup for a toast. Ken halted the proceedings to run to his room and fetch two small cordial glasses for Hoa and his wife to use. While this would have normally been a men-only ritual, Christmas brought out the most tolerant in all of us, so this fine lady was honored to join us in a toast for Christmas. This was very unusual in their culture, but this was a more sophisticated, educated family than most. There were toasts to success, to victory, and to the cause. Hoa then proposed a toast to America,to his advisers, and to an end to the war. That was our Christmas eve for now, as Hoa and his family graciously returned to their house. He would be joining us for dinner tomorrow. The rest of the night was quite solemn and, thankfully, free of any enemy activity to worry about. The Christmas truce had held - in Tu Nghia

at least. I know there were hundreds of cease-fire violations throughout the country, but here it was quiet for now.

We spent Christmas day quietly, feasting as planned on our special turkey dinner with Hoa and most of his staff of officers in attendance. Most of them, politely, ate small amounts of our strange food and of course took us up on a beer offered for lack of anything as safe to drink. That was about it, as everyone retired to their team houses to read, or nap, or to write a special Christmas letter home. Most of us had sent Vietnamese Christmas cards we had found in Quang Ngai City. One of those that I sent now hangs on the wall of our family room. At Christmas time it reminds me of that one Christmas I missed at home but experienced with friends in an adopted home half-way around the world. Most of those friends are probably gone now. I wish I knew.

CHAPTER SIXTEEN

A couple of days after Christmas Major Hoa invited a few of us to dinner at his favorite Chinese restaurant in Quang Ngai City. About 1500 (3 P.M.) we took off in two vehicles for the 5 mile (25 minutes due to traffic and extra caution) trip to the Province Capital. Ken drove his Scout with Dave, the DIOCC adviser lieutenant, and Doc on board while I rode with Hoa, *Dai Uy* Cahn, and two bodyguards in Hoa's jeep. He drove and I rode "shotgun" as was the custom on such jaunts. We left early to allow for a leisurely dinner and enough time to get home before darkness fell over the district. We still respected the difference between the waning hours of daylight and the first hour of darkness in this fragile war zone. Frankly, I feared the city itself (actually a small town by our standards) more than I did the short ride out on the open (newly paved) National Highway 1. Returning to the District Headquarters would be easier on entrance because everyone knew that the District Chief was out on the town and would need a swift entry into the relative security of the guarded compound.

Dinner, as usual, was an extravaganza fit for a king. Our rag-tag little group was seated at a large, isolated table and waited on hand

and foot by three or more waiters and the owner at all times. Several of the other people now filtering in were civilians that I recognized. There were people from the Embassy, USAID, CORDS, JUSPAO, and other acronymed U.S. and Vietnamese operative agencies. One needed a scorecard to keep track of which was which, which was operating according to its advertised charter, and which was a front for the CIA . Sometimes it seemed like all of them were of this last category. Our table seemed to get more attention than the others. Whether this was due to Hoa's influence and earned respect or because we were from the field, in a known hurry, and quite a spectacle for the curious among the city dwellers, I didn't know. But it was nice to be treated like royalty, even if we were those heathens from the boondocks.

This was not my first time here, but I was duly impressed as before with the outstanding bill of fare at this home-owned family restaurant. The owning family was of pure Chinese descent, and, like their counterparts in the Chinese sections of DaNang and Saigon (the Cholon section there) they catered to the elite Vietnamese and visiting Americans with great food! The multiple course meal consisted of : shark fin soup with cream of crab and asparagus, shrimp-and-pork fried rice, an indescribable salad with odd plant life in a ginger dressing, steamed rice with a beef and onion gravy, and a whole pan-broiled fish with tomato-based sauce for each of us. I remember the fish most for the way it looked up at me as I devoured it. Of course the meal was embellished with fresh French bread and lots of beer and wine, plus, for the Vietnamese purist, generous supplies of *nuoc mam* (the special Vietnamese fish sauce) for application to any and all of the dishes as the individual preferred. I was one of the few Americans that loaded up everything with the pungent *nuoc mam* - and when I would sweat (which was often) I smelled like a native! I loved the stuff ! Perhaps I had become a little Vietnamese myself.

The suitable finale' of this meal fit for kings was the dessert of lychee fruit, which was served chilled and had a very heavy pear-like taste. With hot green tea and fortune cookies, this fruit was delectable and the perfect sweet finish to such a feast. We all left table feeling challenged to drag our gorged bodies down the stairs from the second-story home restaurant to our waiting vehicles, but we finally made it, exaggerating our stuffed conditions all the way. Someone remarked that this was one Chinese meal where we wouldn't be hungry in an hour - maybe for days! What a joke. At the rate our activities consumed energy - fuel - we could never get enough food, even in the stifling heat. It's hard to believe that with all the calories we consumed, all of us were losing weight like crazy. This also in spite of the huge quantities of beer we consumed - not for its low alcohol content, but just as a thirst-quencher. You couldn't drink most of the water over here and to drink cokes all day would make short work of any stomach. So beer was the staple beverage of our normal diet. Still, I weighed about 150 pounds and had less than a 28-inch waist by the time my year was over; normal weight for me is around 185. No comment on waist sizes! Anyway, the trip to the Chinese restaurant didn't fatten me up at all.

*   *   *   *   *

The end of calendar year 1969 came and went rather quietly. "When in Rome" you celebrated holidays like the natives, and here the new year was observed as the Chinese Lunar new year, called "Tet" in Vietnam, which would come more than a month after December 31, 1969. The Americans celebrated with a toast to our survival and to the beginning of another decade. In retrospect the "sixties" had been action-packed, to say the least. While some liked to call it the age of Aquarius or the age of enlightenment, I viewed it as the age of rebellion, selfishness, and abandonment by most of the younger generation of the principles that America was built on. To this day I maintain that everything was "upside-down" in the

60's. One of the glaring paradoxes of this era was that while the protestors and draft-dodgers professed to be individuals "doing their own thing", they were actually conforming to their own patterns. The non-conformists were conforming - to some bizarre form of life! But the sixties were over now and it was 1970, and I was three months away from going home and about seven months away from returning to civilian, "normal", life and the civilian job I had left behind almost 3 years ago. What I wasn't realizing at the time was the fact that the job I was doing right now would be the most important thing I would do in my entire life! But there was still work to do here, New Year's or not.

* * * * *

Lots of construction projects dominated the next few weeks in the district, as enemy activity was at a low level in January, probably because they were gearing up for a new "Tet" offensive, and partly due to the presence of the 2nd ARVN units operating in the district, complete with Tu Nghia-based artillery. We took advantage of the lull to complete two major projects - the re-furbishing of the compound's well - our only washing water source - and the building of a real chopper pad for our district headquarters. As a side project, some enhancements to our bunker and team house were also in order. Most of the work would be done by Vietnamese carpenters - some of the most unorthodox but uniquely skilled artisans I had ever had the pleasure and entertainment of watching. This would be a learning experience - one where we learned that it didn't matter if you had the right tools or materials, one could build almost anything if he put his mind and ingenuity to it. Just to see the houses made out of coke cans would bear out the claim that the Vietnamese were the most skillful people at "make-do" of any in the world.

The well project was more like one of sheer labor on the part of the workers who would venture twelve feet down in the existing well to dig deeper and, alternately, shore up the fragile mud walls in preparation for the lowering of yet another hollow concrete ring to be put in place below the others. By definition, each ring would become smaller and smaller, but with the water table as shallow as it was in this coastal district, we shouldn't have to go much further! In fact, all of us were surprised at the depth we were at already! It was intriguing to watch these workers, under the supervision of one of the compound sergeants (Vietnamese, of course) complete their tasks, including the tedious, laborious lowering of the well rings - two of them this time - into place. Of course, all their work was punctuated by the flow of water, not to mention all sorts of creatures - I don't even want to imagine some of them - who lived in the warm, still waters at the bottom. The well was finished in a few days, and many of the workers moved on to more imaginative projects.

The carpenters - sheer geniuses as far as I could tell - were able to add a complete room to our team house without the first blueprint. It was like they understood what we wanted, visualized the finished product, then started to cut out the pieces they needed to complete the job. I was most intrigued with their basic method of cutting lumber or plywood. After marking with a blue pencil with the measurements visualized before, one of these artists would jump up on top of the piece of plywood and proceed to saw vigorously in the direction of his own feet. One of his assistants would steady the work piece and prepare to rescue the cutter on this human table saw. If he didn't, the work would collapse and send the sawyer tumbling head-over-heels. Once "enough" pieces were cut - not measured, just cut - the carpenters began assembling them to the outline of a complete room add-on. After nailing up a few pieces, it was back to the cutting again. This process went on for what seemed like forever until all the Vietnamese jumped back and took a bow for their finished artistry. Actually, the hooch they had built wasn't bad. Most Americans, particularly those schooled in the fine arts of engineering and construction, would doubt the ability of these artists to create what they did without "a plan", but they did it just the same. We were impressed! And, we liked the new hooch too much to make fun of the methods used to raise it, to create it. It was ours now, and it would serve us well as a recreation room and above-ground radio room. No longer would the person on radio watch have to spend all his time in the dank - though friendly and safe - confines of the American bunker. He could be a part of civilization and might get into a friendly poker or hearts game in the process of listening for radio traffic. And, once the new digs were secured with several overhead layers of sandbags, it would be relatively safe to be in here. That little task, the sandbagging, would be complete before nightfall because, sure enough, the bad guys would know about our new building and would try to drop a couple of mortar rounds through the roof if they could. We foiled that idea quickly with enough layers of sandbags to withstand a B-52 strike! Sorry, Charlie!

The biggest project was still ahead. With the help of the U.S. Army Engineers, we would soon have ourselves a first-class, raised, secured chopper pad for the helicopters that we had to land as a regular part of our day-to-day operations here at the district. Unfortunately, due to the cramped quarters of the district compound, the pad would have to be outside our "strong" perimeter defense, which would make night operations less than fun. But, I guessed that anything was preferable to landing these birds right on the highway, which we had been doing long before I had arrived. The best site we could find was indeed across the highway and required a considerable buildup of the land in a rice paddy to bring the landing pad level with Highway 1. This turned out to be a relatively simple task for our Engineer buddies from 3 klicks down the road. Once the plan was known, their heavy machinery made short work of the creation of a flat, built-up area about 50 by 50 feet snugged up against the highway and at the same level. Several crews of our Vietnamese "construction experts" helped by working the topsoil completely flat and emplacing 3 or 4 layers of sandbags all around the exposed sides of the pad. This was done to prevent erosion as well as to discourage planting of bombs in the soft soil around the landing zone.

The crowning glory of this landing pad was the surface, which would consist of a layer of pierced-steel-planking , commonly known as PSP, which creates an ideal landing surface with drainage and protection against the planting of mines at the same time. Many of the classiest runways in Vietnam were laid with PSP, and we had it too - thanks again to our Engineer friends. We now had the most secure, from a technical standpoint, chopper landing and launch pad in the area. Of course because of its position outside our compound it had to be under surveillance night and day, but we had the manpower to accomplish that boring mission. As a double-check, before each day began, we would have one of our PF squads probe the holes in the PSP and carefully check all around the sides for signs of tampering by the bad guys. For those wondering, only once did we have a case of suspected violation of our chopper pad, and that was when a couple of civilians tried to liberate a sheet of PSP! We weren't surprised.

We could hardly resist the temptation to put some kind of special identification on the steel surface of our new pad. After brief discussion, the choice was unanimous. It had to be the infamous Playboy Bunny logo which now adorned the entrance to the American part of our compound. If this was truly "The Playboy Club -Tu Nghia" then we had to advertise the fact to every aircraft that passed within 10 miles of us! After all this time, I can't remember how we did it, but we ended up with a black rabbit's head in a circle of white paint that must have been 10 by 10 feet. All I know is that on my next chopper flight, I could make out the design at 1000 feet 2 klicks away. There did arise a flap with the Province team for a short time about this "breach of security", but our PSA, the colonel who liked us, squelched the complaint in a hurry. Why couldn't we brandish our logo? The 101st Airborne did it with skywriters! Besides, Charlie knew exactly everything he needed to know about us, including my name and my home town. What secrets were we giving away by flaunting our happy-go-lucky logo? So, more visible and obvious than ever, the Tu Nghia Playboy Club was alive and well. Chopper pilots from far and wide, even those just passing through, would be familiar with our blatant signal of "laid-back" American influence in our little district - this microcosm of Vietnamese society with its ever-present sign of America of the "sixties" - the Playboy Bunny! (I was happy - but not surprised - that nobody on our team had voted for the peace symbol - that which had become synonymous with the anti-war mentality. We all believed in what we were doing too much to make fun of this mission of ours!)

One of my more significant returns to the sign of the rabbit was after one of our infrequent heliborne visual recon's (VR's) into the mountains in the western part of our district and further into the well-known enemy haven called Nghia Hahn - smack in the middle of these 300-meter and higher mountains. When we took one of these flights with the District Chief we were risking a lot, but we found it necessary. On one such VR in the past we had spotted an enemy unit of considerable size and had reported it up the chain until the Americal Division dispatched a battalion - 600 men - by chopper to engage the enemy. The NVA unit was driven out, probably keeping them from infiltrating our district and possibly overrunning our compound. On this January VR we didn't spot any large units or fortifications but we did take considerable fire from several isolated locations - just enough to make the young chopper pilots with their beginnings of blonde mustaches sit up and take notice. The door-gunners let loose some heavy fire into the jungled mountains to suppress the enemy fire. The well-known "pucker factor" was up for these guys while Hoa and I, sitting in the doorway, maintained our nonchalant, business-as-usual looks. If the truth was told, I was scared stiff when we detected the 51 caliber machine-gun fire, but I couldn't afford to show it. It was part of the game - plus it kept everyone on a confident note if you looked that way. In times of crisis we look to each other for reassurance, and the one that shows calm confidence first will be believed - yes, followed. To this day, I try to follow the same principles in a business environment. If one is calm under stress, all will be OK . This VR ended with no real remarkable results, so the pilot quickly swung back east, cleared the mountains and then low-leveled (maybe 10 feet off the ground) his way back to Tu Nghia and the comfort of our little life. Our pilots looked relieved, although I would have assumed that this would have been routine and comparatively safe for them. I learned later that they not only never rested, they didn't see any mission as too routine to do their best and to stay very alert. I liked that! Most pilots even took seriously all of our "milk runs" - I actually called them "pig-and-chicken runs" in memory of my first in-country flight in the C-130 full of families and their livestock. These chopper pilots would gently land and unload us on top of the bunny and then high-tail it for Chu Lai. I didn't know it, but my last mountain VR was over.

Later in January, we paid another visit to our Navy friends, the junk-base advisors, in their forlorn digs out by the coastal area of the district. This tiny, helpless-looking compound made me feel good about our spartan but superior living conditions at the district headquarters. These 4 sailors really had it tough and their security was way below par. They must have used up eight of their nine lives already, but they kept up their mission of advising the Vietnamese junk navy in its efforts to provide security at the mouth of the main province river and to interdict the seemingly uncontrollable waterborne passage of the bad guys from district to district.

Our chopper was totally overloaded as it barely escaped gravity in time to avoid the flooded rice paddy adjacent to the pad. Good thing the pad was elevated about 5 feet, because our skids (runners that the helicopter sat on) dipped low enough to pick up some muddy debris before we got enough combination of forward speed and air under us to feel the spinning rotor blades start to lift us up just the slightest bit. I don't think we ever got any higher off the paddies than the original 5 feet until we reached the coast either. This made for a fast ride at 90 knots this close to the deck! (Now that all those shenanigans are over I'd love to try it again just for fun). Easy to say now if you know you've made it. Back then you couldn't worry too much because the alternative - walking the distance through some nasty territory - wasn't too attractive either. At least the fear of a ride like this was over in a few minutes! The overload of this chopper - call-sign "Utility" because of the varied jobs it was called on to perform day by day - was due to the several hundred pounds of canvas we were carrying to the Navy advisors. We had scrounged it for them from the civilians in the city and were giving it to the junk base for temporary cover for their quarters, which had been all but destroyed in a heavy mortar attack a few nights earlier. We had known when it happened because I had tried to coordinate counter-mortar artillery fire from my friends at LZ Snoopy while listening to the pleas for help from the Navy guys. We thought the quick and deadly fire support may have shortened the mortar barrage and could have warded off a potential ground attack at the time. The "squids" were extremely glad to see us!! The Lieutenant - equivalent to an Army Captain - gave me a friendly bear hug when we landed. He asked me to pass on his eternal gratitude to the artillery boys at Snoopy for him. Later he thanked them personally over the radio. Just sitting there in his hooch, I couldn't help but let my mind compare their plight to ours. While they were more isolated and vulnerable to enemy ground attacks, we were always moving around just looking for trouble - and often finding it. This had all the trappings of one of those situations (over a beer) where one group tries to give more credit for bravery to the other. "Man, I couldn't do what you guys do!" kinds of discussions - growing louder with each passing beer. My hat was off to these guys! This was the last time I would see any of them. Two months later - within days of my rotation back to the world - we heard that the junk base was overrun and the fate of the advisors was as yet unknown. Our district had offered to send a relief column but was told that it was too late. The enemy had abandoned the base immediately upon over-running it, but the advisors were nowhere to be found. Province told us they were all right, but I never heard for sure. I never heard the true story before I left - and of course wonder to this day what happened to my Navy friends. I'm sure I'll never know. It's an unanswered question - one of many that linger - and haunt - to this day.

*   *   *   *   *   *   *

Tet of 1970 came rather peacefully. Unlike the now-famous Tet Holiday of 1968, when a major communist offensive kicked off the Chinese New Year holiday season, this holiday began without fanfare. There was, as usual, a truce declared - both sides trying to get the jump - to be the side of peace, law and order. All of the South Vietnamese troops were instantly on holiday to be with their families. I shuddered to think what would happen if a major communist offensive were mounted - how would we get our troops back to work again in time? Of course in our case the troops didn't physically go away to be with their families as they lived right here in our area of operations. But when they were off - they were off! No amount of pleading would be able to muster a majority of our district forces if needed in case of an attack. We would have to grin and bear it and call in the world - now a convenient euphemism for U.S. fire support - if anything happened. On the night of Tet, the Americans in our compound kept a 100 per cent vigil. About all we were treated to was a constant barrage of celebratory firing of weapons and fireworks all over the district. This outburst of fireworks included a battery fire-for-effect from the six tubes of Vietnamese 105 mm artillery temporarily housed in our district compound. Nobody knows where the rounds actually hit as the guns went off, but it was a spectacular display by our standards. Shortly after the barrage was fired our engineer friends from down the road called to ask what the hell had happened and if we were being overrun or something. Fortunately they didn't complain about any of the stray rounds falling into their area as "incoming" or anything like that, but I was holding my breath for that eventuality.

Actually, the night had been punctuated by the kidnapping of 3 of our loyal Hamlet Chiefs by the communists. In return the next night our Phoenix people went out and captured 5 Viet Cong Infrastructure (VCI) operatives - all of whom were killed while trying to escape justice. There would be a great hue and cry about these "atrocities" committed by troops friendly to the Republic of South Vietnam and their American advisers. As usual there would be no stories about the kidnapping, torture, and killing of government officials by the communists. Kind of led us to wonder whose side the world's press corps was on, anyway. As we all grew up we learned exactly whose side they were on - and it wasn't ours!! The reporting of the Vietnam war was the first indication of what the left-wing press could and would do to destroy the very country that gave it its audience and its license to report the news as they saw it. Unfortunately, most of the liberal press reports the "news" as they wish it to be! As a result, the American people will probably never know the truth about what is happening. Lord knows they still don't know the truth about our efforts in Vietnam. The majority of the people never will know the truth - even if they care about it any more.

The next day we received an alert from the Province net that hundreds of cease-fire violations had taken place and that we should be on full alert all day and the next night. We kind of laughed. Our District had lost 3 of its trusted government-supportive Hamlet Chiefs and now the HQ guys were advising us to be careful out here! But we answered in the affirmative - telling the Province intel people thanks for the warning. We'd keep our heads down. The pattern was so familiar. The communists would try to get public sentiment on their side by declaring a temporary truce before every significant holiday and then break their own truce. But the government actions were the only ones reported. It seemed that the bad guys were not only in control of the initiative on the battlefield - they were in control of the reportage' of the war itself. Surely the entire news media couldn't be in the pockets of the communists - or could they? At a minimum we knew that the media was sympathetic with the communist cause. Was this because the plight of the "freedom-fighting" rebels from the '50's was still considered a better story than the government of this 3rd world country trying to make a civilization free from the bonds of a totalitarian socialist system that recognized none of the freedoms that the industrious, entrepreneurial people of South Vietnam so valiantly sought? I think it's clear that the desire for self-determination on the part of the South Vietnamese lost favor with the press of the 60's who were so much in bed with the left-wing it wasn't funny! So, when the "news" of Tet was reported this time it was all about how the evil South Vietnamese government, with the help of the oppressive Americans, had violated the cease-fire so honorably offered by the "patriots" of Vietnam (the communists). In reality , revisionism was handling history even as it was happening. Revision of history didn't have to wait years and years - it was instantly "revised" on national TV broadcasts like that of Walter Kronkite and others. What a tragedy!!

It would have been nice to have been able to speak out and tell the truth about what was happening here, but nobody wanted to hear it. Just like when the hordes of reporters looking for the dirt about "My Lai" had descended upon Quang Ngai Province. Anyone - Vietnamese or American - whose story didn't fit the mold of what the sensationalists wanted to "report" was ignored. If no witnesses were available, testimony could be manufactured. We will never know the real truth about My Lai because of that. In addition, we will never see reported the slaughter of over 6000 South Vietnamese civilians in Hue City by the communists during Tet of 1968. Why?? To see, on the 6 o'clock news some night back in the world, the truth about the local, rice-roots struggle of the free South Vietnamese people to live their lives and the valiant fight of their local government militia forces to provide them the security to do so would have made a great story. But it wasn't to be. The news media were looking for the story about the American soldier smoking dope or torching a village or otherwise acting out the role of "ugly American", just as Ho Chi Minh and his communist party wanted it to be told. Why, it was almost as if the American news media was the puppet of international communism. Could that be?? It sure looked that way to the hundreds of thousands of us who returned home to watch the 6 o'clock news and hear Walter Kronkite say "that's the way it is" when he was totally lying about it!

*   *   *   *   *   *

Tet was over, we had survived, and I was now less than 2 months from my DEROS (date estimated for return from overseas). I would be heading back to the world in less than "60-and-a-wake-up". At once I was excited and also again concerned that my time had gone by so quickly that I had not come close to accomplishing all that I had wanted to. About this time the mail chopper brought my orders for departure. They quoted an exact MAC (Military Airlift Command) flight number out of Than Son Nhut airfield in Saigon - set for takeoff at 2400 hours on 23 March 70. I would be on a freedom bird 6 days before my year was up. The charter flight would be loaded with 250 or more American soldiers holding their collective breaths until the wheels went up for the last time. I showed my orders to the members of my team and they congratulated me for the 6-day drop and promised they would be following along soon. It was so reminiscent of the night at Fort Benning that I had brought back the OCS Company from a night training problem to find 150 copies of my orders for Vietnam waiting on my desk. Then I had waved the stack of orders in front of the assembled Officer Candidates and ordered them to congratulate me, as I was on my way to do the job that Fort Benning had trained me for - and in fact was now training them for. This time there weren't any cheers - just a pat on the back - but somehow I was just as forlorn as I had been on that night at

Benning. Then my innermost thoughts had been: "am I really ready for war?". Now my silent wonderings were more like: "am I ready to give up war??" How would I act without it? Granted these were bizarre thoughts and emotions, but I would venture to say that I'm not the only nut who had these mixed thoughts. Of course, the career officers were known to have said : "this may not be much of a war, but it's the only one we've got!" And they meant it! What was a 3-year reserve officer doing having second thoughts about giving up war and going home to safety? I don't know and probably never will know, but I really felt lost inside. The war would soon be over for me, and I would only be able to relive it vicariously. I was actually sad that my tour of duty was approaching an end!

NOT ME !!

I busied myself with more and more operations and visits to the Regional Force company outposts. We made occasional contact, but nothing spectacular. Dave went on most of these operations with me to further solidify his training and his relationship with our counterparts. He would be taking over the team on my DEROS - just as I had from Ron several months earlier - and so the cycle repeated itself. I really enjoyed these operations as they kept me alert and ready for anything. I didn't want to revert to the bunker mentality - not yet! On one of the operations we once again approached the Hourglass island - the VC stronghold - and again rained countless dollars worth of Uncle Sam's finest ordinance on it, but again failed to mount a ground assault on the island itself. My vow of several months ago to one day set foot on that snake-pit of enemy hiding places was broken. I now knew that no friendlies would ever go in there. The Hourglass would stand as one of the untouched sanctuaries of the enemy - and it was right here before my eyes, only 50 meters across the river! Well, at least we came close. I couldn't venture a guess as to how many tons of hot metal, fire and brimstone from the good old USA had been dumped there over time, but we would now retreat from the area for my last time. Someday, I will return to Vietnam under less hostile conditions and perhaps someday will - cautiously - fulfill my great wish to walk on the island we called "The Hourglass".

CHAPTER SEVENTEEN

Time was getting short for *"Trung Uy' "* (Lieutenant) - *co van truong* (adviser leader) of our little 5-man MAT team. That's me. I was getting close to 30-and-a-wake-up now, and everybody knew it. This last month was usually the one where the "short-timer" felt the most vulnerable. After all this, it would be horrible - and embarrassing - to have survived 11 months of combat and then buy the farm in your last month. It was for this reason that most Army officers spent the later months of their tours in the rear with the gear. Not so with MACV-COORDS. Not so for a Mobile Advisory Team. We were needed in the field until the last possible moment. This was OK with me, as I felt comfortable here. Better the devil you know......etc. Besides, I had some things I wanted to get done and I really didn't want to leave the friends I had made here. Of course, when the actual date to leave came, I would go with all the enthusiasm of any red-blooded American headed back to the USA and his real life. But as long as I was in Vietnam I wanted to stay right here with my friends in Tu Nghia. After all, friends are hard to come by in life, and here in Quang Ngai Province they were also hard to keep!

Combat operations continued as normal through February with sporadic contact here and there, but nothing to write home about. (Actually I had not made it a practice to write home about any of our combat experiences - just as well.) During this time we even ran a few overnight ops. These were not the most comforting maneuvers for a schooled Infantry officer, as the tactics, discipline and security of our Popular Forces units on the move would make Francis Marion - the father of guerrilla warfare - turn over in his grave! Many times I was sure that they brought me close to an early one! It was really not much fun, looking back on it, to be in the middle of a bunched-up (dangerous) formation while one of the PF platoon leaders wants to walk beside you holding hands!! (The hand-holding was just a common gesture of camaraderie to the Vietnamese - nothing to be alarmed about.) At night defensive positions, we were always betrayed by the noise and commotion along the "perimeter" caused by each little PF wanting to cook his late-night snack while we were supposed to be invisible to the enemy. Many nights, if I was able to sleep at all, it was with one eye open at all times. (I think I still sleep with one eye open, but can't prove it.) If we did sleep on a night defensive position, or even on an ambush patrol, it would always be with feet facing North. That way you would be oriented if you were awakened suddenly. In truth, I never slept soundly enough on these operations to be awakened without total possession of all my senses.

No! (handwritten margin note)

Speaking of senses, I have realized, even in later life, what my year in the bush did to my sensory powers. First of all, I developed peripheral vision that must extend to 240 degrees from eyes front. In a combat situation you learned to scan large chunks of the terrain in front of and to the right and left of you with full comprehension of not only the area scanned but the peripheral view that could detect any movement far to either side of the main

FOR COVER (handwritten note)

focal point. I use this sense even to this day in what I believe is the most sensitive and anticipatory form of defensive driving that anyone could possess. Call it paranoia, but I continuously scan the road and the other drivers in both directions, assuming they are going to screw up sooner or later and planning my corresponding evasive moves. Along with the acute vision is an incredible sense of smell and - more important - an uncanny ability to differentiate and identify multiple smells, connecting them to experiences and anticipating accompanying actions. This may sound a little too analytical, but its a reflex - not something I dwell on. This must stem from the constant exposure to extreme smells and the act of trying to sort them out as normal or abnormal and threatening. Most people reminisce over the sound of certain songs as they are heard on the radio. I react to associative stimuli of the sense of smell - of what is normal and what is not - of what is dangerous and what is harmless - almost animal-like. The sense of hearing was raised to superior sharpness in the boondocks as well. One of the things the human mind is capable of doing is to be aware of, and processing, multiple mixed sounds. Sometimes we don't consciously realize it but we are constantly evaluating sensory input. I found that this was a way of deciding actions or at least to categorize and respond to multiple stimuli at once. More simply, identifying the sound of a lone dog barking in a nearby quiet village at the wrong time set off reactions in me that may have saved my life a time or two. Of all these sensory phenomena, they all seem to linger with me to this day. Some of them are probably useful today, but most are just a throwback to my days in-country. I also would guess that these quirks of man are probably shared with countless other Americans who have experienced combat, especially in Vietnam where the war truly was all around you.

Birds cherping AT Night!

*   *   *   *   *   *

About 3 weeks before my scheduled departure date an eerie thing happened to me. Late one night *Thieu Ta'* Hoa came over to our side of the compound and politely invited me out into the open area for a beer, excluding others that were sitting around Ken's hooch at the time. It was obvious that my esteemed counterpart wanted a private chat with the one person he trusted most with military information. Hoa proceeded to break out a map that detailed the western part of our district as well as the district next to ours, which was called Nghia Hanh, where the mountains really became mountains and where none of us or our forces had ventured since before 1967. The district of Nghia Hanh ran up to the fabled central highlands of South Vietnam which provided free run for large NVA (North Vietnamese Army) units who infiltrated through the Ho Chi Minh trail and, eluding the border surveillance of the montagnard camps advised by my friends of the Green Beret, could typically pick their routes of advance. As we squatted papa-san style, Hoa spread his map out over the concrete "patio" of our compound and pointed to a distant valley nestled among the imposing high mountains of this no-man's-land. It was in this small valley, he intimated to me, that the Viet Cong had moved one of their small, brutal prison camps, complete with American prisoners captured in a debacle of the Americal Division farther north in Quang Ngai Province. Unique about this prison camp was the fact - as his Vietnamese intelligence network had it - that there were American soldiers collaborating with the enemy, carrying weapons as if they were prison guards, and actually helping the VC to convince civilians in the area - as scarce as they were - that the communists were right and that the American imperialists and their "puppet" South Vietnamese were wrong. Most intriguing about the intel report was the very detailed description of the traitors as "one black and two white" Americans. While I found the story fascinating, I began to worry that the next shoe was about to drop. Sure enough, it did drop! *AMERICAN ARMY OPERATION ?*

Thieu Ta' Hoa, being the brave soldier he was, made the leap of thought to the next obvious plan of action. He said if I could get him 2 choppers, we - he and I - could take about 12 PRU's (Province Recon Unit) troops - our best - and raid this lightly guarded VC prison camp! Not only would we score a major triumph against the communists by liberating American POW's, we could be heroes by returning 3 American turncoats to justice by capturing them also! My first reaction was analytical. If we could trust this intel from entirely Vietnamese sources, we could very quickly prescribe the appropriate action by the allies. Unfortunately, taking the correct chain-of-command approach would delay any activity long enough to let the prey escape and would leave everyone wondering if the story was true or not.. So, we couldn't wait. We also could not reveal our plan to a soul - nobody. Hoa did not trust anyone but the two of us right now with this information. Of course, when the right time came, we would have to tell the American support forces - like the unsuspecting chopper pilots, for instance - what the exact plan was. There was no way I could get the support we needed without telling the truth of the plan. Hoa agreed that we would give 24 hours notice to the helicopter people, but nobody else. This was getting serious. This was for real and I was getting nervous!

Once again I faced the dilemma that had confronted Ron and me back in July, when our logical reluctance to go on that suicide night march had given way to our sense of face and our loyalty to our counterparts. Going against our better judgment had gotten us ambushed and had almost gotten us both killed - or worse (captured) - when Ron was just a couple of weeks short of leaving country! Now I was almost that "short" and by all rights should have turned Hoa down on this little adventure. Sure! I was going to refuse my friend and lose face by dodging the most important and exciting mission of all? Not a chance! Deep down I was hoping against hope that this mission would somehow never materialize. If it just didn't happen for some reason I could breathe a sigh of relief. Part of me felt guilty for not wanting it to come off, and part of me was thrilled at the thought of possibly succeeding in such a neat operation. It would be just like the movies! But I already had learned that the real thing is never like the movies. The Vietnam experience had taught me these things.

We parted company as Major Hoa assured me that he would find out in one or two nights what the right timing would be. It became obvious that he was thinking only of a night operation! Oh, great! Just another detail to raise the pucker factor. I returned to our hooch and just thought about it for a few minutes. Dave came in with a concerned look on his face and asked if anything was wrong. I told him no, but that we might have one more hairy operation coming up in a few nights - just sit tight.

A couple of nights passed with no more talk about the "special operation". I didn't bring it up, as I never wanted to bug the district chief. He moved on his own time schedule and to wait for his lead in a situation like this was normal for us. Of course, I was getting shorter every day and would just as soon it never happened now, at this late date. A couple more nights went by, and it was starting to get to me now. I finally couldn't resist, and the next time I was alone with Hoa I asked him when we would be going to the mountains. He then told me that he was waiting for one more intelligence report that would confirm that the camp was still there, as there was also one report (or rumor) that it had moved southward and out of our reach. I started to feel a little relieved and a little disappointed at the same time. We might be missing out on this big chance after all. Now a part of me was anxious for this caper to be a reality. I wanted more than anything to pull this off as a parting act to do my part to end the Vietnam war successfully!

But it would never happen. Two more nights passed before *Thieu Ta'* let me know the bad news. The crude VC prison camp had been moved far to the south mountains. Somehow the bad guys, maybe including the 3 Americans who had sold out - for whatever reason - had heard that they were known and may soon be attacked by a force out to liberate the prisoners. I was momentarily heart-broken, then relieved, as surely this would have been not only the most exciting but also the most dangerous mission that I would have gone out on. But it wasn't to be.

*   *   *   *   *

But this isn't the end of this part of the story. Over 10 years later, 1982 I believe, I was routinely watching the evening news when the story came across that an American soldier had just "walked" out of Vietnam - now all communist controlled after the fall of South Vietnam in 1975 - claiming that he had been a POW (Prisoner of War) all those years and had just now been set free by a benevolent Communist government of Vietnam - our former North Vietnamese enemy. The soldier's name was Robert Garwood - soon called "Bobby" by the leering press, as he must have been called by his American buddies long ago. I had no idea at the time what was unfolding, but as the days and weeks rolled by it became evident that there were people around who had known or seen Bobby Garwood in Vietnam - and not under the most flattering of circumstances. I was, of course following the story closely, but was still taken by surprise - no, shock - when one day the news allowed as how there was suspicion about how Bobby Garwood had behaved while a POW in South Vietnam, in one of the jungle prison camps. Rumor and speculation abounded. There was accusation by former soldiers about Garwood helping the VC in conducting the camps, sometimes acting like an armed guard - often just speaking against the American government and its allies.

Before I knew it, there was the news that PFC Bobby Garwood was about to be court martialed by the government for treason, and now the full details of accusations came out in public view. One day I was personally shaken to read in the paper that Garwood had allegedly run with 2 other turncoat soldiers in his stint at these prison camps - one black, one white !! My God!! The article continued that the trio was called "salt-and-pepper" due to their mixed color. I was frozen in place. A sharp chill coursed to my spine. This time there was corroborating evidence to the story I had heard from Major Hoa way back in March of 1970! Americans who had been imprisoned by the VC in South Vietnam reported that the "salt-and-pepper" team had visited their prison camp more than once and that they were obviously working for the communists and were armed with Russian AK-47 assault rifles just like our enemy carried. These apparently were eye-witness reports! I started to get the shakes. Ever since the operation had been called off in 1970, I had wondered - probably doubted - if the story had been true. Now, I realized that it must have been true and here - maybe - was one of the individuals that we would have been going after 12 years earlier - at night, with a small force, and "short" to boot!

The story about Garwood was apparently damning enough to convince the court martial board of officers. A decade or more later, I still hear conflicting reports from fellow vets. Opinions vary widely and it's still a hot topic in North Carolina, where the court martial took place. A lot of the local vets feel that Garwood got a raw deal - that he was a scapegoat. Others have heard other corroborating stories, some from buddies who knew eyewitnesses. One of my friends recently told the story of hearing from fellow grunts in the Americal Division way back in 1968 that they had gotten into a firefight and had actually seen Americans with the VC. At first thinking that the Americans must be prisoners whom the VC would use as shields, they later noticed that the Americans - one black and one white - were armed and were even returning fire! Sure, these could have been exaggerated bar stories, but the description at that time was too coincidental not to be believed. Of course, this didn't prove it was Garwood, but it sure checked out as far as details go. Could there be this much pure coincidence??

It is now obvious to me that the story Hoa had told me had been true, and that the additional details of location that night must be given a lot of credibility. Just think! If we had taken faster action on the word of our spies and informants, we might have pulled off one of the great coups of the war. Not only could we have rescued our American comrades, the real POW's, from a fate worse than death, but we could have also captured 1, 2, or 3 traitors! We could have made history! And we also could all have been dead or - even worse - captured ourselves! Easy to say now, but I really wish we had taken the gamble and acted on instinct. I am also sure now that if the decision time had arrived, I would have gone with my counterpart. Against my better logic, but I would have done it just like Ron and I had done it the night of the fatal ambush, when we lost 40 people in 15 seconds. The only question remaining is who would I have taken with me? After all, we never went on any kind of an operation with just one American. I guess I would have asked Dave to volunteer as my assistant team leader. Probably wouldn't have taken an interpreter along this time, although that would have been against our rules, too.

*   *   *   *   *   *

So, I had missed out on a great opportunity for more excitement. I had thought about our aborted plan later in 1970 , after returning home, when it was announced that a small, hand-picked force of mostly Green Berets had attempted a night attack on a North Vietnamese prison camp at a place called Son Tay - in North Vietnam. The operation, though courageous and perfectly executed, had failed. The North Vietnamese had abandoned the prison, probably in haste. The Son Tay raid turned out to be a wild goose chase. On hearing this I didn't relate my story of our planned raid to anyone at home. At the time very few people wanted to hear "war stories" from Vietnam returnees. Besides, anyone I had told would probably think I was making it up to go along with the current news. Meanwhile I still wondered how it would have been to pull off our little raid. Along with the other possible outcomes loomed the chance that we might have also raided an empty nest.

CHAPTER EIGHTEEN

The last couple of weeks of my tour of duty in Vietnam overflowed with last-minute excitement, reminiscence, and mixed emotions. I was so excited to be going home I could taste it, but I also felt a certain emptiness - like wondering what life would be like after this experience, and, more often, how would this thing go after I left. Would the team I left behind and my Vietnamese friends succeed? Would they win the war in a few months or would it take a few years. I don't think, at the time, that I even considered losing it. I just knew that America would not give up until the South Vietnamese had won their freedom, even if it took a commitment of troops like that in Korea, where Americans were still on duty - helping the South Koreans maintain their sovereignty - almost 20 years after the war in Korea started. Never in my wildest dreams at that time did I think that my country would give up the fight, abandon the cause, and betray our allies in South Vietnam.

I kept going out on operations until my DEROS date to keep busy and, maybe, to hold on to this sense of accomplishment and importance I had attached to the work we were doing here. In reality, I was like a kid at the circus and I didn't want it to end. Each day was increasingly filled with sharpened appreciation of the Vietnamese people we were trying to protect and the young men who served in our Popular Forces platoons and Regional Forces companies and, most of all, with my admiration of my counterpart, Major Hoa.

*   *   *   *   *

One operation focused on the highest point in the populated coastal section of Tu Nghia District, a small fishing village that centered around an old fortified outpost on a hill that couldn't have been more that 25 feet above sea level, but it was really a hill among this vast expanse of flat rice paddy.

There were no usable roads out to this location, and we wanted to be able to start the operation early in the morning. We would not waste time (or take the chance) moving across 5 klicks (kilometers) of the district just to get there. The command group, consisting of myself, Doc, Dave, *Thieu Ta'* Hoa and Tu the interpreter, would chopper out from the district compound at first light. The area would be secured by Regional Forces Company 711 - our lone Montagnard company commanded by *Dai Uy'* (Captain) Hai and his 100 transplanted mountain tribesmen. Right away I knew this was an important operation as the District Chief would command it and he had picked his most effective unit to participate. These Montagnards were tough and tenacious. If we did get into contact with the enemy, I felt comfortable with 711 on my side, even though I was so "short".

The province chopper - "Utility" - arrived at our new chopper pad at about 0630 and promptly picked up our team. We were already hot and sweaty after waiting on the pad in the already abusive heat for almost a half hour. We had to be outside the perimeter and across the Highway to the pad well before the helicopter arrived. Better we wait on him than the other way around. You just didn't want a helicopter sitting on the ground - ever. After takeoff, the breeze that blew through the open passenger area, generated by the 90-knot low-level flight of this bird, was more than welcome. I sat as close to the door as I could. This chopper crew was new to the province run and probably had expected to pick up some ground-pounders whom they could scare just for fun. (Sometimes the young Warrant Officer pilots were like that.) But our group acted as nonchalant as possible with the flight and nobody even reached for a seat belt. This usually taught the pilots that they need not try any tricks with us. We were cool. I actually enjoyed these rides and I knew I would miss them someday.

Less than 10 minutes later, the bird took a sudden jolt from its ground-hugging flight and raced upward in the hot air. The G-forces were pretty hairy. Once we reached about 100 feet altitude I could see that the pilot was looking for a clean place to land. We were there and we wanted to get down as soon as possible. This was the most vulnerable point in any flight. This big bird was a sitting duck for any enemy gunner who wanted to take a pot shot at us. And even a round from an individual AK-47 rifle could do some damage - could even bring the ship down hard. There was no way to land on the hill, so we would have to set down at the base of it, but there wasn't anything but rice paddy. Shortly a puff of yellow smoke could be seen floating up from one of the narow, 1-foot-wide, paddy dikes that separated one hectare-sized paddy from another, just southeast of the hill. How was this pilot going to land on this narrow strip of land? I found out shortly. The Huey swooped down to within about 20 feet above the dike and then started a vertical descent and hover move - not the normal approach. The skillful young pilot then very gently rested the chopper's skids on the narrow dike while running full power. In effect he was hovering under power while just steadying the bird and balancing it on the fulcrum created by the skids' small contact with land. Nice maneuver! We all scrambled out and - bent over with bush hats in hand to avoid the rotor wash - tiptoed hurriedly out of blade range and to the safety of friendly troops who until now had been invisible. It was comforting to see the perimeter 711 Company had set up around this side of the hill for our arrival. Unfortunately, as the helicopter powered straight up, then made for its more conventional takeoff toward the south, we observed green tracer rounds flying around the Huey. Enemy snipers! Just as the chopper blew out of sight, we also observed the vapor trail of a B-40 Rocket that barely missed! By this time I was on my field radio to thank the air crew and at the same time warn them that they were taking enemy fire. They knew! They thanked us for the thrill and promised to see us again. This was a veiled way of reminding us that they would return at the time we had agreed upon when we had talked over the Huey's intercom on the way out. Now we wouldn't mention the pickup or its scheduled time over the open radio. If the enemy heard it - which you had to assume - they would be waiting to try again to shoot down the chopper! So anyway, we now knew that there were enemy close enough and bold enough to have tried to shoot down a helicopter in plain sight of us. This also meant that they probably had been observing us long enough to have been able to try to shoot it down before or during the unusual landing when we had all been aboard. Another one of those familiar chills went through me. We had been extremely lucky - again!

Well, it was still early morning and we had already had enough excitement to make a day! But now we prepared to move out to secure the village on the hill with a human cordon. The District Chief would then lead the command party in to meet with the hamlet and village chiefs and the head of the local People's Self Defense Force (PSDF). This group was truly made up of civilians who were armed and ready to provide some kind of defense some night if the ville were attacked. What was supposed to happen was that every one in this ville would retreat to the old fort and the PSDF would man the perimeter walls with their old shotguns, Tommy-guns, and other ancient weapons. This was the most primitive form of village security I had seen yet, but I knew it was quite commonly used in the central highlands west of us, where most of the population was Montagnard. The first form of this had been the CIDG (Civilian Irregular Defense Groups) started and supported by the CIA in the late 50's and taken over by Special Forces in the early 60's. And it had worked as long as defense was the key word. (Later use of these people in offensive operations with the Green Berets in command proved not to be so successful.)

On further discussion with the villagers and some of their leaders, Major Hoa learned that this PSDF group operated a little differently. They actually holed up in the fort every night themselves. This was not only selfish, it almost ensured that the people they were supposed to be helping to protect would be left on their own. Hoa immediately informed the hamlet chief that he would detail one PF Platoon to begin occupying the area to ensure that the PSDF did their job as it was meant to be done. The bad guys had not given this particular ville as much notice for some reason, so district security had been pulled off. In reality it appeared to me that there was just as much potential for trouble here as in any other part of the district, particularly since it was so close to coastal access. I sensed some political reason for this lack of normal district security. It became obvious that most of the people here were displaced Montagnards themselves and were of "less value" to the government. This didn't sit right. I could not imagine Hoa being this way, but even the best were quite discriminatory. I also wondered why these people didn't pick up and move closer to the 711 outpost where their own kind were in charge and could provide very effective security. But I never got an answer to that. I later would learn that there were different tribes of Montagnards who didn't get along with each other. That might have been the answer that was missing at the time. Anyway it looked as if security would be improved with the addition of a PF Platoon, perhaps only to show us the District Chief's concern.

Now there was the matter of those bad guys who had blatantly tried to shoot down the province chopper. Captain Hai was ordered to move out with two of his platoons to sweep the area from the hill east to the beach, leaving one platoon and a weapons squad behind to maintain security for the District Chief and his entourage of officials. Dave, Tu and I went with *Dai Uy'* Hai to provide fire support if he needed it. I had already asked my friends at the artillery fire base, LZ "Snoopy", to point two of their four 155 mm guns in my directions just in case. The battery commander had come back to me to let me know that he would cover me with all four tubes, "knowing I was short and all". I was grateful for that. Knowing these guys were behind me always made me feel more secure. Our small group moved cautiously around the hill and then in an easterly direction - right across about 150 meters of rice paddies. This was not a good feeling, being exposed on line slogging through knee-deep water and mud, but we had to get to the tree line that separated us from the beach some way. *Dai Uy'* Hai used a slightly different tactic for this vulnerable move that reminded me of the old "fire and maneuver" tactics we had learned at Fort Benning, but this time he was doing it with two platoons instead of two fire teams or two individuals. One platoon on the right of the line would move forward, well spaced apart, about 15 meters while the other platoon on the left would crouch and cover the advance - prepared to lay down a base of fire on the enemy if the other group took fire. Then, of course, they would switch. The covering platoon would now leap-frog by moving 30 meters to end up 15 meters ahead while the other group covered. This process would be continued until we reached the tree line, where the troops could switch to a wide wedge. I was reminded of my very first combat operation across similar territory about ten months ago. I felt just as tense but somehow more confident in myself and the group I was working with. The first group was about 30 meters short of the tree line when a few shots rang out from the front. It was almost half-hearted and probably was intended as a delaying tactic as the few bad guys made it for the coast. On the other hand, this could have been a clever trap. I had heard of more than one situation where friendlies were suckered into chasing a few enemy stay-behinds only to run into a well-organized ambush by superior enemy units. Often a few local yokel VC guerillas would act as bait to lure a friendly unit into a large North Vietnamese Army setup. My friend Captain Hai was as cautious as I was about walking into a trap. He grabbed Tu and told him to ask me for artillery on and beyond the tree line. I had already raised the artillery boys on my radio and was ready to "walk" the rounds from this tree line clear to the beach if that would ensure that the bad guys weren't able to ambush us! An amusing thought occurred to me at this point. For the next week or so maybe everywhere I went I would walk artillery in front of me, even if I was in Quang Ngai City. Sure! But it made the point.

We moved cautiously as the artillery moved about 200 meters ahead of us all the way to the coast. After each set of rounds I would give the command to "add 100",which moved the next barrage 100 meters more toward the water. Never did we see any further sign of the enemy, but we did succeed in clearing the area. This type of clearing operation was not unusual in Vietnam. Some units called it reconnaissance by fire but they would use direct-fire weapons en masse' instead of artillery. Often you would find a stray enemy casualty or so, but generally it just chased them away to fight another day. This didn't help in reducing the numerical threat of the enemy, but it did provide a psychological edge - if only temporarily. The problem was that the Viet Cong and the North Vietnamese possessed the most formidable weapon in this war of the sixties - patience! Our enemy could wait until Hell froze over, if necessary, for the right moment. For them it had been a war of the forties, fifties, *and* sixties and they could keep it up through the seventies if necessary. We Americans - and some of our South Vietnamese allies, for that matter - were not as patient. If you're an American soldier, you want to get it done and get it over with. You've only got a year to get it done. If you're a South Vietnamese officer or official you can wait, but not as long as the northern aggressors can. In this case, the bad guys that had taken shots at our helicopter would now hide out for a while. If they knew we would be picked up this afternoon, they would have been waiting for the bird to come in low and slow for maximum exposure. Otherwise they would wait for days, weeks or months for the next opportunity to do some real damage to the Allied effort.

Captain Hai and his troops were ready to move back into the ville and to take the customary "siesta" - lunch and a nap - that they had earned with their hard morning's work. We arrived in time for this ritual and enjoyed it as usual. The Montagnard troops kept watch during siesta so the majority could rest comfortably. The lack of activity during this break in the action (recognized by both sides) was eerie, as usual, but we felt more comfortable with the Montagnards surrounding us rather than some of the units I had worked with during my tour. I knew they wouldn't let us down - ever.

After siesta the district chief ordered 2 Popular Forces platoons to join us here in the village. About two hours later they arrived after a march across 5 kilometers from the district compound. One of the platoons was detailed to stay in the village to help the People's Self Defense Force learn how to defend their village more actively - things like not running for cover while leaving the villagers behind,for example. The second PF platoon would provide security for us to move across land back to the district Headquarters. Major Hoa wanted to march out rather than to be picked up by chopper, so I cancelled "Utility's" pickup. I think to this day that he was concerned about the sniper fire this morning and didn't want to endanger a U.S. helicopter and his advisors. He felt it was safer for all of us to go back on foot. The only trick would be to get to the compound before night fell. If we left immediately, we could just make it. The 711 Company could provide added security for half the trip, then we'd bolt for home with just the 30 PF soldiers surrounding us. It worked, but I would have preferred to have the 711 Company's Montagnards around me all the way home. Of course this would not happen because these "savages" were not allowed to move as a group anywhere near the district town. This was how the Vietnamese treated their strongest fighters. Too bad.

Our troop arrived back at the team house without serious incident just before dark. Another successful operation completed........ and we were all still alive and well ! This called for a celebration. Breaking out the beer was the first order of business, then inviting Major Hoa over to join us was my job. Actually we celebrated with just a quiet beer in Ken's hooch, where he was playing his reel-to-reel tapes for background music under the slowly rotating ceiling fan that looked like it had been salvaged from an old Bogart movie. It sure was nice to have these few creature comforts provided by the big 30 kw diesel generator that the district team had scrounged from somewhere long ago. Along with the luxuries, the generator provided us with the ring of perimeter floodlights that consumed a large part of its electrical capacity. These big floods bathed the entire perimeter of our compound so that the front line troops guarding us could see out nearly 100 meters as if it were daylight. I felt secure and at home in the Tu Nghia compound. This was home and it felt safe enough for even a short-timer like me. It might not have been so safe, but it seemed that way, and that was what counted at this point!

At this little gathering I could sense fatigue in Major Hoa. He had lived a hectic life since taking over the district. He left us early to supervise the deployment of nightly patrols and ambush teams. (These offensive patrols were vital to the security of the district HQ and nearby villages and refugee camps.) Then perhaps he would get time to spend with his family. Before departing Hoa smiled at me and asked "how many days?" I answered "*moui*", 10 in Vietnamese, and the Major just shook his head as he grasped my hand, turned, and disappeared into the compound yard. My eyes tried to follow him, but suddenly he was headed back into our little compound and was slightly startled but happy to see me standing outside still. As if remembering to say something he had meant to say before, Hoa almost sheepishly asked if I would go out on another operation with him and his troops tomorrow morning. Of course I would. Wouldn't miss it! Would he need helicopters for any part of it? Not this time, he smiled. I didn't think he wanted to get into that sniper thing we had run into today. I would find out in the morning why we wouldn't need the choppers.

*   *   *   *   *   *   *

Next morning, early, a mixed bag of PF's, PRU's(my bodyguards) and the Command group consisting of the district chief, Doc,Tu, *Dai Uy'* (Captain) Khanh and myself assembled in the compound yard. *Thieu Ta'* Hoa showed me on my field map where we would be going and what our main objective would be that day. It was one of those "walks in the sun" that were legend in Vietnam. A walk in the sun involved a show of force but only rarely - accidentally - would they ever include contact with the enemy. It really was intended to show the villagers that government troops were in fact there to protect them. Outside the compound 3 PF platoons were gathered, eating as usual, and preparing their individual gear for the operation , "securing" lots of the baseball-type frag grenades to their web gear with rubber bands as usual. The grenades set up this way used to scare me, but now I just laughed and anticipated watching a grenade's most prevalent use on one of these walks in the sun - fishing. (A grenade dropped in one of the many streams that wound through Tu Nghia District would, when detonated, bring lots of fish - stunned - to float on the surface, ready to be scooped up and cooked for lunch.) At about 0630 the group departed straight across the highway, embarked upon a huge circling movement that would cover a semi-circle about 3 kilometers in radius around the eastern part of the district. Geometry told me that this would be a 10-klick tactical movement - about 6 miles. The objective was to create a presence and to possibly encircle a few stray guerillas or VC Infrastructure operatives as we searched through every hamlet in our path. We did accomplish this, finding about a dozen very questionable characters who didn't have the right papers. These were whisked back to the district compound for processing as P.O.W.'s - Prisoners Of War

Just before noon our column made its way back to the hamlet of La Ha (4), where we would be treated to a fine lunch in one of the most secure areas in the district. Just one catch! This was the very same hamlet where, 7 months ago, Ron and I and a group of 80 PF's had been ambushed at night. We had lost half our people that night in this most secure hamlet, primarily because the hamlet chief had failed to warn us. The new hamlet chief brushed over that incident, but made sure we knew that he had not been in charge at the time, which we already knew. He then invited us inside his hooch, which was set up more like a miniature town hall and probably served as one. I was very leery about being trapped in this mud and grass structure with limited escape routes. I could just see and feel the shock of an explosive satchel charge being thrown into the town hall, a.k.a. this hamlet chief's modest home, while we socialized over lunch!

My fears were wasted. This turned out to be one of the nicest lunch meetings I had had while in the district. Just to be sure of security, 6 of the PRU (Province Recon Unit) bodyguards sat - awake and on guard - outside the door, giving me a much-needed sense of comfort. I genuinely relaxed for an hour or so and enjoyed the company, the camaraderie, and the food. Just the ambiance of being among friends in a foreign land was enjoyable. The food, as usual, consisted of the staple - *Pho'*, the noodle soup that I had grown to love - along with sticky rice and extra cut-up chicken and duck parts. Medium-cold Korean and Japanese beer was served instead of the Vietnamese beer called "Ba Moui Ba" - Vietnamese for the number 33 - which our hosts knew was not one of our favorites. The Hamlet Chief brought out the best for this lunch! Our meal was augmented by hard French bread and some kind of appetizer wrapped in leaves that I identified as tough, cold pork. It tasted more like the dog we had often eaten with the Montagnards, but plenty of *nuoc' mam* would help to disguise the flavor if not the chewiness.

It seemed that nobody wanted to end this pleasant break from the everyday war. We used up almost the entire siesta time around the lunch and meeting table. It was hot as the devil in this hooch, but I had learned to live with the environment pretty well after all this time. At least there were openings on two sides that admitted just a slight breeze and no longer frightened me with their vulnerability to a casual hand grenade that could have been tossed in. I spotted one of the PRU's outside each open side. I was beginning to feel much more comfortable that real progress had been made in this particular ville. It should have been that way. After all, we were less than a kilometer from the district headquarters. But later, as we strolled around socializing and taking pictures of and with the little kids, I still could not get the mental picture out of my mind - the remembrance of that night back in July when the ambush had almost been my last operation. Someday I will return to this spot just to prove that I can survive it again. I have to go back!

The hospitality of the La Ha (4) hamlet chief and his villagers was overwhelming. There also was not the usual curiosity with the two strange-looking Americans. They had seen us before and didn't fear a clash with the bad guys would ruin their day, so there was no threat implied by our presence here. The kids were, of course, all over us as usual. They all wanted a picture taken and we obliged, taking several of ourselves posing with them. I had been in some villages where the parents would not let us take pictures of their children, fearing the old superstition that the camera would steal the soul of the subject being photographed. None of that superstition was evident here today. Everything was just as friendly and open as it could be. I was almost embarrassed with all the fuss over us. It appeared that the villagers had all been told to treat us with warmth and enthusiasm so that we would no longer fear coming here and, in return, would once again shower them with America's wealth. The wealth thing was sort of out of my control, but the point about improved security had been made.

Siesta ended and it was time to saddle up and complete the swing back to the district compound. As we made our way down the same rice paddy dike where we had been caught in the night ambush, I again had that eerie feeling. I even glanced furtively into the same paddy where I had spent 3 dark hours hunkered down in the mud and paddy water while artillery illumination rounds popped continuously over our heads, giving us that false sense of daylight and safety while we longed for the real rising of that beautiful, protective ,life-giving sun. Tu and I looked at each other like old warriors, both thinking the same thing - we had survived but what about the others? Major Hoa saw my hesitation at the site of that disaster and immediately came to my side, shook his head and muttered "very bad". That was all he would say about a very low point in his reign as district chief. I certainly couldn't blame him for his feelings about this place. Perhaps, though, today's happy visit would help him like it had helped me. We moved on, as we had to move on.

Our last stop on this operation before returning to the compound was to sweep through the La Ha refugee camp, the new home to hundreds of transplanted refugees from the western mountains of our district. Again our sweep was to show the strength and protective nature of our forces. It was all politics. I was reminded of the squalor these poor people lived in. Their lives were in shocking contrast to the relatively happy lives of the people who still lived in the villages of their birth. The refugees were brought here for protection, but they felt like it was more for their control by the government. For this reason they were extremely vulnerable to any communist propaganda that could be smuggled in by the local VC infrastructure that could be moving throughout the camps at will.

There could have been some in there on this very day. We were able to spend a few minutes in the nearby market place. This local market was certainly a different environment, as busy vendors bargained with shoppers until a mutually good deal would be consummated. Everything from live piglets to paintings to American military gear was for sale or trade. I bought a miniature china tea set for a souvenir. Then it was back home to the team house after a long operation. Another day disappeared from my remaining time here, but I felt like we had accomplished something on this "walk-in-the-sun". If nothing else, I had come to grips with my emotions about La Ha (4) - at least for now.

CHAPTER NINETEEN

One day of my last week in Tu Nghia District was reserved for a
last trip to Quang Ngai City, the Province Capital. Since my MAT
team and I were attached to the Province Team, I had to clear
some paperwork and officially "check out". I picked a day to do this
when there were no major operations so that I could spend some
time in the city markets looking for souvenirs. I had no idea if this
would be my last chance to shop so I figured now was the time. I
wasn't sure what I wanted, but anything that would help bring home
the unique culture of this place, and of my once-in-a-lifetime
adventure, would do. Dave would go with me to meet with the
province team, and Doc wanted to join me on the shopping spree.
He was getting "short" by now himself and wanted to pick out some
things too. We didn't take an interpreter but we did take the jeep
with its permanent radio mount just in case. The 5+ mile ride was

relatively safe now, so we didn't need an escort, but we all carried full weapons - I had my M-16 and the .45 in its shoulder holster. No point in getting lax on security now!

Our stay at the Province HQ was short, just enough time to sign a few papers so that I could be taken off the Advisory Team 17 Morning Report as of 22 March and transferred to Headquarters MACV in Saigon for my one day of out-processing. Now the mystery of the DEROS process was clearer. The team admin sergeant had made some of the arrangements which he now explained to me. I would catch the small Air America courier plane out of Quang Ngai airfield to Danang about noon on the 22nd, then turn around at Danang Air Base on the next Air Force C-130 Hercules transport to Saigon's Tan Son Nhut Airport and MACV's nearby transient facility, where I would spend one last night in Vietnam in relative comfort and security. The 23rd would be spent on more paperwork and then just waiting until the midnight charter flight that would start the 24-hour journey home. I could hardly believe it, but as I listened to the admin guy recite these concrete plans for my departure I realized that it was all for real. The year that was once viewed like it would last a lifetime would be over in no time at all ! Only the memories - good and bad - would last that lifetime.

At my Province out-processing I was given copies of orders for the award of the Air Medal and the Bronze Star Medal. The 2nd Lieutenant who delivered them to me also gave me the written citation that describes the actions for which the individual was being awarded each of these decorations. I could tell that Ken, my District Senior Adviser and day-to-day boss, had written them. They were very complimentary of my achievements as the MAT Team leader. The Bronze Star was for meritorious achievement in operations against enemy forces and the Air Medal was for over 100 air missions in a hostile fire zone. All those helicopter rides, medevac's, VR's, and a few heliborne combat assaults (small ones with my PF forces) got me the Air Medal. There were no actual medals or ribbons given to me at this point. These would be issued to me either in Saigon or at my new stateside duty station. The two decorations plus the Vietnam Campaign Ribbon and Vietnam Service Medal, I guessed, were common for adviser officers to receive when their tour was completed. But back in June I had received orders for and proudly wore the Combat Infantryman's Badge, still said to be the most coveted award in the Army. What you had to do to get your CIB was to spend three months in an Infantry assignment and get into at least 3 firefights with a hostile ground force. I call it "getting shot at and missed". It doesn't sound that hard to get, but those of us who have it all still seem to feel a little bit special for having faced an enemy on an up-close-and-personal basis. For career Army officers it's an absolute must, but for me it just represented something that I will always be extremely proud of. I even wear a replica of the CIB in the lapel of my suit in business environments. It often evokes questions from those who had never seen one, but I really wear it so that those strangers who know and recognize it might strike up a conversation with me as their fellow veteran. That happens all the time. I meet veterans everywhere I go that way.

There was one thing missing, so I asked the Lt. about it. I knew that most advisers also received the Vietnamese Cross of Gallantry with Palm Leaf. This was given in recognition of joint operations with indigenous forces and the U.S. Military Assistance Command (MACV) was authorized to award it in behalf of the South Vietnamese government. The Lt. shrugged and said there was nothing here about that, but I thought I saw him grin in Dave's direction - almost as if to wink knowingly. I felt a little slighted. It may sound petty, but decorations are important to us as a recognition of our service and/or special achievements. Even 3-year soldiers like myself wanted to be recognized by our peers. Sometimes the medals and badges are all you get. But I dropped it, figuring that it was another Army SNAFU and would be taken care of later. A very pleasant surprise would actually take care of it sooner than I expected.

That was about it for the Province out-processing. It would have been customary for the Province Senior Adviser, the Lieutenant Colonel, to hold an exit interview with me, but he was out in the field this day. Just to make sure he covered a checklist item, he would order me to come back on another day just for the 5-minute meeting. Oh, well, this was the Army after all. Was the checklist more important than my safety? Actually, I later finagled it so that I could stop off briefly on my way to the Quang Ngai airfield on the day of my departure. This would allow me to make the visit with the Colonel very brief. My strategy would work.

Doc was waiting out in the jeep in the province compound when Dave and I came outside. He was sleeping, but with one eye open, and jumped at our approach - ready to go shopping. We motored back to the downtown area where all the shops and restaurants were clustered along the paved Highway 1 that ran right through the city. We had learned that there was one parking area that was without any suspicion as to loyalty and the safety of your vehicle. It cost a bundle to leave our jeep there, but it was worth it. We knew there were armed guards and that even our radio would be safe. This service was there mostly for the many American civilians who worked out of Quang Ngai City. They always felt secure here, even travelled alone on many occasions - something nobody on our team would ever do! The three of us, with weapons, would feel relatively comfortable moving through the bazaar of shops looking for good buys on all sorts of trinkets. We could then have a leisurely lunch, then head back to Tu Nghia in early afternoon. Our 3 hours of guarded parking cost 200 ("200 P") - a little less than 2 dollars. That was a bundle! (Everything was relative.)

All of our shopping was done in *piasters*, the South Vietnamese currency, but every merchant begged us to pay in greenback dollars or at least U.S. MPC (Military Pay Certificates), the play money that was used in American installations. Nobody was supposed to have greenbacks at all and MPC were not to be given or traded in with Vietnamese nationals. We had each always carried a good supply of P's in case of any kind of needs in the local economy - even bribes for our safety if necessary. I could shop all day and maybe use up most of my supply of the Vietnamese currency. Then I wouldn't forget to exchange it for "real money" just before I left country. I would try to bring home just a sample or two just as a conversation piece.

The fun part was about to begin. The three of us stayed together and barreled right into the bazaar , looking for who-knows-what. We found availability of almost anything a person could buy! Anything! It was like entering one of our modern-day "flea markets" where many of the goods were homemade, but even more looked stolen. For example, when you could buy a pair of U.S. issue jungle boots here, but couldn't get a pair from the official American or Vietnamese "supply" systems in country, you could bet that these were stolen or bought (illegally of course) from our "supply" people. So here we were, right in the middle of what was called the "black market". But, by this time I had grown to expect just about anything in this fantasy world. The trick was to figure out if it had always been this way or if the American presence had caused it - or perhaps the French before us, or the Japanese before them, or the Chinese before them...and so on.

What was more remarkable was the fact that so many different vendors had so many of the same items and would start their pricing at about the same level. Then we would try to bargain them down - it was the only honorable way. You never paid "list price". And the difference between the first asking price and the final negotiated amount was always huge. You would almost think that the art of the deal and negotiation was more important than the merchandise or the money itself. Something that started out at 800

P - less than 7 bucks - could be bought for maybe 150 P if you worked at it. On top of that, even the ending price would show some consistency between vendors. So, we figured out, they all had the same starting price and the same "walk-away" price - their bottom line. In between, the haggling would range all over the place, and the novice negotiator would pay lots more than minimum. (Anyone who has ever crossed the border from Southern California to Tijuana, Mexico for a little shopping - haggling - would understand). This was all quite entertaining, but none of us really bought much - perhaps a few small ivory, wooden, or lacquered carved figurines and such. I was afraid to touch the jewelry, fearing it might be just junk. Besides, I had been buying jewelry all year and sending it home as a result of Ken's numerous trips to Thailand and the famous Thai gem sellers. All the sapphire, ruby and emerald stuff he had picked up for us was quite authentic and beautiful - and well worth the prices. So, at the Quang Ngai City market, I actually bought very little, but the game of shopping was entertaining anyway.

There was still time to grab some lunch at the little sidewalk cafe at the market before everybody closed up for siesta. Yes, siesta would close down all the shops, too, but the restaurants would feed us even after 1 PM. A few of the shop-owners ate here, too. They were a little more relaxed here about timing, but they wanted to get their midday rest just like everybody else. So we ate our *Pho'* (noodle soup) fast and then saddled up for the short drive back to Tu Nghia District, arriving just in time for our gate guards to wake up and let us in. Now it was 2:30, everybody was waking up, and here we were having missed out on our own customary nap. There was no way I would be able to "sleep" all of that night with one eye open as was my usual way without the daytime siesta I had become so accustomed to. So, without too much concern, the 3 of us decided that we had it coming, so we would nap until suppertime. You see, we had assimilated lots of the characteristics and habits of our hosts. Once again...."When in Rome......

Next day, there being no operations to go out on, Dave and I
decided to make a run down QL 1 to pay my last visit to some of
our American friends at LZ Snoopy, the artillery fire base, and then
at the engineer base, closer to our compound, on the way back . A
couple of the new district replacements, the sergeant and corporal
who had replaced Johnny and Rich on the district team, insisted on
following us in their jeep, too. They happened to be 2nd tour guys
and knew what their presence would mean to me as the shortest
guy in the area. Each of our jeeps had radios for instant contact
with any support we might need. We flew (up to 40 mph!) down the
newly-paved national highway to the next district , Mo Duc District,
and the beautiful mountain (*Nui Dep*) where the artillery guys had
built LZ Snoopy. This was a pretty good haul, about 15 klicks (9
miles), and seemed like it took forever even though we were riding
only about 20 minutes in all. (Before it was paved the trip would
have taken an hour - and I wouldn't have thought of driving it. We
would always go that far by chopper.) There was the usual traffic of
civilians on foot and in every other conceivable mode of transport -
all rushing around doing something very busily. Everyone around
here seemed to have a purpose. Rural South Vietnam never struck
me as a place for loiterers.

 The other thing I remember about this trip - more so on the return
that afternoon, was the renewed appreciation I had for the
incredible beauty of this country, particularly from the highway
looking west toward the foothills and mountains. At long distance
the breathtaking vistas belied the fact that in the expanse between
us and that western horizon there were thousands of bad guys
here and there that were always trying to kill us and our friends and
trying to take their country away from them. But, in the serenity of
this pleasant ride, I momentarily forgot about the context of war.
What a beautiful place! I also tried to superimpose my mental
pictures of a typical locale back in the world, and I couldn't do it! It

wasn't that I couldn't remember what Main Street, USA looked like - I just couldn't imagine what it would be like to be back on that Main Street again. It all seemed so foreign - so distant - to me now. I felt like I belonged in this rural setting in Vietnam and it felt so natural to me that it was scary. Oh, I still wanted to go home. Who didn't?? But I wasn't sure I was prepared to re-adjust. Little did I know then how prophetic those fears were - for me and thousands like me.

At LZ Snoopy I made the rounds with the artillery battery commander, taking the opportunity to shake the hand of and thank each and every one of these great guys whose constant, untiring, and selfless fire support had saved our lives countless times. I tried to find the words to thank the technicians in the fire direction center and the grunts who manhandled the giant howitzers and humped their huge shells and powder bags. All of them sweated like bulls to get maximum rounds out to the targets, the ones I would call in, with speed and - most important - pinpoint accuracy. They all said - to a man - that it was their job and that they loved doing it. Fire missions and hard work beat the hell out of sitting around killing endless waiting hours, so the more fire we asked for the better they liked it. It was their job. This was what they had come here to do! They all said that as long as guys like us were willing to do what we did, they were proud to support us. How many times had I heard - or said - that before? The one other thing that I noticed, again, was that the enlisted men on this fire base felt very comfortable communicating with officers like Dave and me on a one-on-one basis. This was unusual, even in Vietnam. The separation between officers and enlisted men is always there and is a fact of life, but at LZ Snoopy I felt as comfortable with all of these men as they did with me. I guess our relationship had been built during the many firefights we had fought together - remotely. They had joined us - vicariously - in battle. We had all become brothers in war. I had once learned - to my surprise - that in the middle of a fire mission the fire direction controllers would always let the men on the firing line know who they were hustling to shoot for. I had been told that when the gunners were told that it was "Mike 1-1 in trouble" they would hump just a little bit faster. I guessed that they knew that we were always up against it with our inexperienced troops and that without the artillery, we would be a couple of Americans all alone and in beaucoup hot water somewhere out there. Maybe they felt sorry for us. I think they also worked harder because we always went out of our way to give them lots of feedback every time. Apparently, some of the American units they supported didn't show their appreciation as much as we did. To me it was elementary that if you showed your appreciation to those who supported you, they would work harder for you. And we really did mean it, too. They had helped us escape so many jams that we loved these guys! This "mutual admiration society" may seem corny, but it was for real. This was the brotherhood of war.

Our next stop at the Engineer compound, nearer our district HQ, proved to be quite different, but it was important to me anyway. After all, without these engineers, we would never have seen QL1 paved and as safe as it was now (in the daylight, of course). We also wouldn't have our now-famous chopper pad. And we wouldn't have as many friends as we really did. Dave and I spent all of our time with the officers on this farewell visit, with just casual and friendly waves to the enlisted men. It was just different here, but our team's relationship with the engineers was just as significant to our efforts as any relationship we had. We were always grateful for their hard work and their support.

If it seems like we were always indebted to someone else for their support of our efforts, it's only because that's exactly what it was all about! We, as the front-line advisers, really couldn't do anything. We could only be as helpful to our counterparts as the people and groups behind us would be. Given the totally informal "system" of support and supply, we could mainly count on the support of those units we had courted heavily. Fortunately, they all seemed to be willing to help us. From the engineers to the artillery guys to the medevac "dust-off" pilots to the "slick" (troop-carrying and utility chopper) crews to the Air Force FAC's in their puddle-jumping prop airplanes directing the hellfire-breathing jet air strikes from Marines and Air Force and all the way to the USS New Jersey - it seemed like we had coaxed a grand array of Americans to do our bidding to help us bring technology to the beck and call of our South Vietnamese brethren. And so be it. Pragmatists that we were, it was whatever worked that we would try to duplicate. Everything we did seemed to be a "field expedient" - the Army term for using your initiative and ingenuity. That was us - in spades! I thought we had all used up our last initiative cards by the time my tour was half over, but our friends kept helping us - and we kept improvising.

*　　　*　　　*　　　*　　　*　　　*

It was the now the last full day before my scheduled departure from Tu Nghia. Needless to say, I didn't go out on today's operation. Dave and one of the new guys handled it. I stayed in the district compound to get my gear in order, but I closely monitored all Dave's radio traffic in case they made contact on the operation and he needed some support from here. It wasn't the first time that Dave had taken an operation on his own - and it certainly wouldn't be the last - so I felt completely confident in his abilities. He had learned a lot over his first months here, and I felt perfectly fine turning over the team and "my" district to him. Their operation was uneventful this day - one of those frequent "walks-in-the-sun" that could be so frustrating - and everyone returned to the compound shortly after siesta.

At about 1500 (3 pm), Major Hoa came over to our team house to ask me to get a chopper, that there was something he wanted to check out from the air off in the western part of the district. He had had a report of some unusual activity out there and had been ordered by the Province Chief to personally check it out. I called up the chain and - lo and behold - was told that "Utility" would be available about 1700 hours for a short time. Hoa was delighted! He then asked me if I would go with him one last time - "one more VR" he called it. It would be a short flight out near the mountains, a couple of circles for observation of the "activity" and back to the compound. I couldn't resist and I'm certainly glad that I didn't. The ride was uneventful and pleasant. Our visual recon didn't turn up much of anything unusual. Must have been false intelligence reports. On the way back I made it a point to relax and enjoy the ride. Hoa and I sat opposite from each other in the left side doorway - he on the front-facing seat and me sitting Indian-like on the floor. The chopper cruised along at about 500 feet, much more docile than it had been on the low-level (15-foot altitude) run outbound earlier. Even the door-gunner on our side relaxed his guard, cleared his M-60 machine gun, and just let it hang loose in its cradle. It was like everybody was in stand-down mode and was enjoying the flight for a change. For the crew it was their last mission of the day. For Hoa it was just another of many flights he would take with American friends. For me it was the last time I would fly in a helicopter for at least the next 40 years or so. I would miss it - very much.

*   *   *   *   *

Flying in a "Huey" helicopter is really a thrill. It was the workhorse of Vietnam and in a way symbolizes the entire war. This workhorse was actually a thoroughbred race horse. But, for all its glory earned in millions of missions of every kind, perhaps two of the most poignant images of our abandonment of the Vietnam war and our South Vietnamese friends involved those unmistakable Huey's. One was of course the film of the last Air America chopper plucking people from the roof of the CIA compound during the fall of Saigon in 1975. (That's right! It wasn't the US Embassy, as most of the poorly-informed journalists - even the famous ones -think it was.) The other image is perhaps for some of us the most disturbing of all. That's the one of the Hueys being pushed over the side of an aircraft carrier's deck and into the South China Sea - a symbol of our abandonment of everything to do with Vietnam, our efforts there, and the technology with which we should have been able to support a victorious South Vietnam. That image cries out for the futility of the way we stumbled into and through this war and the final act of giving up - of throwing in the towel.

*   *   *   *   *

So this last aerial visual recon was over and we were back safe in the Tu Nghia District compound with darkness bringing a close to my last day as MAT team leader. As we trudged back from the "Playboy" chopper pad to our inner compound Hoa told me he wanted me to be sure and be available for his flag-raising ceremony the next morning. Every working day, the flag of the Republic of Vietnam - official name for South Vietnam - was raised at 8 a.m. to start the work day in the little offices in the district headquarters. There would be a ceremony on special days and there had been one when Ron had left to go home, so I knew it was my turn. I told Hoa that I'd be there for sure, but also that I looked forward to his taking part in the small and quite private gathering of our team tonight - my last night in the team house. I was pretty sure I was about to be roasted, but that was part of the fun of a going-away party. I would have been disappointed if they didn't roast me! They did.

Ken announced a small drop-in for "Trung Uy'" in his hooch after dinner. All members of the MAT and district teams were invited - about 9 Americans - along with *Thieu Ta'* Hoa to celebrate my DEROS. Toasts included the usual barbs and clever remembrances of every goof or faux pa'. It was as if someone had kept a detailed diary when I wasn't looking. A couple of plaques were presented and the speeches that accompanied them were hilarious by our standards. This was all in good fun and, again, I would have been disappointed if they hadn't done it. Hoa seemed to get a special kick out of the way we treated each other in good humor. He laughed in all the right places, too, as he understood English as well as he spoke it and, after so many years of working with the Americans, he understood our humor and a lot about our culture. If he ever made it to the U.S. he would have no trouble adapting to life in America. This quiet evening was perfect - including the temporary interruption by a couple of mortar rounds dropped routinely into our perimeter. Same old harassment. The mortarman probably had gotten word that I was leaving and wanted to give me his version of a going-away present. No problem. I beat everybody to the bunker, which brought on even more laughs at my expense, but I didn't care. I could be as paranoid as I wanted to be. I was leaving tomorrow and wasn't about to buy the farm on my last night. The party broke up shortly after that, but about 2 a.m. our friendly bad guy dropped about 10 more rounds on us - all right in the compound. I had been first into the bunker again. In fact, I had been awakened by the sound of the first mortar round sliding down the tube from 200 meters away and by the time it gave off its first tell-tale "thump" I had yelled "incoming" and was in the bunker before the first round even landed.

The night still wasn't over for me. After the mortar attack there was about 3 hours time before the safety and security of daylight would come. I would stay awake for the duration. For the first time my "short" status really got to me. I would stand "guard" until first light so that nothing happened on my last night in-country. I guess I thought that if I was awake I was automatically safe. It worked. First light came and reminded me of my agreement to participate in the flag-raising ceremony. I got dressed in my least-faded set of fatigues and then completed my packing for the long journey home that would start at noon today. I could hardly believe that this was happening! It just had to be a dream! But it was for real. I was about to leave what had been my home for the past year. At my age a year was a long time, and I almost felt that this way of life was all I knew - and once again a part of me didn't want it to end. Without this I might be lost. Nothing I could ever do would compare with this wonderful experience and I was about to give it up and

WHAT ?!

say goodbye to my friends. The only thing that let me do it was an even stronger desire to get home. It was a good thing. I might have stayed in Vietnam!

CHAPTER TWENTY

The flag-raising at Tu Nghia District HQ was normally routine and
unceremonious, but this day it was to be a special happening. An
American adviser was leaving Vietnam to go home to "the world",
as we called it. That was me, Mike 1-1, who would be turning over
the leadership of the MAT Team to Dave and heading back home. I
was asked by *Thieu Ta'* Hoa, Tu Nghia District Chief, to be a part
of the ceremony, and I guessed it was so that he could recognize
me in front of the troops and District officers and employees. Well,
recognize me he did! At the appropriate time Hoa asked me to
step forward from my front line position in the formation, then
summoned his right hand man, *Dai Uy'* (Captain) Kahn, who bore
a black velvet pillow with a large ribboned medal on it. I glanced out

of the corner of my eye as Hoa gave a short speech and read a
citation - in both Vietnamese and English - to his assembled troops
and my team. This was one of the few times I had seen an actual
formation way out here, so it was an important occasion. It
became obvious that the District Chief was awarding me the *I Receive both*
Vietnamese Cross of Gallantry with Bronze Star, a special
decoration awarded only directly by Vietnamese Officers. This was
different than the Cross with Palm Leaf that I had wondered about
before, as it was routinely awarded to most Americans by the U.S.
in behalf of the South Vietnamese Government. I was extremely
proud to be awarded this honor directly by the Vietnamese and
especially by my good friend Major Hoa. Needless to say, I was
very touched by this turn of events, and very proud of the honor.
Most of all, I was thankful to have had the experiences that brought
this decoration and to have earned the respect of my friends of the
Vietnamese government that we were trying to advise and support.
Major Hoa proudly pinned the medal on my jungle fatigue jacket,
stepped back and saluted. Then he stepped forward and warmly
shook my hand and thanked me for what I had done for his district
and his country. Now I felt more guilty than ever to be leaving a job
undone!!

As the flag of The Republic of Vietnam (South Vietnam) was raised
for the last time that I would see it raised over Tu Nghia District I
felt, strangely, fulfillment and inadequacy at the same time. I was
satisfied that we had done the best we could to bolster the fragile
government and the local armed forces of South Vietnam through
our advisory and support efforts, but at the same time I was
concerned that "our best" wasn't good enough. Had we really
positively affected the ability of our allies to secure their country?
Would the local militia forces we had trained be able to protect their
villages while the regular ARVN army went out to take on the North
Vietnamese Army in division-sized pitched battles? With the
relentless draw-down of U.S. troops and support, and the inevitable
cut-off of all financial support from the U.S., would the ARVN and
its government be able to conduct a country and a war? Without

the continued U.S. presence like that in Korea (the American public probably wouldn't stand for that) could the South Vietnamese keep the North Vietnamese Army from over-running their country?? All these questions troubled me greatly but it was supposed to be my turn to go home and "forget about it". I knew full well that I could never "forget about it"! These questions would haunt me for decades. *IN 1968-69 I KNEW iT WAS OVER IF/WHICH THE AMERICANS LEFT!!!* * * * *

I know now that we were fooling ourselves if we really thought that the South Vietnamese could resist forever the onslaughts of North Vietnamese Army troops without our support. The South Vietnamese at the time had the 5th largest army in the world. Unfortunately, their North Vietnamese invaders had the 4th largest and were backed by both the Russians and the Communist Chinese (both of which they feared and detested but accepted support from). Ironically, it was the threat of a major land war in Asia - or even World War III - that had caused our government, particularly during the Johnson years, to fail to make a full commitment to winning in Vietnam. Johnson and his advisors, such as the inept but influential McNamara (Secretary of Defense) were terrified that the Russians or at least the Chicoms would come into the Vietnam war in a big way and that an all-out nuclear confrontation that could end the world might happen on Lyndon Johnson's watch. This same fear caused virtually all U.S. officials to condone the gradual, agonizing buildup of U.S. involvement which, starting in 1970, Nixon would have to reverse in order to be a hero. This lack of commitment eventually culminated in the loss of South Vietnam, whose fate was sealed when the weak-kneed Congress, threatened by the protest movement in our own country, voted in 1974 to suddenly cut off all aid to South Vietnam. What happened in Vietnam a few short months after Congress deserted our allies is history. At the time, it was also inevitable.

*　　　*　　　*　　　*　　　*　　　*

Once the formal part of the ceremony was completed, I took the opportunity to go around and shake the hands of each of the 40 or so Popular Forces officers and soldiers assembled for this honor. I felt like they really wanted to say their goodbyes as did I. Many of these men had been the main forces involved in many firefights and we had become "brothers" because we fought together. That's just the way it was in a combat situation. Each handshake was prolonged by broken English (theirs) and broken Vietnamese (mine) so by the time this ritual was over it was time to take off for Province headquarters to officially sign out and to meet with the Province Senior Advisor for the obligatory exit interview. Dave and Tu would drive me and my gear to Province and then to the Quang Ngai airfield to catch the Air America shuttle plane while Hoa, Ken and DIOCC - the Phoenix adviser - would meet us at the airfield just before noon for a final sendoff. The rest of my team would say goodbye to me right here. I had a special goodbye for Doc, who had been with me almost from the beginning of my tour. We had grown up together over the past months, and I wished him the best and safe trip home as he would be following me out of country in less than a month. Sergeant L would be going home in about 3 months, so he was just getting to the "short" stage. I knew he wouldn't slack off a bit, though. He was an excellent soldier and team player. The 5th member of my team , Sergeant A, was out on an in-country R&R and we had said our goodbyes before he had left.

All the goodbyes being taken care of we piled my worldly goods, including a "hold-baggage" crate, into the beat-up old jeep we called "Tramp" and headed for Province HQ at the Quang Ngai City soccer field. Here I would routinely sign out with the duty sergeant and then meet with the Lieutenant Colonel who was the Province Senior Adviser (PSA), or the counterpart to the Province Chief, a full Colonel (Dai Ta') who was actually my counterpart Hoa's boss.

The PSA greeted me with a gruff handshake and in a few minutes let me know that he knew through word of mouth, both American and Vietnamese versions, that I had done an exceptional job with my MAT team, particularly in the trusting relationship I had built up with not only my District Chief, but with other officers as well. I felt highly complimented. For people who count to have trust in me and to have it so recognized was all the reward I needed. I thanked the PSA for his comments and for the opportunity to make a difference, but I had to confess to him my over-riding feeling of guilt at leaving a job undone. He told me to rest assured that all advisers felt that way and that we shouldn't. All in all it was an outstanding short encounter for a young officer. I was treated with respect and appreciation - perhaps because the Colonel knew I was really a "civilian" who had volunteered to do a small part in the Army when needed and not a "lifer" out to get my ticket punched by coming to Vietnam. I think he respected me for this. When it was time for me to get hopping over to the airfield, he thanked me for serving. That was enough for me. I wished him luck for his remaining time here and, with a handshake instead of a salute, left the office.

Dave cranked the old jeep and started out of the Province compound. This would be my last trip through Quang Ngai City. Normally one would want to slowly take in the sights for memory's sake, but I asked Dave to step on it and get me to the airport fast! He laughed and implied that I wanted to get out of town in a big hurry. I told him that I knew I wouldn't miss the plane, I just wanted to make sure I got there in time to spend a few minutes with Hoa, who I knew would be there by now, before Air America was ready to take me out of here on my long journey back to the world. We came screeching in on two wheels, almost crashing into the Butler Hut that served as a combination airfield control office and pilots lounge. (Dave was a better adviser than he was a driver!) On the other side of the hut I noticed first the Air America twin-engine Beechcraft Queen-Air retractable sitting on the tarmac in its red, white and blue glory. He was early!! The second thing I noticed was Ken's scout vehicle and 4 people standing around it. Ken, Hoa and the DIOCC had been joined by the Air America pilot who later would be understanding enough not to rush me away from my small going-away gathering. In fact, he became part of the send-off. The Air America pilots were civilians, working for the CIA and were quite the swash-buckling "soldier's-of-fortune" (mercenaries) who were paid well to do things regular Army or Air Force pilots could not - or would not - do. They were a pretty loose bunch. While this pilot filed a flight plan back to Danang just for the record, my send-off began with a toast of rice wine for everybody. Each of my friends had to make a toast with Hoa saving his till last. The pilot re-joined us and got in on the last two swigs of rice wine, raising his cup high, and was ready to go whenever I was. It seemed to me that if we continued toasting too long I would lose my pilot to the rice wine and we'd never get off the ground, so I used my discretion to get the show on the road. There were warm handshakes and even grown men hugging - again the last left for my special friend *Thieu Ta' Hoa*. With that I jumped on the 7-passenger plane and the pilot roared off in the direction of the short runway. We took off in no time as I stared back and waved at my friends - close friends whom I would probably never see again. All of a sudden my pilot - I was the only passenger this time so I call him "my" pilot - turned the plane around in a tight circle and flew back across the runway that we had just taken off from. I could see the small gathering by the Scout looking and pointing up at us. As we crossed the runway at about 200 feet the pilot dipped one wing and then the other in fast repetition - a kind of wave or salute to those on the ground. They waved back and we roared out of the area. I could look back and still see that Hoa was still waving with one hand while his other arm was apparently wrapped around Dave - his new counterpart on the MAT team. Life would go on, but I knew Hoa had the same sense of loyalty to me as I had to him. I knew that there would be a tear in his eye - just like the one I now struggled to suppress. To Hoa, I was gone now, and he would now be that much closer to Dave as the team leader - the new "Mike one-one". I was glad they had begun this relationship. Dave could pick up right where I had left off. I know they made a great team - almost as great as the one I had had with my Counterpart.

I could now turn my head to the front of the aircraft in the direction of my new journey The most significant, exciting year of my life was almost over, and I was about to start the odyssey that would carry me through a whole new and differently rewarding kind of life for at least the next 3 or 4 decades. But for all of that time, my experience in Vietnam would have a profound effect on me. The war, and the incredible experience, would be with me for the rest of my days. At the time I pondered the question of how I would ever do or be involved in anything quite as significant as the Vietnam War. And, at the time, I was sure I knew the answer. Nothing would ever compare to this experience. Sometimes I wish that I could re-live it!

*   *   *   *   *   *

The Air America plane went "feet-wet" all the way back to Danang, just like we had done on my first trip to the Province and District almost a full year ago. In a little over an hour the fast "Queen-Air" was making its final approach into Danang airfield. As we glided ever closer to the long concrete strip, I kept my eye on the lone pilot - partially out of curiosity and partly to make sure he was doing everything right. It looked ok for me, but just before we were to touch down the plane groaned in acceleration and struggled back to climb attitude just over the runway. We were doing a fly-by at the 10,000 foot Danang airfield, or Aerial Port, probably the busiest airfield in the entire world at the time. I thought there might be a flight of jet fighters behind us that we had to get out of the way of, just like the Pan Am freedom bird from Hawaii had had to do. This time, however, there was nobody behind us in trouble. Were we the ones in trouble? The pilot glanced furtively back at me as he started a big circular second approach to the main runway. I was beginning to wonder and worry about this caper. I could just see myself surviving a year in combat and then buying the farm in a routine Air America milk run mishap! I watched like a hawk this pilot's every move. I thought I noticed a change in his approach procedure, and then I was sure of it! This time I saw him reach down, grab a knob marked "GEAR" and slide the manual control all the way down. He was lowering the landing gear on our airplane! It only took a split-second to figure out why we had done the fly-by. This guy had been about to land this bird with the gear retracted! The first time around he had forgotten to lower the landing gear! How could an experienced pilot do this? Of course he had no co-pilot, by Air America's normal - and scary - procedure, but I still couldn't believe he could forget to lower the gear!

This time around the aircraft landed safely and taxied up to the transient terminal that Air America always used. After everything was shut down, I just sat there and waited for my pilot to walk past me and out of the airplane. He would have to face me sooner or later. He got up and walked past me to open the door. I noticed a sheepish grin on his face. Then he confessed to me that he had just forgotten to lower the gear because he usually flew the fixed-gear Porter airplane - the other Air America standard - and never had to lower any landing gear. I failed to see the humor in this and I knew he could tell that. I also noticed him eye-balling my shoulder-holstered .45 caliber automatic pistol with wide-eyed fear. I think he thought I would shoot him for what he had almost done to me. Some field troops would have done it! Somehow, I found the humor and just laughed as I grabbed my gear and sauntered off the plane and across the tarmac - never looking back at what could have happened. For sure, I had just left the most embarrassed pilot in the world. I would bet that he never made that mistake again. To this day, every time I fly on a scheduled, professional airline, I wonder if the pilot and co-pilot have followed their checklist properly. I hope so. I would never want to lose it due to simple pilot error. What a waste that would be! I also would lay odds that my Air America pilot tells the story on himself these days - if he's still alive - and wonders if that grunt adviser - me - has ever forgiven or forgotten. These are the stories we tell over a beer now, the "funny" ones.

*　　　*　　　*　　　*　　　*　　　*　　　*

So, my journey home did not lack excitement, and it had just begun! What would happen next?

The next leg of my journey included what should have been a routine C-130 Hercules flight from Danang to Ton Sun Nhut airfield in Saigon. As it turned out, this C-130 had to be the oldest and most shot-up aircraft in the Air Force's inventory. It was rigged with the usual jump seats (straps) and it's open-air cargo hold was more "natural" than most because the tail ramp just wouldn't close all the way. As we took off, the shuddering and shaking was unbelievable; I was sure we weren't going to get off the ground. But we did. An hour later we started a brutally sharp descent into the army airfield at Qui Nhon in Binh Dinh Province, about 1/3 of the way between Danang and Saigon. This sea-level airfield near a huge American base camp was nestled between mountains and the coast. Naturally the prevailing winds dictated that we had to take the final approach over the mountains, which meant a sudden drop in altitude after we cleared the last mountain between us and the airfield. I sensed that the sudden drop was also an evasive maneuver to avoid enemy anti-aircraft gunners - and it surely was. A safe but bumpy landing brought a sigh of relief to all hands, but this relief too was short-lived. This joyride would be continuing very shortly - how could the airframe take such continual punishment without falling apart? Don't ask! The C-130 scurried to a stopping point protected by a steel revetment. There we exchanged some cargo and added more passengers, many of them South Vietnamese civilians. It reminded me of the flight north on a similar C-130 almost 11 months earlier. I think the same giant pig was on this aircraft, bound for the market in Saigon, now stuffed head-first into a conical bamboo basket. What a sight! Anyway, I felt right at home with a pig's business end staring me in the face and me slouched into one of the strap jump-seats on the C-130, headed for Saigon and whatever lay ahead of us. Seated next to me was an obviously green soldier who was in awe of the goings-on in this U.S. Air Force aircraft. I smiled and told him to get used to it. He had a long time to go. I couldn't help but remember how I felt when the eternity of one whole year was staring me in the face. I tried to convey to this FNG (.... New Guy) the fact that, before he knew it, he too would be headed back to the world - without adding those other five words: "if he lived that long". Now I wished I could wave a magic wand and deliver this young guy from whatever lay ahead of him. Then I thought that if I could do that, I could have willed far more blessings to occur, such as a win in this war and safety and success for my team and for my "counterpart", Major Hoa. Ever since that moment, I have wondered if these hopes had come true.

As the lumbering C-130 Hercules made its way to the ready line for take-off, I closed my eyes in my own form of prayer that we at least would become airborne without the plane falling apart or being shot out of the sky by a lone Viet Cong gunner. (Was I paranoid, or was it just that when you get this close to the promised land you assume the worst is going to cut you off from salvation?) Fortunately we were taking off at 1230 hours, which meant Charlie would be at lunch break - siesta - now, so our chances of being shot down were next to zero, so that narrowed my short-timer's fears to that of mechanical failure or general metal fatigue in the giant transport's wings or tail or fuselage. Neither failed this time and we got airborne and shuddered our way toward Saigon - another miracle! My fears may seem inordinate, but I was used to being attacked by the clever communist enemy and now I was short! I had a right to be paranoid about any form of sudden death!

Before I knew it we were making our final approach into Tan Son Nhut Airfield just outside of Saigon, the Pearl of the Orient and home to USMACV and its "Pentagon East" Headquarters. This was also my jumping off point to leave Vietnam, so I held it in a form of reverence. It was here that I had arrived almost 365 days ago, and it was this place that I would watch fade away from the window of that great Freedom Bird that would take off in a little more than 30 hours, at 2400 hours on 23 March 70 – the final day of the year of my life. As usual, I was thinking "I wish it could happen all over again". That thought often occurs to me – sometimes daily – many decades later. I know it will always be that way for the rest of my days.

Finis

Made in the USA
Columbia, SC
20 May 2020

97771475R00159